day trips from columbus

third edition

getaway ideas for the local traveler

Sandra Gurvis

travel

Guilford, Connecticut

Special thanks to Pattie Stechschulte, researcher extraordinare,
who helped with the update of this edition.

All the information in this guidebook is subject to change. We
recommend that you call ahead to obtain current information
before traveling.

To buy books in quantity for corporate use
or incentives, call **(800) 962-0973**
or e-mail **premiums@GlobePequot.com.**

Copyright © 2002, 2004, 2009 Morris Book Publishing, LLC

ALL RIGHTS RESERVED. No part of this book may be reproduced or transmitted in any
form by any means, electronic or mechanical, including photocopying and recording, or
by any information storage and retrieval system, except as may be expressly permitted in
writing from the publisher. Requests for permission should be addressed to Globe Pequot
Press, Attn: Rights and Permissions Department, P.O. Box 480, Guilford, CT 06437.

Day Trips is a registered trademark of Morris Book Publishing, LLC.

Text design: Linda R. Loiewski
Layout: Joanna Beyer
Spot photography throughout © Shutterstock/Michael Shake

ISSN 1536-3589
ISBN 978-0-7627-4773-3

Printed in the United States of America
10 9 8 7 6 5 4 3 2 1

In loving memory of my
parents, who enjoyed
their travels in Ohio

contents

north

day trip 01

the roller coast

day trip 02

lake erie islands

day trip 03

it's history

northeast

day trip 01

state parks

day trip 02

amish country

day trip 03

christians, indians, and presidents

day trip 04

ohio's innovators

day trip 05

old stuff and new thrills

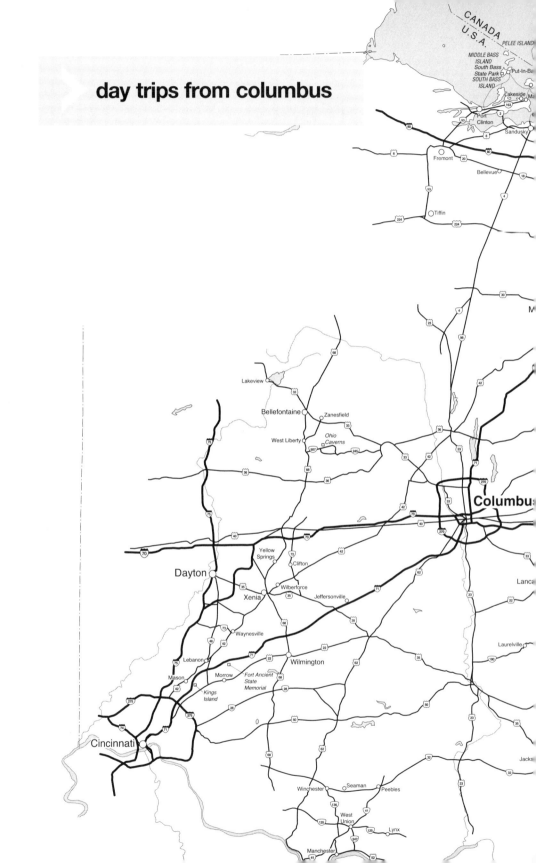

day trips from columbus

day trip 04

arts and science

west

day trip 01

simply capital

day trip 02

fun in the sun and snow

day trip 03

another alternative

day trip 04

a wright outing

introduction

I have lived in Ohio all my life, but I also have journeyed throughout the United States and overseas. Whenever I return, I am again reminded how much can be found within the borders of my home state. Not only are many cultures represented here, from Amish country to the Underground Railroad to the ethnic neighborhoods of Cleveland, but you can also experience a vast array of cuisines, learn about the manufacturing of baskets or glass, romp on the shores of Lake Erie, and encounter one of the largest concentrations of amusement parks in the Midwest. Museums and cultural entities abound, making science, rock and roll, dead presidents (not the green kind), and pioneer exploration fun and relevant for both children and adults.

Along with a rich history of elegant and quaint homes, farms, covered bridges, and unique communities, there are wonderful shopping and recreational opportunities. Clusters of outlet stores can be found in Ohio and in nearby Kentucky, while small towns such as Yellow Springs and Dresden offer an eclectic array of goods. Columbus, Cincinnati, and Cleveland have malls galore, from upscale to discount. You can go horseback riding, learn how to care for animals, and explore Native American heritage by visiting their ancient burial places and witnessing live reenactments of their lives and times. Ohio's state park system has a wonderful assortment of lodging as well as camping, fishing, hiking, boating, and other sports opportunities. And most things are reasonably priced, making tourism here a bargain compared to more heavily trodden areas.

Ohio is a state for all seasons. The clement spring and summer provide an abundance of outdoor options, while winter offers skiing and ice fishing. The fall foliage, particularly in spots such as the Hocking Hills, is magnificent. The color lasts several weeks, providing quite a window of time to visit during this moderate and generally sunny period.

But perhaps Ohio's greatest appeal can be found in the people. Most are pleasant and genuinely willing to help but mind their own business if that's what you want. They'll say, "How are you?" and mean it, without ulterior motive or desire to impress. So if you ever need anything, ask. You'll generally get more assistance than you originally bargained for. People who come from out of state are amazed at how quickly they feel comfortable and accepted.

In the middle of this "old shoe" is Columbus, which is about two hours away from the farthest points north, south, east, and west. In recent years, Columbus has pretty much shed its "Cowtown" image; transforming into "C-Bus," an urban, multicultural and—dare I say it?—sophisticated small city. Because of its central location, Columbus/C-Bus/Cowtown-no-more offers rich access to the state's many and varied pleasures. Therefore, most of the entries in this book are within Ohio's borders.

So if you like to relax, enjoy, and explore new and old cultures and pastimes, this is the place for you. You needn't spend a fortune on gasoline or deal with the hassle of flying on an airplane. Good food, nice people, lots of things to see and do inexpensively—what more could one ask?

driving tips

Ohio state troopers and local police are notorious for cracking down on speeders and reckless motorists. They also strictly enforce seat belt and drunk driving laws. So although drivers from other states might find it frustrating to be surrounded by seemingly pokey vehicles that go no more than 5 miles per hour over the posted limit, they may quickly learn the reason when they receive additional points on their licenses and hefty fines. The good news is that many of Ohio's major interstates and highways have a 65 miles per hour speed limit.

Law enforcement is also quick to help those in distress. If you're lost or having car trouble, call the State Highway Patrol at (877) 772–8765, and they'll dispatch someone to provide assistance.

Also be on the lookout for the dreaded orange barrels; those mean road construction and possible delays. It's especially wise to stay within posted speed restrictions, as fines may be more than doubled for offenders. Signs often designate alternate routes. Although these detours may require more actual driving, they save aggravation and, in some cases, travel time.

ohio quirks

This state has its idiosyncrasies. For instance, the term "deli" is very loosely interpreted here. In Ohio a deli is generally one cut above a fast-food eatery and serves mostly sandwiches, soups, and prepackaged salads. It's nothing like what you'd expect in New York, Los Angeles, and other big cities. One exception is Corky & Lenny's in Cleveland (see Northeast Day Trip 6); Columbus, Cincinnati, Dayton, and even Athens have their versions.

Ohioans have a sense of humor (some might say an inferiority complex) about their lack of mountains and ocean. If you hear someone refer to Mt. Parnassus, it's a very steep slope at Denison University in Granville. Mt. Campbell (actually Campbell Hill according to the map) near Bellefontaine, a mere 1,550 feet above sea level, is the highest elevation around. "Buckeye Ocean" is a pond-turned-lake, while "Surf Ohio" generally refers to waterskiing or other wet 'n' wild activities on Lake Erie or one of the artificial bodies of water.

how to use this guide

In the interest of accuracy and because they are subject to change, hours of operation, attraction prices, and credit card designations have been omitted. Most places take credit cards, although some may accept certain types and not others. If you have questions, contact the destination for specifics. Whenever possible, Web addresses have been included so you can obtain more information on the Internet.

pricing key

Accommodations:

$—inexpensive, less than $75 for a room

$$—moderate, between $75 and $125

$$$—expensive, $126 and up

Most rooms are for two people, but if you want to be certain of whether the pricing applies to a single or a double room, you will want to call the establishment. Many of the properties listed are bed-and-breakfasts. When making reservations, always check to see if accommodations include a private bath and what type of breakfast is included, particularly if you have food allergies. Also let proprietors know if you're bringing children or pets, and find out if they have animals themselves.

Restaurants:

$—inexpensive, $10.00 and less for entrees

$$—moderate, between $10.00 and $25.00

$$$—expensive, $26.00 and up

highway designations

Interstates are prefaced by "I" (for example, I–270) and are generally multilane divided highways.

U.S. highways are two- and three-lane undivided roads and prefaced by "U.S." (for instance, U.S. 68).

State highways are paved and divided and prefaced by "SR" (for example, SR 256).

County roads can be paved or even gravel and are prefaced by "CR" (e.g., CR 10).

where to get more information

This book attempts to cover all bases and interests, but those looking for additional material can contact the following agencies by phone, mail, or the Internet. Regarding the latter, when checking out the various destinations, be aware that online reviews may be contradictory and conflicting. Everyone's experience can be different, and the Internet allows for a forum for these diverse opinions. So call the place directly and be conscious of ratings such as AAA and the Better Business Bureau. Many of the areas have chain hotels and restaurants, which are generally not included in the listings in each chapter. Along with a roundup of festivals and celebrations, the back of the book provides the addresses and phone numbers of chambers of commerce and/or convention and visitor bureaus. Here are some additional resources:

general information

Ohio Department of Development, Division of Travel and Tourism
77 South High Street, P.O. Box 101
Columbus, OH 43216
(800) 282–5393
www.discoverohio.com

bed-and-breakfasts

Ohio Bed and Breakfast Association
5310 East Main Street, Suite 104
Columbus, OH 43213
(614) 868–5567
www.ohiobba.com

ohio state parks

Division of Parks and Recreation
2045 Morse Road, C-3
Columbus, OH 43229
(614) 265–6561
www. www.ohiodnr.com

historic sites

Ohio Historical Society
1982 Velma Avenue
Columbus, OH 43211
(614) 297–2300 or (800) 686–6124
www.ohiohistory.org

help us keep this guide up to date

We would love to hear from you concerning your experiences with this guide and how you feel it could be improved and kept up to date. Please send your comments and suggestions to:

editorial@GlobePequot.com

Thanks for your input, and happy travels!

north

day trip 01

north

>>> **the roller coast:**
sandusky • cedar point

If you like going around in circles, the Sandusky–Cedar Point area is the place for you, what with all the merry-go-rounds and roller coasters. Several of the few remaining hand-carved antique carousels in the United States can be found here, along with Top Thrill Drag-ster, until recently the world's tallest and fastest roller coaster. Although it was displaced by Kingda Ka at Six Flags in New Jersey, Cedar Point keeps reinventing the wheel, offering new scream machines, other wild-to-mild rides, and entertainment galore. Why else would people keep gyrating back?

sandusky

Sandusky is about 110 miles from Columbus, a straight shot north from I–270 to U.S. 23 to SR 98, which turns into SR 4 about halfway at Bucyrus. With its small-town charm, late 1800s limestone architecture, and easy accessibility, Sandusky is a great place to get your feet wet in the vast and varied tourist attraction that is Lake Erie.

where to go

The Merry-Go-Round Museum. 301 Jackson Street, Sandusky, OH 44870. Talk about life imitating art: The museum is housed in a former post office shaped like a horseshoe (carousel horses, get it?). The city of Sandusky also issued four commemorative carousel stamps in 1988. There's a real working 1936 merry-go-round inside, a colorful medley

Lake Erie

MIDDLE BASS
ISLAND
South Bass
State Park
SOUTH BASS
ISLAND

Peter Island

Put-In-Bay

Buckeye
Island

Marblehead

Port
Clinton

Cedar Point
Amusement Park

Sandusky

Fremont

Bellevue

Milan

Tiffin

Mansfield

Lucas

Perrysville

Loudonville

Millersburg

Bellefontaine

Zanesfield

Ohio

West Liberty

Granville

Newark

Frazeysburg

Dresden

Columbus

Buckeye
Lake

Clifton

Lancaster

Wilberforce

Jeffersonville

Rockville

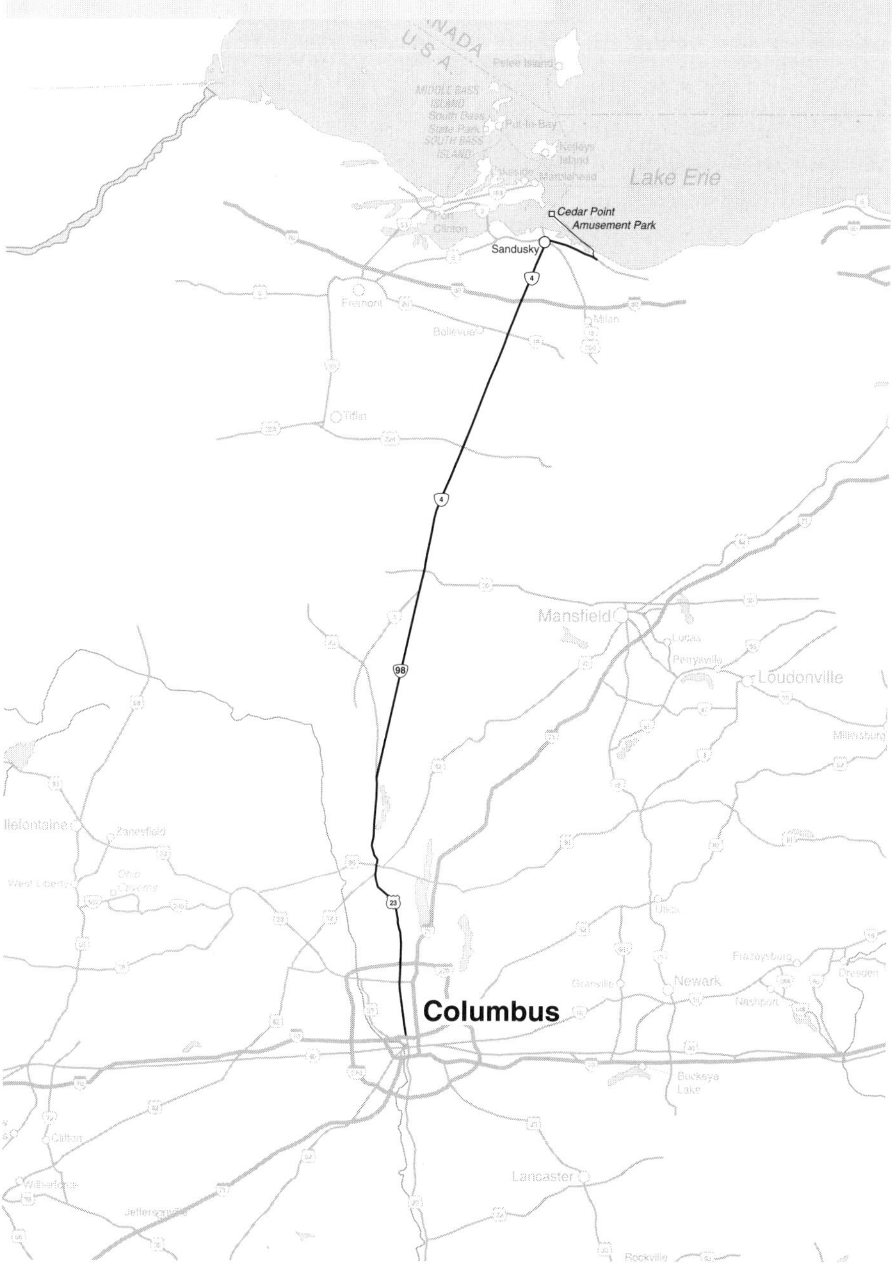

of animals and chariots from various manufacturers and eras. You'll also find the tools, workbenches, and other implements of master artisan Gustav Dentzel, in addition to his partially chiseled steeds. Other acquisitions include works by well-known carousel crafters such as Daniel Muller, M. C. Illions, and Charles Loof; a primitive horse that was part of the first merry-go-round in the United States; and a stained-glass replica of one of the stamps. Hours vary according to season. Admission is charged. (419) 626–6111; www.merrygo roundmuseum.org.

Maritime Museum of Sandusky. 125 Meigs Street, Sandusky, OH 44870-2834. This nautical but nice collection boasts artifacts, photos, and maps, providing a rich sense of the area's maritime history, including fishing and ice-harvesting activities. Displays include locally constructed vessels from different eras, and there's even a boat-building class. The gift shop offers books, prints, and clothing relating to the Sandusky area. Hours vary according to season. Admission may be charged. (419) 624–0274; www.sanduskymari time.org.

Eleutheros Cooke House. 1415 Columbus Avenue, Sandusky, OH 44870. This Greek Revival jewel boasts an ornate collection of glassware, porcelain, and antique furnishings from several eras and an elaborate garden with a working greenhouse. Built in 1843–44, it was moved to its present location in the 1870s and reconstructed, then completely redecorated in the early 1950s. Open Tuesday through Saturday, April through December; other times by appointment. Admission is charged.(419) 627–0640; ohsweb.ohiohistory .org/places/nw03/.

Follett House Museum. 404 Wayne Street, Sandusky, OH 44870. The archival research center for the Sandusky Library, this collection also has fascinating Civil War artifacts from a former confederate officers' and soldiers' prison on nearby Johnson's Island, in addition to Victorian housewares, toys, furnishings, and clothes. A standout is a Baltimore-style quilt made in the 1840s. A visit to the widow's walk on top provides a panoramic view. Open April through December; hours vary. Free. (419) 625–3834; www.sandusky.lib.oh.us/ follett_house/.

where to eat

Cedar Downs. 1935 Cleveland Road, Sandusky, OH 44870. This establishment has the distinction of being the state's only offtrack-betting enterprise. Along with putting on the feedbag for Italian and American cuisine and local favorites, you can also play the ponies "live" by watching televised events at Churchill Downs, Gulf Stream, Santa Anita, Saratoga, and others. Horseplay never tasted so good. $$–$$$. (419) 627–8573; www.cedardowns otb.com.

DeMore's Fish Den. 302 West Perkins Avenue, Sandusky, OH 44870. Home of the giant perch sandwich and featuring Lake Erie pickerel (aka walleye) and perch by the pound, this spot reinforces the tenet that it's better to feast on fins than to be fish food. Casual dining on an outdoor patio also provides prime people-watching. $–$$. (419) 626–8861.

Cameo Pizza. 702 West Monroe Street, Sandusky, OH 44870. Since 1936, this family-owned eatery has been serving up pizza with "Mama's" secret sauce and dough made daily. Along with the obvious, they also serve wings, fried chicken and shrimp, salads, and sandwiches. A wide variety of sizes, crusts, and toppings are available. $–$$. (419) 626–0187; www.cameopizza.com.

Toft's Dairy. 3717 Venice Road, Sandusky, OH 44870. This family-owned operation has been in the area since 1900 and makes its own products. The ideal place for a cone or confection after a hard day of touring. $. (800) 521–4606; www.toftdairy.com.

where to stay

Cottage Rose. 210 West Adams Street, Sandusky, OH 44870. There's a modicum of privacy in this second-floor accommodation, which features two bedrooms, a bath, and a study. It's a bargain, considering the prime location, and you can stay as little or as long as you'd like. The home is furnished with antiques, so parents with younger children might want to consider an alternative. $. (419) 625–1285.

Wagner's 1844 Inn. 230 East Washington Street, Sandusky, OH 44870. Listed on the National Register of Historic Places, this beautiful Italianate-style B&B is filled with antiques. Three spacious guest rooms have private baths, and you're close to Lake Erie and Sandusky attractions. $$. (419) 626–1726; www.lrbcg.com/wagnerinn.

Big Oak. 2501 Campbell Street, Sandusky, OH 44870. Furnished with family heirlooms, this Victorian farmhouse was built in 1879 and boasts several small gardens. The hosts, James and Jeanne Ryan, have also provided plenty of games and books, along with insider tips for visiting the area. Only one of the four bedrooms has a private bath. Breakfast brings Dutch Babies, an egg puff served with strawberries. $–$$. (419) 627–0329; www.thebigoakbb.com.

cedar point

The largest amusement park in the world—take that, Six Flags New Jersey!—a trip to Cedar Point requires planning. A short hop from Sandusky, it's almost impossible to miss. Simply follow the signs for Cedar Point Causeway. Other parks have mushroomed around Cedar Point as well.

where to go

Cedar Point Amusement Park. One Cedar Point Drive, Sandusky, OH 44870. For over a decade, Cedar Point has been the "Golden Ticket," according to the trade industry magazine

Amusement Today. And the one-and-a-half-square mile behemoth keeps growing. Recent acquisitions include Planet Snoopy, several rides and entertainments specifically geared for the younger set; Maverick, its seventeenth coaster, two-and-a-half minutes of cardiac arrest, er, speed, wild turns and the world's first Twisted Horseshoe Roll; and the maXair ride, a 70 mph whirligig suspended in midair. Not having fun yet? They've also added the Cedar Point and Lake Erie Railroad, an authentic steam-powered journey through the park; a parasail/Jet Ski experience; a paddlewheel excursion, and more. So there's something for everyone, from couch potatoes to daredevils, and all ages and gradation in between. Open daily mid-May through the first weekend of September; weekends September through October. Best times to visit are Tuesday through Thursday in May and June. Admission is charged. (419) 627–2350; www.cedarpoint.com.

Soak City Water Park. One Cedar Point Drive, Sandusky, OH 44870. Here you can get in touch with your inner tube. This eighteen-acre complex next to the Point has slides such as the mammoth Zoom Fume, a wave pool, rafting rivers, and three children's play areas. Or you can go Main Stream with a calm tube ride or get jolted and jarred while traveling down Renegade River. Along with a twenty-one-and-over swim-up bar, the entire family can enjoy picnic shelters for land and food breaks. Open daily from the end of May through the first weekend of September. Admission is charged. (419) 627–2350; www.cedarpoint.com.

Challenge Park. One Cedar Point Drive, Sandusky, OH 44870. Not had enough towering coasters and terrifying rides? Throw yourself into the stomach-churning Skyscraper, a giant propeller consisting of two spinning arms going 55 mph, 160 feet above the ground. You can also purchase a video of this lunch-losing encounter for posterity. For a near-roadkill experience, there's the Rip Cord, a super-bungee that involves being tethered to an aircraft cable, hoisted up a 15-story launch tower, having the rip cord released, and speeding toward the ground at 65 mph, stopping a mere 6 feet from certain pulverization. A race park, a raft of video games, and miniature golf round out the head spinning array of offerings. Open daily mid-May through the first weekend of September; weekends September through October. Fee depends upon option chosen. (419) 627–2350; www.cedarpoint.com

Kalahari Resorts. 7000 Kalahari Drive, Sandusky, Ohio 44870. Those surfing for a less frenetic safari can catch the waves (literally) at huge pools, a lazy river, tube slides, body slides, family raft rides, interactive play areas for the little fishes, and many other offerings both indoors and out. Almost a country itself—a small one anyway—it's one of America's largest indoor waterparks. Be a dictator for a day (or more) by taking advantage of cabanas with amenities like flat-screen TVs and iPod docking stations; African-themed hotel guest rooms and suites; restaurants; and spa services. Get your feet wet on the Wild Wildebeest and Zimbabwe Zipper, then go have them massaged and pedicured. Open daily; outdoor waterpark open Memorial Day to Labor Day, weather permitting. Admission is charged. $$$. (877) 525–2427, www.kalahariresorts.com.

Ghostly Manor. 3319 Milan Road, Sandusky, OH 44870. Why wait until Halloween to get your fright on? This haunted mansion features state-of-the-art technology, with lots of gore, skeletons, and dead things grabbing at you from behind dark corners. An intense and very noisy 3D motion simulator ride allows you to choose your favorite movie or select them all for a discount. There's also a roller skating rink (disco ball included) and Halloween gift shop with "scary" good deals on masks, skull T-shirts and other necessities. The haunted mansion is not recommended for children 9 and under, so if you have kids that age who misbehave at Cedar Point, this might be an alternative to "time out," as long as you're willing to pay for therapy later on. Hours depend on the attraction chosen. Admission is charged. (419) 626–4467, www.ghostlymanor.com.

where to eat

Listed here are some of the many restaurants located on or near the Cedar Point property. Unless otherwise designated, most are only open when the park is operating. Unless otherwise noted, call (419) 627–2350 for more information.

Bay Harbor. A bit more upscale and also next to the waterfront, the Bay Harbor serves a wide variety of fresh seafood, fish specials, steaks, and chops. Although open year-round for dinner, it's closed for lunch. No swimsuits, cutoffs, or tank tops allowed. $$$. (419) 625–6373.

Breakwater Cafe. Adjacent to the Sandcastle Suites, this waterfront site serves up three squares ranging from pasta to steak, all with a terrific view of Lake Erie. Selections are available for kids, and there's a lounge for the adults that serves cocktails along with great sunsets. $$.

The Coffee Shop. This spot, located in the Hotel Breakers, is ideal for a quick meal or late-night snack. You can choose from breakfast, sandwiches, pizza, and more. Early birds might get to meet the Peanuts gang (during the season only). $$.

Famous Dave's Legendary Pit Bar-B-Que. Stop by the Cedar Point marina for award-winning St. Louis-style ribs and other BBQ delights. A variety of luncheon and dinner entrees ranging from deluxe salads to chicken and burgers to desserts are available, as are adult beverages. $$. (419) 609–2054.

Tomo Hibachi Sushi at Cedar Point that's not the walleye from Lake Erie? This newest entry (and entrees), also at the Hotel Breakers, appears to have "caught" on, with both cooked and raw menu items. Tables are set up hibiachi-style, so the cook can prepare the food in front of you. They may go so far as to squirt sake into your mouth, as long as you can show your ID. $$.

vino ohio

Believe it or not, many wines actually originate in Ohio; it's estimated the state has some 2,200 acres of grapes, and counting. And with well over 100 wineries, the state's $75 million industry is expanding as well, recession be darned. Oddly, many wineries can be found in the northern corner of the state, where the winters are most notorious. So you don't have to travel to California or Italy to visit wine country; according to the Ohio Wine Producers Association (33 Tegam Way, Geneva, OH 44041, 440–466–4417, www.ohiowines.org), there are six wine trails to choose from, including those in the far northeast corner of Ohio, in the Columbus area, in the Akron/Youngstown region, and in southeast and southwest Ohio as well. Below is just a taste of the many in and around the Lake Erie region. Bottoms up!

- **Firelands Wine Co.** *917 Bardshar Road, Sandusky, OH 44870. After a hard day at Cedar Point, a glass or two of vino sounds awfully tempting from Ohio's oldest and largest winery, whose history dates back to the Revolutionary War. The wines are comparable to their French and Italian counterparts without the attendant travel and potential for snobbery. Along with an extensive list offering everything from Gewürztraminer (bless you!) to rose, Firelands has garnered numerous awards and accolades for their Pino Grigios, Reislings, and cabernets. This is one sample sale that should leave you smiling. Please allow 1 to 1½ hours for tour and tasting. (419) 625–5474, www.firelandswinery.com.*

- **Mon Ami Restaurant and Historic Winery.** *3845 East Wine Cellar Road, Port Clinton, OH 43452. Here you can truly "wine and dine." Built in the 1870s as a winery, it has expanded into two restaurants. Along with tastings, you can tour historic cellars and learn the secrets of making your own. Then chow down in the more casual Chalet or dine formally. Offerings range from Lake Erie catches to steak to pasta. (800) 777–4266; www.monamiwinery.com.*

- **Heineman's Winery.** *P.O. Box 300, 978 Catawba Avenue, Put-in-Bay, OH 43456. Established in 1888, this business has been "all in the family" since then. Along with receiving a complimentary glass of the award-winning wines (or grape juice for the kids), you can also visit Crystal Cave, at 30 feet wide, arguably the world's largest geode. Made of bluish white celestite crystal, it was accidentally discovered a few years after the winery opened. Two for the price of one! Admission is charged. (419) 285–2811; www.heinemans winery.com.*

- **Kelleys Island Wine Company.** *418 Woodford Road, Kelleys Island, OH 43438. Spend a relaxing few hours sampling the fruits of European hybrid grapes. In addition to a nifty gift shop with gourmet and wine accessories, it also features a deli with cheese and sausage platters, sandwiches, pizza, and wraps. (419) 746–2678; www.kelleysislandwine.com.*

- **Pelee Island Winery.** *455 Seacliff Drive, Kingsville, ON N9Y 2K5. Open since 1979, this popular attraction not only bills itself as Canada's largest estate winery, but also hosts tours, tastings, and events, including barbecues, live bands, and (Canadian) holiday celebrations. The pavilion and vineyards are located on Pelee; the production facilities are in Canada. You can purchase their ever-expanding vintage online or on-site. Open May to mid-October. Admission charged for tours only. (800) 597–3533; www.peleeisland.com.*

where to stay

Greentree Inn. 1935 Cleveland Road, Sandusky, OH 44870. This hotel is about as close to the Point as you can get without actually staying on the grounds. There's something for all in the family: an indoor heated pool, whirlpool, and fitness center, plus a bowling alley with arcade games and snack bar. Bonus: Glitter Glow bowling, a laser light and sound show in the evenings. It's also home to Cedar Downs restaurant and sports bar. $$–$$$. (800) 654–3364.

Great Wolf Lodge. 4600 Milan Road, Sandusky, OH 44870. In case you get really stuck for something to do—not likely if kids are involved—this hotel/indoor water park combo offers 271 luxury suites, a 4-story atrium lobby, two restaurants, and planned kids' activities to give Mom and Dad a respite. For the youngsters (and perhaps not-so) there are seven slides, five pools, two hot tubs, a twelve-level tree fort, and about one-hundred arcade games. So it can be snowing outside—or worse—and everyone can have fun. $$$. (800) 641–9653; www.greatwolflodge.com/sandusky/waterpark.

Cedar Point Resorts. Except for Castaway Bay which is year-round, the lodgings listed here operate seasonally. The mailing address is One Cedar Point Drive, Sandusky, OH 44870. Unless otherwise noted, the phone number for reservations is (419) 627–2106. Call ahead for special weekend packages that can provide discounts.

- **Castaway Bay.** 2001 Cleveland Road, Sandusky, OH. Every day is Friday—yes, there's a T.G.I. Friday's on site—and it's a Caribbean-themed waterpark, too! A short drive from the main park, the 38,000-square-foot waterganza does it up Cedar-Point style with a water coaster, wave pool, slides, children's areas and a 6,000-square-foot game room in case you have any spare change left over. Many of the remodeled guest rooms include connecting rooms and suites with a private patio or balcony and all have a refrigerator and microwave. $$$.

- **Hotel Breakers.** Those looking for the turn-of-the-twentieth-century leisurely ambience need search no further. The hotel, which is rapidly approaching its first one hundred years of operation, also has amenities such as an indoor pool, a beach, and several restaurants. With 650 rooms, it's the second largest hotel in Ohio. A variety of accommodations is available, from single rooms in the main hotel to large suites with Jacuzzis in the recently added Breakers East and Tower. $$$.

- **Breakers Express.** Although it's geared for the budget-minded family, this nicely maintained property offers a game room, coin-operated washers and dryers, and an outdoor pool shaped like Snoopy. Pricewise, it's also the best deal on the Cedar Point property. $$-$$$. (419) 627–2109.

- **Sandcastle Suites Hotel.** It's water, water, everywhere, although you can get to the Point from this far-from-the-madding-crowd property by walking. There's plenty of beach, along with tennis courts, volleyball court, sundeck, and outdoor heated pool. Each suite has its own screened-in patio or balcony. $$$.

- **Camper Village.** For those who prefer to bring their own—RV accommodations, that is. Each site has electricity, a charcoal grill, and a picnic table, along with a nearby convenience store for those last-minute supplies. An outdoor pool, recreation area, and arcade are close by and the beach and the park are within walking distance. $.

day trip 02

north

lake erie islands:
port clinton • put-in-bay and middle bass island • kelleys island • pelee island • lakeside and marblehead

What's up, dock? Plenty, particularly if you like fishing and boating. The Lake Erie island area is a sporting paradise, even during the cold months, when ice fishing happens. Thanks to high nutrient levels and warm temperatures, its shores teem with walleye, smallmouth bass, yellow perch, freshwater drum, crappie, white bass, and more. Don't forget to purchase a fishing license (among other places, at the Ohio Division of Wildlife, 305 East Shoreline Drive, Sandusky), and be cognizant of the daily limits, which vary according to type of fish.

The area's also chock-full of bird brains: herons and egrets as well as migratory warblers to the tune of more than 300 species. Prime spots include Kelleys Island and South Bass Island. For information on "Wing Watches" and hotels accommodating birders, contact the Erie County Visitors Bureau at (800) 255–3743; www.shoresandislands.com.

There are also enough restaurants, shopping, and historical sites to keep even the most seasoned traveler occupied. You can party at the bustling town of Put-in-Bay and on Kelleys Island, or have fun with the whole family at parks, monuments, and museums. Once you arrive, getting around the islands is made easy by a variety of bike and golf-cart rental companies, which are usually located within walking distance of the ferry.

getting there

First, however, you need to reach the island of your choice. Short of purchasing or renting a boat, ferries are the only option. Some depart directly from Sandusky, while others

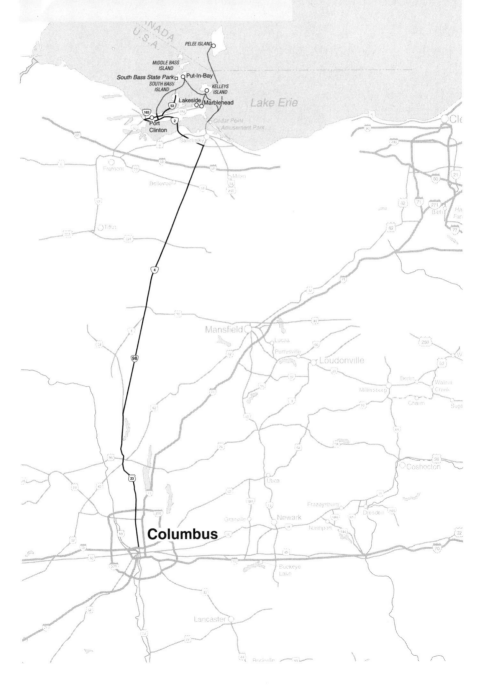

north day trip 02

PELEE ISLAND

MIDDLE BASS ISLAND

South Bass State Park Put-In-Bay
SOUTH BASS ISLAND   KELLEYS ISLAND

Lakeside Marblehead

Lake Erie

Port Clinton

Cedar Point Amusement Park

Cle

CANADA U.S.A.

Fremont

Bellevue

Tiffin

Mansfield

Lucas
Perrysville
Loudonville

Coshocton

Utica

Frazeysburg
Dresden

Granville   Newark

Columbus

Buckeye Lake

Lancaster

embark from Port Clinton (west) or Marblehead (east) just over the Bay Bridge, which splits off at Route 2. Most of the ferry services listed below operate seasonally and may not run as frequently during wintertime. Call ahead to check schedules, many of which are also available online. Ferries accepting autos and other vehicles are also noted. All charge a fee.

Goodtime I. Take Route 4 North into downtown Sandusky. Left onto Water Street, then right on Jackson Street. Right on Shoreline Drive and the dock is straight ahead on the left. Free parking. Departs from Sandusky, Ohio Tuesday through Saturday on a daytime island hopping cruise, as well as other specialty cruises. Also available for private charters, and seasonal special excursions. (800) 446–3140; www.goodtimeboat.com.

Jet Express. 3 North Monroe Street, Port Clinton, OH 43452. Hydrojet catamarans provide transportation to downtown Put-in-Bay. (800) 245–1538, www.jet-express.com.

Miller Boat Line. End of SR 53 north off SR 2 at Catawba. Mailing address: P.O. Box 239, Put-in-Bay, OH 43456. Auto/ passenger trips to Put-in-Bay, South Bass Island, and Middle Bass Island. (800) 500–2421; www.millerferry.com.

Passenger and auto transportation to Kelleys Island every half hour can be found via the following:

Kelleys Island Ferry. 510 West Main Street, Marblehead, OH 43440; (419) 798–9763; www.kelleysislandferry.com.

port clinton

A key link in the Lake Erie chain, mainland-bound Port Clinton serves as a base for many excursions. The town has its own unique charm, however. The top of a restored lighthouse sits in the marina, and a picturesque stretch of sandy shore located along the main drag is a popular beach. The downtown area is also undergoing revitalization, so you might be able to get a cappuccino and bagel while waiting for the ferry.

To get to Port Clinton from Columbus, head north on U.S. 23 to SR 98, which turns into SR 4 at Bucyrus, then head west on SR 2.

where to go

African Safari Wildlife Park. 267 Lightner Road, Port Clinton, OH 43452. Want to start your seafaring adventures on land? Here you can view giraffes, zebras, and other exotic animals from your car, ride on a camel, and even watch a pig race and other shows featuring critters. Open daily April through October. Admission is charged. (800) 521–2660; www .africansafariwildlifepark.com.

Shore-Nuf Charters. Drawbridge Marina. 247 Lakeshore Drive, Port Clinton, OH 43452. Flexible offerings allow for "walk-ins" (individuals who want to fish on a boat) as well as charter groups of twelve or more. Schedules vary, but most activities take place April through October. Fee is charged. (419) 734–9999; www.shore-nuf.com.

Fisherman's Wharf. 83 North Madison Street, Port Clinton, OH 43452. This family-owned and -operated business not only has a bait and tackle store for all the necessary supplies but also offers several different kinds of boats for larger groups and smaller expeditions. Call for schedules and times, which vary according to season. Fee is charged. (419) 734–0488; www.wecatchfish.com.

Island Adventures Family Fun Center. 280 SE Catawba Road (Rt. 53N), Port Clinton, Ohio 43452. Choose from 18 holes of miniature golf, a go-kart race course, a bumper-boat lagoon complete with water pistols, sifting for gemstones and fossils and more. Ideal for those with short attention spans. Open weekends in May; varying hours June–Aug. Fee is charged. (419) 732–2020; www.island-adventures.net.

Monsoon Lagoon Water Park. 1530 S. Danbury Road, N. Port Clinton, OH 43452. It's Port Clinton's answer to Soak City, with over 300,000 square feet of water, water everywhere. Choose from six waterslides, including the three-stories-tall Typhoon Rush Slide Tower. The Adventure Island Tree House boasts 105 water play stations on 17 different levels. Kids can splash and play in the Little Squirts Play Pool, while those over age twenty-one can soak their cares away in an adult pool with a swim-up bar. Open May–Sept. Hours vary. Admission is charged. (419) 732–6671; www.monsoonlagoonwater park.com.

where to eat

Rum Runners Sports Bar. 102 Madison Street, Port Clinton, OH 43452. This trendy renovation of a longtime watering hole features burgundy, black-and-yellow décor and broadcasts of various sporting events on multiple flat-screen TVs. Some of the original ambiance remains, such as a bullet hole in the ceiling courtesy of a circa-1880s sheriff. The menu is a lineup of the usual suspects of chicken strips, wings, nachos sandwiches and more. $$. (419) 734–0100; www.islandhouseportclinton.com.

New Island House Restaurant and Lounge. 102 Madison Street, Port Clinton, OH 43452. Another alternative is "old school" at this fine dining, white tablecloth establishment. The varied menu includes locally raised beef like NY strip and filet mignon as well as lighter offerings. And it wouldn't be "Erie" unless the menu had perch, walleye, shrimp, and other seafood and fish. $$–$$$. (419) 734–0100; www.islandhouseportclinton.com.

The Garden at the Lighthouse. 226 E.Perry & Adams. Formerly a lighthouse keeper's home, this scenic eatery overlooking Lake Erie has become a favorite with locals and tourists alike. Attire is anything goes, and can range from jeans to formal although full frontal nudity is usually relegated to Put-in-Bay. An extensive wine list and menu are complemented by daily specials. Great service and decadent desserts also keep 'em coming back. $$$. (419) 732–2151.

where to stay

Island House Inn. 102 Madison Street, Port Clinton, OH 43452. Designed to be the most elegant "gentleman's hotel" in Lake Erie, this circa 1886 structure has been completely renovated with upscale touches such as plush beds and flat-screen TVs and is now a "condotel" where guests can own individual rooms for personal use or rental. Room sizes vary from double to king suite; choose from a variety of packaged trips, from romantic escape, island hopper, adventure and more. Two restaurants (Rum Runners Sports Bar and New Island House Restaurant and Lounge) complete the self-contained experience. End of September through mid-May, $–$$; mid-May through mid-September, $$–$$$. (419) 734–0100; www .islandhouseportclinton.com.

Our Guest Inn and Suites. 220 E. Perry Street, Port Clinton, OH 43452. This unique setup offers a smorgasbord of accommodations, including standard issue with queens or doubles, Jacuzzi suites with fireplaces, even Victorian homes with vintage-era furnishings. There's a heated outdoor pool, restaurant, and in some spaces, full kitchens. Many rooms have microwaves and refrigerators. Special packages, such as bird watchers, women's weekends, and romantic getaways are also available. $$–$$$. (419) 734–7111; www.our guestinn.com.

put-in-bay and middle bass island

Put-in-Bay, on South Bass Island, started out as a sheep ranch in the 1850s. Along with several other Lake Erie Islands, it became a center for grape growing and wine making and by the turn of that century, a popular visitor destination. It was also the site of a key battle during the War of 1812, where U.S. troops were led by Commodore Oliver Hazard Perry. Today Put-in-Bay is party central, with plenty of bars and other adventures to choose from. In contrast, Middle Bass Island's tranquil atmosphere and rugged, natural landscape is so laid back you might have to pinch yourself to make sure you're still breathing, especially since Middle Bass Island State Park is in the process of being renovated and there's not much to see—yet. So you pretty much have to make your own fun.

where to go

Perry's Victory and International Peace Memorial. Near the ferry ramps. Mailing address: Bayview Avenue, P.O. Box 549, Put-in-Bay, OH 43456. If he who dies with the tallest monument wins, then Commodore Oliver Hazard Perry comes in third in the United States, thanks to his victory over the Brits in 1813. In order to get to the top of this 352-foot-high structure, you need to climb thirty-seven steps on a winding circular stairway to an elevator. But the view is worth the effort, especially on a clear day. A newly constructed visitor center offers interactive displays, memorabilia, a video theater, and live Web-cam shots of the monument, among other things. Open daily from mid-May to mid-October, other times by appointment. Admission is charged. (419) 285–2184; nps.gov/pevi.

Kimberly's Carousel. Delaware Avenue, Put-in-Bay, OH 43456. A must for the young, no matter what age. With band organ music and a red-and-white-striped top, this Allen Herschell machine is one of the last operating carousels in the United States with all-wooden horses. It's also decorated with various scenes from around the area. Rides cost only $1.00, although that can be subject to inflation. Open seasonally. (419) 285–2212.

Aquatic Resource Center. Located at Peach Point, off West Shore Boulevard. Mailing address: P.O. Box 38, Put-in-Bay, OH 43456. Operated by the Ohio Division of Wildlife, this attraction offers live fish exhibits, hands-on displays, children's activities, and (of course) free fishing on the dock. Open May through August; closed Monday. Free. (419) 285–3701 or 424–5000.

Stonehenge Estate. 808 Langram Road, Put-in-Bay, OH 43456. This restored farmhouse and winepress cottage is nestled on seven acres of landscaped grounds and furnished with antiques, photographs, and memorabilia. Visitors get a sense of wine growing during the 1800s, plus there's a cool gift shop with kaleidoscopes, bronze sculptures, porcelain signs, antique crafts, and more. Open daily during the summer. Admission is charged. (419) 285–2585; www.stonehenge-put-in-bay.com.

Lake Erie Island Historical Society. 25 Town Hall Place, P.O. Box 25, Put-in-Bay, OH 43456. Founded in 1985 by folks interested in preserving their heritage, this 6,000-square-foot center not only offers a wide variety of exhibits but provides several educational programs. Displays cover ice sailing and fishing, wineries and vineyards, ships, lighthouse lenses, ferryboat history, and more. Models, postcards, photographs, and original documents help bring the past to life. Hours vary; call ahead during the off-season. Free, but donations are welcome. (419) 285–2804; www.leihs.org.

Perry's Cave and Family Fun Center. P.O. Box 708, 979 Catawba Avenue, Put-in-Bay, OH 43456. This attraction has something for everyone. Discovered in 1813 by Commodore Perry, it's historically significant: His men drank from the underground lake to help cure their ills. Geologically, it's 52 feet below the surface and remains a steady 50 degrees, no matter what it's like outside. Walls, ceiling, and floor are heavily encrusted with calcium carbon-ate, the result of centuries of drippage, a sort of eternal Chinese water torture. After-hours lantern tours are also available, and as an added bonus, you can sift for real gems! Finds may include rose quartz, topaz, moonstone, ruby, and more. Open daily during the summer. Admission charged. (419) 285–2405; www.perryscave.com.

Chocolate Museum. 820 Catawba Avenue, Put-in-Bay, OH 43456. Here you can indulge yourself while pretending to learn about history; the history of chocolate-making that is. Okay, so it's really an excuse to sample 100 different kinds of chocolate, including several sugar-free varieties for "dieters" (yeah, right). Coffee happens as well, including espresso, cappuccinos, lattes and mochas for double or triple the caffeine. Alcohol can also become involved with martinis, mudslides, and more at the so-called "chocolate bar." Open May–Sept. Free. (419) 734–7114; www.chocolateohio.com.

Island Tour Train. 2071 Langram Road, Put-in-Bay, OH 43456. This one-hour narrated tour of Put-in-Bay hits the high spots—Perry's Cave Family Fun Center, Heineman Winery, Crystal Cave, and Perry's Victory and International Peace Memorial. You can get off and on at the various attractions and explore them at leisure. Once that's out of the way, it's onto the bars. . . . Open May until the end of the season. Fee is charged. (419) 285–4855; www.put-in-bay-trans.com.

where to eat

The Round House Bar. P.O. Box 60, Put-in-Bay, OH 43456. The history of this restau-rant, established in 1873, is as circuitous as its design. Some claim it was built in Toledo, while others insist it was constructed on the island. In the 1940s the circular bar was cut in half so the owner/piano player could play facing a full audience. The rollicking ambience is accentuated by red decor and murals painted by a late local artist known as Canoe Bob. $$. (419) 285–2323; www.theroundhousebar.com.

The Skyway Restaurant and Lounge. P.O. Box 717, Langram Road, Put-in-Bay, OH 43456. This restaurant caters to all preferences and budgets, from inexpensive lunches to elaborate clambakes. The martini menu includes variations such as saketinis and chocolate raspberry flavors for those who prefer liquid lunches or dinners. Dinner offers a full range of gourmet soups and appetizers, in addition to entrees. $–$$$. (419) 285–4331.

The Boathouse Bar and Grill. Hartford Avenue. Put-in-Bay, OH 43456. With the same name and approximate location, this new structure offers outdoor seating, a view of the park and downtown, and a menu that is sandwich and local-catch intensive. Six original vessels are also hanging around at various points on the ceiling and above the bar, with the latter being a relatively rare "Iron Clad," which was used by the current owner's grandfather. $$. (419) 285–5665; www.theboathousebarandgrill.com.

Axel & Harry's Waterfront Grille. 1618 Bayview Avenue, Put-in-Bay, OH 43456. Tired of the maddening crowd? Put-in-Bay's take on fine dining serves up fresh seafood, steaks, and wine on a spacious patio overlooking Lake Erie. There's also live entertainment of the rehearsed kind, as opposed to the performance art that happens frequently at other Put-in-Bay bars. $$$. (419) 285–2572; www.axelandharryswaterfrontgrille.com.

Beer Barrel Saloon. 1618 Delaware Avenue, Put-in-Bay, OH 43456. Or take advantage of the free show at the world's longest bar, which has 56 beer taps and a seating capacity of 1,200. Be aware, however, that once you shoulder your way inside, you may encounter women who arbitrarily pull up their shirts and bare their breasts. Hey, maybe that's why it's always so jam-packed! $–$$. (419) 285–7281; www.beerbarrelpib.com.

J. F. Walleye's Eatery and Brewery. 1810 Fox Road, Middle Bass, OH 43446. A recent fire gutted the original structure, and they rebuilt with a vengeance. The snazzy-looking interior includes cathedral ceilings and light wood decor, as well as an extended menu covering salads, sandwiches, pizzas, wings, and all manner of bar food. Karaoke fans can breathe a sigh of relief: The owner plans on continuing that long-running tradition. $$. (419) 285–2739; www.jfwalleyes.net.

Hazard's Restaurant and Microbrewery. 1223 Fox Road, Middle Bass, OH 43446. When worlds collide, the result can be extremely eclectic. Along with bamboo walls, outside torches, and a tiki bar, this eatery has oak doors and wooden furnishings from Cleveland's old Municipal football stadium. $$. (800) 837–5211; www.sthazards.com.

where to stay

Perry Holiday Hotel. 99 Concord Avenue, Put-in-Bay, OH 43456. With restaurants, tennis courts, public docks, a nine-hole golf course, and more, this fifty-two-unit hotel will round out any getaway. Plus you can walk to just about every attraction, restaurant, and shop on the island. $$–$$$. (419) 285–2107; www.perryholidayhotel.com.

Park Hotel. P.O. Box 60, Delaware Avenue, Put-in-Bay, OH 43456. The good news: The rooms in this restored Victorian hotel have been individually decorated and air-conditioned, and there's a large front porch where you can sit and watch all the activity downtown. The not-so-good news: There are separate men's and women's bathroom facilities on each floor, harking back to those college dorm days. $$–$$$. (419) 285–3581; www.park hotelpib.com.

Islander Inn. 225 Erie Street, Put-in-Bay, OH 43456. This hotel caters to all ages and stages of life. Its H2O diversions include a kids' pool with a slide, a swim-up bar, a water-fall, and a thirty-person Jacuzzi. Satellite TV and a lunch counter complete the offerings. $$–$$$. (877) 500–7829; www.islandinnpib.com.

St. Hazards on the Beach. 1223 Fox Road, Middle Bass, OH 43446. Those searching for the Caribbean need look no further. With a fountain of dyed blue-green water, artificial palm trees, a pool, and a restaurant, this is about as close as you can get to Jimmy Buffet-tland without jumping aboard an island-hopper. Villas, cabins, and campsites are available; one-bedroom chateaus accommodate up to six people. You must furnish your own linens and towels; cabins lack a private bath. Villas, $$–$$$; chateaus, $$–$$$; cabins, $–$$; campsites, $. (800) 837–5211; www.sthazards.com.

Bayshore Resort. 328 Toledo Avenue, Put-in-Bay, Ohio 43456. The only lakefront hotel at Put-in-Bay, this relatively new accommodation covers almost three acres. All rooms have water views and there are two heated swimming pools, a poolside tiki bar, and a 30-person Jacuzzi spa (talk about getting up close and personal with strangers!). Those looking for a fine dining experience on site will find it at the Waterfront Restaurant and Grill. Or it's a short walk to Put-in-Bay and all its attendant delights/revelries. $$$. (866) 422–9746; www .bayshoreresortpib.com.

kelleys island

Kelleys Island lurks somewhere between wild 'n crazy Put-in-Bay and slo-mo Middle Bass. The largest of the Lake Erie Islands is dominated by natural areas, with rocky shorelines, beaches—which may or may not be pristine, depending on the time of year and who is inhabiting them—forests, vineyards, and historical homes. The pace of life is unhurried and at times golf carts and bicycles outnumber cars. Shopping is low-key too, heavy on the tchotchkes and other assorted knickknacks and restaurants/nightlife consist of mostly casual places, some with Karaoke. What better diversion from texting, Twittering, and Facebook?

where to go

Glacial Grooves. North side of the island, off Division Street, near Kelley Island Camp-ground. Fans of erosion might enjoy this. One of the largest and most easily accessible geological phenomena of its type, this limestone bedrock was formed about 18,000 years ago by passing ice, resulting in a 400-foot-long, 35-foot-wide, and, in places, 10-foot-deep incision in the earth. The limestone contains marine fossils between 350 and 400 million years old. Open year-round, daylight hours. Free. (419) 797–4530.

Inscription Rock State Memorial. South shore of the island, by East Lakeshore Drive. Looking for more excitement? This flat-topped limestone rock has faint pictographs of men, birds, and animals. Archaeologists believe they were inscribed by Erie Indians between 400 and 800 years ago. Eroded by the elements, the rock is now protected by a roof and has a viewing platform. Open year-round, daylight hours. Free. (419) 797–4530.

where to shop

Anneliese's Treasure Chest. 212 Division Street, Kelleys Island, OH 43438. Here you can browse for gifts and memorabilia, including the popular Kelleys Island afghan, while listening to an old player piano. Selections include nautical items and the work of local artists. (419) 746–2821; www.kelleysisland.com/treasurechest.

Kelleys Cove. 108 West Lakeshore, Kelleys Island, OH 43438. Specialties include Cat's Meow designs, Harbor Lights collectibles, and Ben Richmond art, along with depictions of Lake Erie in other media. Bonus: You can purchase fishing licenses and supplies here and rent a condo, if so inclined. (419) 746–2622; www.kelleysisland.com/kelleyscove.

Vi's Island Treasures. 125 Division Street, Kelleys Island, OH 43438. The newest, just-remodeled addition to the local gift array features everything from gold and sterling jewelry to sunglasses, with frogs by Kitty Critters, snowmen by Willaraye, American Chestnut figurines, clothing, nautical gifts, McCall's candles, and more. (419) 746–2268.

where to eat

The Village Pump. 103 Lakeshore Drive, Kelleys Island, OH 43438. A favorite with both locals and "summer people," this watering hole offers hand-dipped onion rings, perch by the pound, and other specialties. Brandy Alexanders and mudslides made with ice cream are a favorite of the over-twenty-one set. $$. (419) 746–2281.

Bag the Moon. 109 Lakeshore Drive, Kelleys Island, OH 43438. Along with daily specials, popular offerings include ribs, steak, and perch. Thanks to live entertainment and sing-alongs, the whole family can party, although only those of legal age can partake of their signature strawberry shots. $$. (419) 746–2365.

The Kelleys Island Brewery. 504 Lakeshore Drive, Kelleys Island, OH 43438. Located dockside, it's grub with a view, including handcrafted beer; full breakfast, lunch, and dinner menus; and friendly people, not to mention great ice cream. $–$$. (419) 746–2314; www .kelleysislandbrewpub.com.

The Casino Restaurant & Marina. 104 Division Street, Kelleys Island, OH 43438. Take a gamble and dock here, by boat, foot, or other vehicle. There's a full menu, indoor/outdoor dining with great sunset views, and the "Casino Royale" cocktail, James Bond not included. The place really comes alive after sunset, with a hopping bar scene. Let the games begin! $–$$. (419) 746–2773; www.kelleysislandcasino.com.

where to stay

Kelleys Island State Park. North side of the island, 920 Division Street, Kelleys Island, OH, 43438. Along with a sandy beach and prime fishing and bird-watching, this park has about 150 campsites, although only a few provide electric hookups. Shower- and bathhouses are located throughout. It's first come, first served and fills up quickly during weekends and peak season. $. (419) 797–4530; (419) 746–2546 seasonally.

Kelleys Island Venture Resort. 441 West Lakeshore Drive, Kelleys Island, OH 43438. This property combines the hominess of a B&B with the privacy of a hotel. Choose from a variety of suites, from the first-floor "Glacier" with a divided living room and sleeping area to the luxe Cunningham, three bedrooms and two baths with a fully equipped kitchen. Tucked amid landscaped rock garden and waterfall are a swimming pool and hot tub combo; spectacular views abound, and include Lake Erie, Marblehead Peninsula, and, on a clear day, Cedar Point. $$–$$$. (419) 746–2900; www.kiventureresort.com.

A Water's Edge Retreat B &B. 827 E. Lakeshore Drive, Kelleys Island, OH 43438. Sail away to this classic B&B which has been featured on the *Today* show, in *Travel & Leisure,* and the *Chicago Tribune,* among many others. A Victorian atmosphere with antiques and period furniture combine with the necessities (the hosts refer to them as "conveniences") of a private bath; central air and a gourmet (read: fattening) breakfast feast provide a chance to get acquainted with fellow travelers. Spend the rest of the day walking or running off the calories exploring the island and swimming, hiking, kayaking, and more. Bonus: a cruise is included on a 35-foot-yacht with a Master USCG captain. $$$. (800) 884–5143; www .watersedgeretreat.com.

pelee island

Those looking to wander farther north can cross over into Canadian waters to Pelee Island. Unlike the other Lake Erie Islands, "wild life" here usually involves four-legged activity rather than two. Florida Keys, only with a winter coat and no Key West, this sedate 10,000-acre playground offers bicycling, water sports, and hiking. Fishing and bird-watching opportunities abound in such easily accessible places as Lighthouse Point (northeastern tip of Pelee) and Fish Point (southwestern spit), site of the Pelee Island Bird Observatory, a major stopover for black-crowned night herons and other winged travelers. Romantics wanting to visit Hulda's Rock should probably read the poem about the Indian maiden found at www .pelee.org. Otherwise it's just another big stone sitting the middle of the water. And don't forget to bring your passport/identification papers, in case ICE (Immigration and Customs Enforcement) thinks you're making a run for the border!

where to go

Pelee Island Heritage Center. 1073 West Shore Road, Pelee Island, ON N0R 1M0. Although its goals are lofty: "to research, collect and preserve the evidence of the Island's (and neighbors') human history, to protect the community's natural heritage, and to educate the public" there's some pretty interesting stuff here. These include exhibits with artifacts from the first settlers, the history of ice travel and commercial fishing, the battle of Pelee

Island, womens' contributions, shipwrecks, and more. Open daily, May 1–Oct. 1. Fee is charged. (519) 724–2291; www.peleeislandmuseum.ca.

Kite Museum. Located in the Pelee Island Heritage Center. Rather than go fly a kite, the curator and his family decided to display some 4,900 of them. Kites of various sizes shapes, colors and manufacturers are stockpiled into several rooms and include early twentieth century Stieffs and paper kites; kites used in advertising; as well as those from England, Asia, and the Far and Middle East. The museum opened in 2008, so they're looking for more rare birds to add to the high-flying collection. Fee is included in Heritage Center admission. No phone; info@thekitemuseum.com; www.kitemuseum.com.

where to eat and where to stay

The Gathering Place. West Shore Road, Pelee Island, ON N0R 1M0. One of the Island's original limestone structures, this historic bed-and-breakfast provides a library, fireplace, and screened-in porch, as well as access to the beach. $$–$$$. (519) 724–2656.

It's Home. 1431 East Shore Road, Pelee Island, ON N0R 1M0. This relaxing bed-and-breakfast offers four bedrooms, a private sitting room, and full and continental breakfasts. You can chill out on the patio and watch the water, or participate in one of the island's many birding events. $–$$. (519) 724–2328.

The Anchor and Wheel Inn. 11 West Shore Drive, Pelee Island, ON N0R 1M0. This combo restaurant/B&B accommodates a wide range of budgets. Along with the inn itself—six private rooms with two shared bathrooms—there are cottages, a guest and a beach house, even camping. The Caribbean-themed restaurant is a popular local watering hole and includes a tiki bar and full-service menu. Accommodating visitors since 1899, when it was a boardinghouse, the present iteration was opened in 1977, which in these times, is testimony enough. $–$$$. (519) 724–2195; www.anchorwheelinn.com.

lakeside and marblehead

Circle back to the Western tip of the U.S. mainland and you'll find Lakeside and Marblehead. Dubbed the "Walleye Capital of the World," Marblehead, which is encompassed by the area's Western Basin, harvests 80 percent of all that species caught in Lake Erie. You can also find, on the south side of Bayshore Road, a battle marker for the War of 1812. One of the few remaining Chautauquas—retreats for a Methodist-based adult education movement founded in the late 1800s—Lakeside continues to be a popular draw for individuals and families seeking spiritual and intellectual renewal. Along with plenty of waterfront activity, this small town boasts a symphony and theater.

where to go

Marblehead Light House. 110 Lighthouse Drive, Marblehead, OH 43440. The oldest continuously operating lighthouse on Lake Erie, this 67-foot masonry and limestone landmark has been "beaconing" ships into Sandusky Bay since the early 1820s. Among its fifteen keepers were two women, including the widow of Benajah Wolcott, the original keeper. It's been restored several times and has been automated since 1958. Also surrounding the lighthouse are lakeside daisies, a tiny and rare protected species. Open Monday through Friday, June through September, and some Saturdays. Admission may be charged. (419) 734–4434.

Johnson's Island Confederate Officers Prison. 414 West Main Street, Marblehead, OH 43440. Off the causeway, from the southern edge of Marblehead Peninsula. Now a cemetery for the 201 soldiers who died there, the prison housed 9,000 Confederate officers, soldiers, and civilians during the Civil War. It originally consisted of thirteen barracks and a hospital, artifacts from which are scattered around local museums and historical societies. Open year-round. Small fee charged to cross the causeway. www.johnsonsisland.org.

where to stay

Hotel Lakeside and Fountain Inn. 236 Walnut Avenue, Lakeside, OH 43440. This property, on the National Register of Historic Places, offers a unique combination of the old and less-than-antiquated. Built during the Victorian era, the refurbished Hotel Lakeside has hosted two presidents, among other luminaries, and has many of the same furnishings used during that period. The newer Fountain Inn provides fifty-six rooms with private baths, carpeting, and air-conditioning. $$–$$$. (419) 798–4461, (866) 952–5374; www .lakesideohio.com.

Idlewyld Bed and Breakfast. 350 Walnut Avenue, Lakeside, OH 43440. This B&B has fifteen rooms, some with private baths. A large gathering/dining room is also available for workshops, meetings, or retreats. Includes a full English breakfast. $–$$. (419) 798–4198; www.idlewyldbb.com.

Keystone Guesthouse. 202 Maple Avenue, Lakeside, OH 43440. Although it was built in the late 1800s, this inn boasts full suites with kitchenettes and central air. It's also within walking distance to just about anywhere in town. $–$$. (419) 798–4263; (614) 204–6203.

Rainbow House Guest Cottage & Tea by the Sea Tea Room. 115 West Second Street, Lakeside, OH 43440. The charmer offers a combination of themed guest rooms with names like Lilac, Sunflower, and Summer Breeze, and afternoon tea with assorted dainty sandwiches, fruit, sherbet, desserts, and (but of course) tea. $. (419) 798–4255; www.rainbowhouse.us.

South Beach Resort. 8620 East Bayshore Road, Marblehead, OH 43440. Tired of B&Bs and all-night revelers? Then South Beach Resort may for you. Tucked away on a quiet part of Sandusky Bay, it consists of a four-story inn and eighteen cottages spread over eight and a half acres. Rooms have Jacuzzis and waterside views and cottages offer plenty of room for families. Other perks include a private beach, marina, three heated pools, tennis, volleyball, and even a sun deck built to look like a pirate ship for the kiddies. Fishing, slips for docking your boat, and a spa with massages are available. $$$. Hotel (419) 798–4900; cottages (419) 798–5503.

day trip 03

north

>>> it's history:
milan • bellevue • fremont • tiffin

This region's eclectic assortment highlights nineteenth-century pacesetters, railroad chronicles, a U.S. president, and glassmaking history mixed in with shopping and restaurants. Each town has a unique personality.

milan

Although it's mostly known as the birthplace of Thomas Alva Edison, this bright idea for a town was originally founded in 1816 as Merry's Mill, and by the middle of that century it was second only to Odessa, Russia, in wheat exportation. Milan also has the distinction of being a center of shipbuilding, a major hub for the formation of wagon trains heading west, and the home of Isaac Hoover, the area's most successful potato farmer. Hoover created and manufactured the Hoover Potato Digger (not to be confused with the vacuum cleaner of the same name, which was invented several miles east in North Canton).

This sparklingly maintained New England-inspired burg offers a nifty square with museums, shops, and nearby parks for hikes and more. It's less than 100 miles north of Columbus: Take I–270 north to U.S. 23 to SR 98, which turns into SR 4 at Bucyrus, then head east on the Ohio Turnpike (I–80/90) until you get to U.S. 250, which bisects the town shortly after turning south off the Turnpike.

north day trip 03

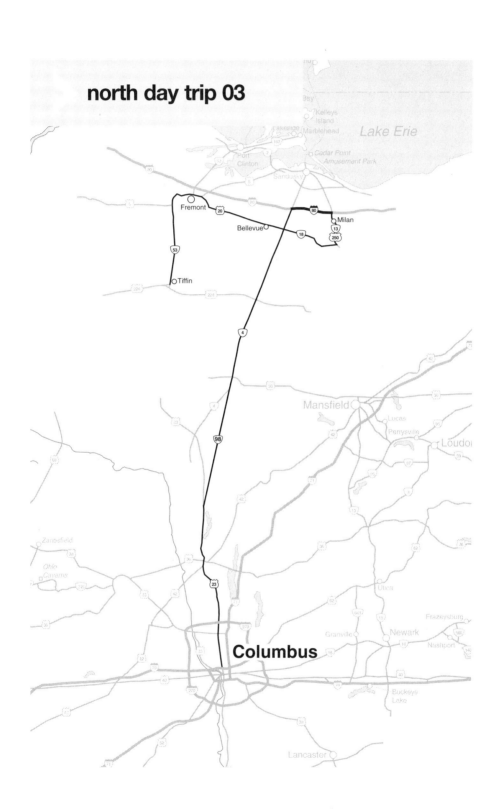

where to go

Edison's Birthplace. 9 Edison Drive, Milan, OH 44846. February 11, 1847, was a date that changed Milan—and the world—forever. It was the day that Thomas Edison, originator of the phonograph, the lightbulb, and many more time- and labor-saving devices, was born. The museum contains rare examples of the man's early inventions, documents, and family photographs. Although the family sold the house in 1854 and moved away, Edison's sister purchased it several decades later, and Edison himself became the owner in 1906. Much of the family's furniture was lost in a fire, but it has been restored as closely as possible to its original appearance, thanks to the donations of friends and relatives. Open Tuesday through Sunday, April through October; by appointment only from November through March. Closed in January. Admission is charged. (419) 499–2135; www.tomedison.org.

Milan Historical Museum. 10 Edison Drive, Milan, OH 44846. Constructed about the same time as the Edison home, this complex consists of several buildings housing an impressive collection of glassware, dolls, and Civil War memorabilia. The fully furnished Sayles House boasts a weaving room, children's playroom, and cellar, and the Edna Roe Newton Memorial Building contains an accumulation of goodies from one world-traveling Milan family. You will also find a blacksmith shop, a carriage shed, and a fully stocked circa 1850 general store. Open Tuesday through Sunday, April through October, with special events on holidays. Small donation requested. (419) 499–2968; www.milanhistory.org.

where to shop

Sights and Sounds of Edison. 21 South Main Street, Milan, OH 44846. It's horns aplenty at this antiques store that focuses on old phonographs. Those with an ear for Victors, Panel Horns, and Edison Music Masters will find a veritable cornucopia of styles. (419) 499–3093.

Effie's Attic. One Main Street on the Square, P.O. Box 509, Milan, OH 44846. Among other things, they also peddle teddy bears, collectible and antique dolls, seasonal items, and furniture and reproductions. (419) 499–2491.

where to eat

Pollyanna's Tea Room. One Main Street on the Square, P.O. Box 509, Milan, OH 44846. With a name like that, it has to be cheerful. The menu alone should incite a smile: Along with made-from-scratch soups, chicken salad, and a specialty sandwich or salad, you can choose from such exotic blends as caramel tea, chai spice, and blue lady (grapefruit with marigold and mallow flowers). $. (419) 499–2491.

where to stay

Coupling Reserve. 11618 SR 13 (Mud Brook Road), Milan, OH 44846. Mailing address: Erie Metroparks, 3910 East Perkins, Huron, OH 44839. This is one sleeping experience you're not likely to forget. Stay in a gen-u-ine heated railroad car in a twenty-acre pastoral setting. You can also go canoeing, hiking, and sledding during the winter. Except for the occasional mouse or other small critter, you won't be bothered by noisy neighbors. $. (419) 625–7783.

bellevue

Hop back on U.S. 250 south to U.S. 20 west and you'll run into Bellevue in about a half hour. Along with a railroad past and present, which includes modern-day railroad yards that still contribute to its economy, this town is home to a diverse assortment of attractions.

where to go

Seneca Caverns. 15248 East Township Road TR 178, Bellevue, OH 44811. Also known as "The Earth Crack," this unusual natural wonder, which was formed whole rather than from erosion, was discovered in 1872 and has seven different levels. At the bottom, 110 feet below the surface, you'll find Ole Mist'ry River, a crystal-clear stream that is part of a vast underground system. Bring a light jacket—it's 54 degrees year-round—and expect to do lots of walking. Open daily Memorial Day through Labor Day, weekends in May and September through mid-October. Admission is charged. (419) 483–6711; www.seneca cavernsohio.com.

Sorrowful Mother Shrine. 4106 SR 269, Bellevue, OH 44811. Established in 1850 as a place to honor the Virgin Mary, these peaceful 120 acres have been visited by countless believers as well as others seeking peace. Paved walkways winding amid trees lead to the various Stations of the Cross and replicas of Lourdes and Sepulcher grottoes. There's Mass twice a day, as well as a cafeteria and religious gift shop. Open daily; closed Christmas through New Year's and on other major holidays. Donations welcome. (419) 483–3435; www.sorrowfulmothershrine.com.

Bellevue Heritage Museum. 200 West Main Street, Bellevue, OH 44811. With continu-ally changing displays, this attraction offers something different with each visit. Focusing on items, photos, and other memorabilia relating to the town, it gives you a sense of what the community, past and present, is like. Open Sunday, Memorial Day through Labor Day; call for other times. Free. (419) 483–5359.

Mad River & NKP Railroad Society Museum. 233 York Street, Bellevue, OH 44811. Get on board for this growing accumulation, one of the state's largest collections of railroad memorabilia. Explore the many vintage cars, including the Wabash F-7 diesel engine, a PRR mail car, and the first domed model built in the United States, among others. Stationary artifacts include a watchman's tower, a depot, and a section house, which doubles as a gift shop. Uniforms, lanterns, and locks are also on display. Open daily from Memorial Day to Labor Day, and on weekends in May, September, and October. Admission is charged. (419) 483–2222; www.maderivermuseum.org.

Lyme Village. 5001 SR 4, Bellevue, OH 44811. This cluster of buildings spans one hundred years, beginning in 1830, although most focus on life in the nineteenth century. Some have been restored, while others contain displays. Highlights include a Victorian mansion built by John Wright, a one-room schoolhouse, a log church and homes, a post office, hardware store, and more. Open daily except Monday from June through August, Sunday only in May and September. Call for other times. Admission is charged. (419) 483–4949; www.lymevillage.com.

where to shop

Maplewood Gallery.1012 East McPherson Highway, Clyde, OH 43410. A few miles west of Bellevue, this 14,000-square-foot facility peddles the works of local woodcrafters, painters, sewers, and other artisans. Antiques, glass, collectibles, fine art, and other treasures can also be found. Spacious aisles and uncrowded displays add to the shopping experience. (419) 547–9175.

where to stay

Bellevue Hotel and Suites. 1120 East Main Street, Bellevue, OH 44811. This recently renovated property contains indoor and outdoor pools, whirlpool and sauna, game area, and some in-room Jacuzzis. Dinner and complimentary coffee for breakfast are also available. $$–$$$. (419) 483–5740.

The Victorian Tudor Inn. 408 W. Main Street, Bellevue, OH 44811. Although it was called "the prettiest in the city," over a hundred years ago by the *Bellevue Gazette,* this refurbished manse is still loaded with extensive art, period antiques and fine furnishings from all over the world. Plus, it has the all-important private bath, cable TV (155 channels!), wireless Internet and more. Choose from five bedrooms in four suites or an extended-stay executive apartment. The host, a retired university dean, is a hometown boy who returned to fulfill a dream of operating a B&B and has the inside scoop about what to see and do. $$$. (877) 434–1949; www.victoriantudor.com.

fremont

A few miles west on U.S. 20 is Fremont, home of the nation's first presidential library. There's also lots of good eating to be found here, judging by the large number of restaurants. Routes 53 and 6 also pass through, and it's a favorite stop off the Turnpike (exit 91).

so much POTUS, so little time

Although other states may have quality—or lack thereof, depending upon your political views—Ohio certainly has quantity when it comes to the U.S. presidents. It's the home and/or birthplace of eight POTUSES; more, if you count the theories of Nick Pahys, Jr., founder of a museum honoring John Hanson, a man who he believes was the first president of the U.S. (see below). More legitimate sites include the birthplace—as opposed to the tomb—of U.S. Grant (1551 State Rt 232, Point Pleasant, 800–283–8932, http://ohsweb.ohiohistory.org/places/ sw08/index.shtml) and William Howard Taft (2038 Auburn Avenue, Cincinnati, 513–684–3262, www.nps.gov/wiho/index.htm), along with the home of James A. Garfield (8095 Mentor Avenue, Mentor, 440–255–8722,www.nps.gov/jaga/index .htm). Call or check Web sites for hours and admission fees first.

- **William McKinley Presidential Library, Museum and National Memorial.** 800 McKinley Monument Drive NW, Canton, OH 44708. Okay, so not everything has to do with the twenty-fifth president, even though this attraction bears his name. But there is a classic Greek memorial honoring McKinley as well as animatronic figures of him and his wife describing their personal effects, the largest accumulation of McKinley memorabilia in the world. You can also observe live plants and animals on Ecology Island, encounter a robotic dinosaur at a natural history display, and learn about the outer limits at Space Station Earth.(330) 455–7043; www.mckinleymuseum.org.

- **One and Only Presidential Museum.** 6585 Howard Road, Williamsfield, Ohio 44093. Here John Hanson is celebrated as the first POTUS elected under the 1781 Articles of Confederation. That Washington guy was actually the ninth, and the first president elected under our current Constitution eight years later, in 1789. The first floor serves as a combination souvenir shop selling Presidential Museum root beer in bottles and a general store, while the second floor consists of a cluttered confusion of photos, books, and assorted items about the various presidents, including a room dedicated to the presidents born in Ohio. (440) 344–0523, www.oneandonlypresidential museum.com.

- **Rutherford B. Hayes Presidential Center.** Spiegel Grove, Ohio 43420. The first Presidential library in the U.S., this thirty-three-room mansion is filled with the family's original furnishings. There are carriage and guest *houses, with the latter being decorated in ornate Victorian style. The museum itself consists of more than 10,000 objects and items on loan. With over a million manuscripts, the library also has all of R.B.H.'s diaries and letters in addition to first-source Civil War information. Perhaps this is where the oxymoron "government paperwork" originated as well. (419) 332–2081, www .rbhayes.org.*

- ***Warren G. Harding Home.*** *380 Mt. Vernon Avenue, Marion, OH 43302. Back in 1920, when Harding was on the campaign trail, huge masses of people made the pilgrimage to his Victorian-style residence to hear him orate, not unlike a certain recent inauguration. Harding's home contains nearly all of his and wife Florence's original possessions, including but not limited to cracked leather chairs, a microphone used during the inauguration, and the presidential briefcase as well as Florence's hats and clothes, kitchen utensils, and family portraits. (740) 387–9630, (800) 600–6894; http://ohsweb.ohiohistory.org/ places/c03.*

The quaint downtown, with its shops, galleries, and eateries, is good for a few hours' worth of wandering. The area is well-known for Eshleman Fruit Farm, 1 mile northeast of U.S. 20 in Clyde on SR 101 (753 East Maple Street, 419–547–9584; www.eshlemanfruit farm.com). June through October—when it's open—reap fresh-grown sweet cherries, blueberries, peaches, and apples, along with educational tours and wagon rides for groups and individuals.

where to go

Fremont Speedway. 19101 Orchard Drive, Elmore, OH 43416. Mailing address: 2111 Hayes Avenue, Fremont OH 43420. Those who enjoy going in circles might appreciate races at the "Track That Action Built." 410 and 305 winged sprint cars and trucks go wheel-to-wheel (as opposed to neck-and-neck) around the one-third mile of semi-banked clay oval track. Open since 1951, it has seen speed racers such as Steve Kinser, Sammy Swindell, Brad Doty, Doug Wolfgang, and current NASCAR stars Jeff Gordon and Dave Blaney. It recently became one of the first dirt track facilities in the United States to install softwalls, ensuring the drivers' safety and reducing damage to cars. Gates open at 4:30 p.m. on Saturday, April through September. Admission is charged. (419) 333–0478; www .fremontohspeedway.com.

where to eat

Here is a sampler of Fremont's many restaurants, several of which are family owned and have been around for decades:

818 Club Restaurant. 818 Crogan Avenue, Fremont, OH 43420. This casual eatery has been serving up American cuisine for more than eighty years. Specializes in lunches and dinners. $–$$. (419) 334–9122.

Grate's Silver Top. 3939 North SR 53, Fremont, OH 43420. Looking for a drink or a quick meal? A full-range bar-food menu (wings, nachos, sandwiches) and drinks make this a solid watering/feeding stop. $. (419) 334–9250.

Whitey's Diner. 216 East State Street, Fremont, OH 43420. Famous for hearty breakfasts, this reasonably priced eatery serves up large portions, no matter what the meal. $–$$. (419) 334–9183.

Chud's Grill. 1103 Napoleon Street, Fremont, OH 43420. Lunch features soups, salads, and sandwiches, while steak, chicken, and fish are what's for dinner. $$. (419) 332–9565.

where to stay

Fremont has a variety of chain hotels to choose from; basically the only games in town. They are, in no particular order, Hampton Inn & Suites, 540 E CR 89, (419) 332–7650; Comfort Inn & Suites, 840 Sean Dr., (419) 355–9300; Holiday Inn Fremont–Port Clinton Hotel, 3422 Port Clinton Rd, (877) 863–4780; and Days Inn Fremont, 3701 N Street Route 53, (419) 334–9551. All addresses are Fremont, OH 43420 and prices are commensurate with the chain's usual offering. Hopefully, there won't be any surprises!

Bartlett's Old Orchard Motel. 2438 West State Street, Fremont, OH 43420. Built in 1949, this old-school–style motor inn has twenty-one rooms, about half of which have double beds. But the price is right and the staff is friendly. $. (419) 332–4307.

tiffin

About 20 miles south on SR 53 is Tiffin, a glassmaking center from 1888 until 1980. You can view its "sparkling" history in museums, factories, and various other exhibits, and purchase a piece for yourself in one of many shops.

where to go

Crystal Traditions of Tiffin. 145 Madison Street, Tiffin, OH 44883. Watch glassblowing artisans at work, demonstrating sand carving, acid polishing, and other aspects of this delicate craft. The showroom offers crystal giftware as well as bargains on seconds, discontinued items, and closeouts. Open Monday through Saturday. Free. (888) 298–7236; www.crystaltraditions.com.

Tiffin Glass Museum. 25 South Washington Street, Tiffin, OH 44883. A full display of all original Tiffin Glass, this collection focuses on popular lines, stemware, lamps, optics, and colors. More than 2,000 pieces, arranged in oak cabinets, trace the factory's evolution and its many owners. Open year-round, Tuesday through Saturday; other times by appointment. Donations welcome. (419) 448–0200; www.tiffinglass.org.

Seneca County Museum. 28 Clay Street, Tiffin, OH 44883. Dating from 1853, this Greek Revival house museum is filled with displays relating to the history of the county. Highlights include a carriage house with antique fire equipment and horse-drawn wagons as well as (of course) Tiffin Glass. Open Tuesday, Wednesday, and Sunday afternoons; other times by appointment. Admission may be charged. (419) 447–5955.

St. Paul's United Methodist Church. 46 Madison Street, Tiffin, OH 44883. Built in 1874, this structure has the distinction of being the first public building in the world to be wired for electricity. Bonus: Thomas Edison gifted the brass chandelier. Call for appointment. Donations are welcome. (419) 447–1743; www.gbgm-umc.org/st_pauls.

Ritz Theatre. 30 South Washington Street, Tiffin, OH 44883. This historic 1928 vaudeville and movie palace has been completely refurbished and now attracts top acts as well as local productions. Standouts include 30-foot hand-painted murals and a 1,200-pound Czechoslovakian chandelier. Open Monday through Friday. Free. (419) 448–8544; www.ritztheatre.org.

where to shop

Jeffrey Jewelry. 2449 West Market Street, Wolf Creek Shopping Complex, Tiffin, OH 44883. Here you'll find diamonds, gemstones, watches, gold, and more. Extensive offerings include Lladro, Hummel, Swarovski, and Lenox. (800) 553–7607.

where to eat

Pioneer Mill of Tiffin. 255 Riverside Drive, Tiffin, OH 44883. Located along the banks of the Sandusky River, this former gristmill, built in 1822, serves a variety of foods in a casual atmosphere. Whether you're waiting for the specialty, prime rib, or other orders, you can check out the waterwheel, which still supplies electricity to the complex. $$. (419) 448–0100; www.pioneermilloftiffin.com.

Clover Club. 266 South Washington Street, Tiffin, OH 44883. This popular watering hole is considered by many to be a lucky find; not only is it a good place to catch a game and a drink but also an inexpensive, tasty meal in a clean, fun atmosphere of an Irish pub. It's frequented by locals, out-of-towners, and businesspeople alike. $$. (419) 448–9142.

where to stay

Fort Ball Bed and Breakfast. 14 Clay Street, Tiffin, OH 44883. Built in 1894, all parts of this Queen Anne Revival house are open for guests' use. Some rooms have private baths; others are shared. $$. (888) 447–0776.

Mad River Railroad Bed and Breakfast. 107 West Perry Street, Tiffin, OH 44883. Decorated with antiques and period furnishings, this Victorian home is located next to a walking/bike path, formerly the site of the area's first railroad. Most rooms have private bath and TV. $$. (419) 447–2222; www.madriverrailroadbnb.com.

Tiffin Motel. 315 West Market Street, Tiffin, OH 44883. It may look like a throwback to the '60s but the Tiffin Motel is definitely twenty-first century with free Wi-Fi access, microwaves and fridges in every room, and a nearby Denny's. Perhaps more importantly, the 24-room property appears to be clean and well-kept, albeit no-frills. But with rooms averaging $40–50 a night, what more could you ask? $. (419) 447–7411; www.tiffinmotel.com.

northeast

day trip 01

northeast

state parks:
mansfield • lucas • perrysville • loudonville

Two of Ohio's most charming and diverse state parks are located within a few miles of each other. Malabar Farm State Park is the world-famous home of author and celebrity-monger Louis Bromfield and offers a variety of programs and entertainment. Mohican State Park is a popular year-round recreational and outdoor mecca.

mansfield

Mansfield itself has several natural—and not so natural—attractions. Carousel buffs can tour a manufacturing facility (Carousel Magic, 44 West Fourth Street; 419–526–4009; www .carouselmagic.com), ride the first new hand-carved wooden merry-go-round built since the early 1930s (Richland Carrousel Park, 75 North Main Street; 419–522–4223; www.richland carrousel.com), and do related shopping. From Columbus, take I–71 north to exit 169, SR 13, and turn left toward Mansfield, about 70 miles total.

where to go

Oak Hill Cottage. 310 Springmill Street, Mansfield, OH 44903. Built in 1847, Oak Hill remains one of the most outstanding examples of Gothic homes in the United States. It has seven gables and five chimneys, and Louis Bromfield played there as a child. It was the inspiration for Shane's Castle in the Bromfield novel The Green Bay Tree. Open April

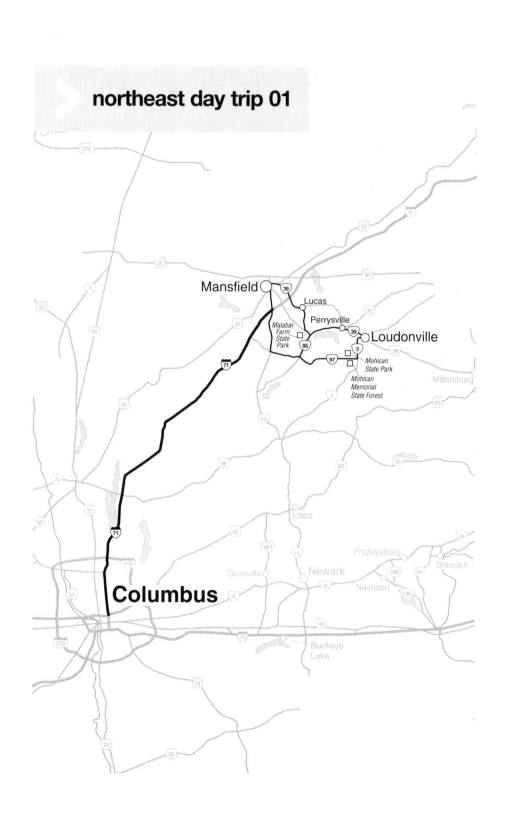

northeast day trip 01

Mansfield

Lucas

Perrysville

Loudonville

Malabar Farm State Park

Mohican State Park

Mohican Memorial State Forest

Millersburg

Utica

Frazeysburg

Granville

Newark

Nashport

Dresden

Columbus

Buckeye Lake

through December; other times by appointment. Admission is charged. (419) 524–1765; www.oakhillcottage.org.

Living Bible Museum. 500 Tingley Avenue, Mansfield, OH 44905. Although this attraction claims to be nondenominational, you should at least believe in *something* when you come through the door. Life-size dioramas chronicle Creation to Judgment, with special effects and audio commentary. There's a wax museum depicting miracles of the Old Testament and a collection of rare bibles, woodcarvings, American folk art, and a Christian art gallery. Open daily, April through December; weekends only the rest of the year. Admission is charged. (800) 222–0139; www.livingbiblemuseum.org.

Ohio Bird Sanctuary. 3774 Orweiler Road, Mansfield, OH 44903. This wildlife rehabilitation facility focuses on species native to Ohio. You can view our feathered friends at a birds-of-prey exhibit or hear their songs in an aviary. Hikes through marsh and old-growth forests also offer opportunities to glimpse them au naturel. Open Wednesday, Saturday, and Sunday; restricted winter hours. Admission is charged. (419) 884–4295; www.ohio birdsanctuary.org.

Ohio State Reformatory. 100 Reformatory Road, Mansfield, OH 44906. A different kind of cage, built in 1886 for those other birdbrains, juvenile offenders. Despite the castlelike appearance, the original cell blocks and administration offices convey a grimy grimness. It was also the location of four major movies and is in the process of being converted to a museum with tours, a library, and special events. One tour Tuesday through Friday and two tours Sunday, mid-May through October. Admission is charged. (419) 522–2644; www .mrps.org.

where to shop

Carrousel Antiques. 118 North Main Street, Mansfield, OH 44902. Housed in a restored Victorian building, more than forty antiques dealers offer a wide selection of merry-go-round collectibles and more from various periods (419) 522–0230.

Beeology. 4886 Ritter Road, Mansfield, OH 44813. Buzz over to a straight-from-the-hive selection of candles, soaps, hand creams, honey, and more. The owners, avid beekeepers, are busy as guess-what, maintaining some 100 hives in a two-county area and teaching seminars at Malabar Farm. Leave the harvesting to the guys in the protective suits and enjoy the fruits of their (and the bees') labors. (419) 886–3431; www.beeology.com.

Richland Mall. 2209 Richland Mall, Mansfield, OH 44906. Anchored by a Sears, Macy's, and JCPenney, this mall, with more than fifty stores and food offerings has weathered tough times, buyouts, and store closings. However, like the love of shopping, it endures, offering everything from accessories at Ashcroft & Oak to women's apparel at Victoria's Secret and a whole lot in-between. (419) 529–4003; www.richlandmallshopping.com.

lucas

Two of Ohio's most charming and diverse state parks are located within a few miles of each other. From SR 13, in Mansfield, drive 2 miles east on Hanley Road, then turn right at Little Washington Road. Bear left at the fork onto Pleasant Valley Road. Go about 6 miles, then turn right at the entrance to Malabar Farm State Park, which is the main attraction in Lucas.

where to go

The Big House, Malabar Farm. 4050 Bromfield Road, Lucas, OH 44843. Although the original structure is more than 150 years old, it was remodeled extensively in 1939, when best-selling author Louis Bromfield and his family moved back to his native Richland County from France. He brought the world with him in the form of famous personalities who visited him frequently, most notably Humphrey Bogart and Lauren Bacall, who married there in 1945. If going down the famous staircase to the tune of the "Wedding March" on the player piano doesn't snag your imagination, then the original furnishings, which have been unchanged since Bromfield's time, probably will. Some pieces are antiques from the 1700s. Open daily during summer hours; weekends during fall and winter. Call for appointment other times. Admission is charged. (419) 892–2784; www.malabarfarm.org.

Malabar Farm Market. 3650 Pleasant Valley Road, Lucas, OH 44843. In addition to being an internationally acclaimed man of letters, Bromfield was quite the agriculturalist. His ideas about conserving soil and sustainable farming are still in use today and are at work on the 914-acre estate, which includes the Bromfield Resource Center, an agricultural library with more than 2,500 documents. Highlights include a smokehouse, dairy barn, and petting farm. An organic produce business sells its products from May to October. You can also go fishing, hiking, ice-skating, cross-country skiing, and horseback riding (you supply the horses); wagon tours are available from time to time. Open weekends in January and February; daily except Monday the rest of the year. Depending on options chosen, admission may be charged. (419) 892–2784.

Fowler Woods State Nature Preserve. On Olivesburg-Fitchville Road. From Malabar take SR 13 north to Noble Road. Go east on Noble Road, then south one-quarter mile on Olivesburg-Fitchville Road in Lucas. Mailing address: Ohio Department of Natural Resources, 1435 Township Road, 38W, Tiffin, OH 44883. This 133-acre woodland is a mixture of old-growth woods, swamp forest, and, in the spring, abundant wildflowers. It's also a naturalist's paradise, with frogs, nesting birds, and breeding amphibians. Best times to visit are during spring, winter, and fall; mosquitoes are prevalent during summer. Open daylight only. Free. (614) 265–6453.

where to eat

Malabar Inn Restaurant. 3645 Pleasant Valley Road, Perrysville, OH 448. There are plenty of good eats here, in the form of "farmhand dinners" (meat loaf, pot roast, potpie) as well as healthier fare (salads, vegetable lasagna, vegetarian plate). Call for winter hours. $$. (419) 938–5205; www.malabarfarmrestaurant.com.

where to stay

Hostelling International, Malabar Farm. 3954 Bromfield Road, Lucas, OH 44843. Those looking for lodging on the Malabar Farm grounds will find "such a deal" here for less than $20 a night. Not only can you participate in the various programs but some private rooms are also available. Closed December and January. $. (419) 892–2055.

Angel Woods Hideaway. 1983 Pleasant Valley Road, Lucas, OH 44843. Visitors have a selection of several "theme" chambers, some with shared baths. Other amenities include common room with fireplace, game room, in-ground pool, hot tub, and exercise areas. $$. (888) 882–6949; www.ohio-bed-breakfast.com.

perrysville

From Malabar Farm in Lucas turn right onto Pleasant Valley Road and follow to the stop sign. Turn right onto SR 603 and go about one-half mile, then turn left onto SR 95, which leads to SR 39 and Perrysville.

where to go

Mohican Memorial State Forest. 3060 CR 939, Perrysville, OH 44864. Adjacent to Mohican State Park, the forest separated from the park in the late 1940s. This truly untouched terrain offers more than 20 miles of hiking and riding trails, free camping sites, a nature preserve, a war memorial shrine, and a snowmobile trail, conditions permitting. And unlike the park, hunting is permitted. Open daily. Free. (419) 938–6222.

where to eat

Bromfield's. Mohican State Resort and Conference Center. 1098 Ashland CR 3006, Perrysville, OH 44864. Breakfast, lunch, and dinner consist of a wide variety of offerings, including steaks, seafood, Italian, salads, soups, and sandwiches. There's a kids' menu and Saturday BBQ/Sunday brunch as well. $$. (419) 938–5411; www.mohicanresort.com.

where to stay

Mohican State Resort and Conference Center. 1098 Ashland CR 3006, Perrysville, OH 44864. A National Gold Medal winner for state parks and recreational excellence, this lodge offers private rooms, many with lake views and balconies, coffeemakers, indoor and outdoor pool, exercise room, and quick access to all park facilities. Children under eighteen can also stay free in the same room. $$–$$$. (419) 938–5411; www.mohicanresort.com.

loudonville

Just a few miles from Perrysville, Loudonville can be reached via SR 39.

where to go

Mohican Canoe Livery and Fun Center. 3045 SR 3 South, Loudonville, OH 44842. Okay, so it isn't white-water rafting, but it is for all ages. Canoe trips down the Mohican vary in length and do offer occasional faster waters in addition to a gentle current. Choose from return transportation via bus, van, or a narrated train ride on "The Doodlebug." Open daily, April 1 through October 31. Admission is charged. (800) 662–2663; www.canoemohican .com.

Mohican State Park. 3116 SR 3, Loudonville, OH 44842. Formerly the hunting grounds of the Delaware Indians, this scenic wonder offers glistening waterfalls, glorious gorges (especially at Clearfork), towering hemlock forests, and the Mohican River, which supports diverse animal and plant life. Recreational opportunities abound, including fishing, hiking, picnicking, and camping. Open daily. Free. (419) 994–5125 ext. 10; www.mohicanstatepark .org.

where to eat

Rader's Restaurant. 3355 St Rt 3, Loudonville, OH 44842. Billing itself as the "Mohican Area's Largest Family Restaurant," Rader's specializes in pies and quality home-cooked food, as well as a daily salad bar. Brunch buffaloes take note: Friday and Saturday see a breakfast buffet. $–$$. (419) 994–5115.

Sojourner Café. 267 W Main St. Loudonville, OH 44842. Although it may look fast-food on the outside, Sojourner offers a full menu with specialties such as chicken pot pie, seasonal lasagna, even New York–style cheesecake. An extensive wine list and classy decor complete the don't-judge-a-book-by-its-cover experience. $$. (419) 994–0079.

River Room Lounge. 424 W Main St, Loudonville, OH 44842. Hankering for a pizza? Along with a couple of dozen types of brew (Bud to Zima) and a few selections of wine, you can order your pie with pepperoni, veggies, and more and "double cheese" it for about $1 more. Subs, burgers, and other assorted bar foods are also on tap, for under $5. Such a deal! $. (419) 994–7447; www.riverroomlounge.com.

where to stay

Mohican State Park Cabins and Camping. 3116 SR 3, Loudonville, OH 44842. Choose your amenities. You can pitch a tent or park an RV at one of 153 campsites with electric, sewer, or water hookups, or forget the gear and utilize a rented tepee. It's first come, first served, and communal showers and modern restrooms are included. Or you can opt for a cozy cottage with two bedrooms, a fully equipped kitchen and bath, living room, gas log fireplace, cable TV, and more. Camping, $; cottages, $$–$$$. (419) 994–4290.

Blackfork Inn. 303 North Water Street, Loudonville, OH 44842. Visitors can choose from two properties: the mailing address, an 1865 Italianate Victorian town house with six guest rooms and two suites, all with private baths, or an 1847 former saloon that's now a small antiques shop with two guest suites. Furnished with lots of Victoriana along with a large collection of Ohio-related books. $$–$$$. (419) 994–3252; www.blackforkinn.com.

Landoll's Mohican Castle. 561 Twp. Rd. 3352, Loudonville, OH 44842. Channel your inner "knight" in a royally appointed suite or cottage reminiscent of the golden era of chivalry with the requisite modern touches. Overstuffed furniture and ornate decorations juxtapose with Jacuzzis, heated floors, and built-in kitchenettes. The 1,100-acre estate boasts 17 bridges set amid brooks and wooded valleys; trails accommodate both hikers and golf carts. With a misty waterfall and cave-like entrance, the castle's indoor pool offers a tropical take on your getaway. $$$. (800) 291–5001; www.landollsmohicancastle.com.

day trip 02

northeast

>>>

amish country:
millersburg • berlin • wilmot •
walnut creek • sugarcreek • charm

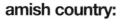

"Wilkummin" to the twenty-first century. By many accounts, Ohio has the largest concentration of Amish and Mennonites in the world. And they're well organized and savvy when it comes to tourism; many even maintain Web sites. They also have religion: Holmes County alone, our destination for this trip, contains nearly fifty churches, which has to be some kind of record for such a sparsely populated area. Not surprisingly, many things are closed on Sunday, making that traditional day of worship a less-than-ideal time to visit.

The other main activities in Amish Country are shopping, eating, and just kicking back. Specialties of the area—and many of its primary industries—include cheese, chocolates, quilts, furniture, country crafts, and every manner of baked goods. So don't be surprised if you come back from your trip with your clothes tighter than when you left.

If you're lucky, you might glimpse the "Plain People" going to services, a meeting, or school in a large group. Given their old-fashioned attire and hairstyles and the untouched rural topography, you may feel as if you've stepped back in time at least one hundred years. You're most likely to see them on one of the county's many back roads or near Old Order strongholds like Charm. However, it's best to refrain from making a fuss over them and taking pictures.

You might find yourself behind a black buggy clop-clopping at 5 or 10 miles per hour—slower if the horse-drawn vehicle is pulling farm equipment. Because the roads have lots of auto and truck traffic, with speed limits of up to 60 miles per hour, wait until you have a clear view to go around it; never pass at the top of a hill, which might result in a horrific

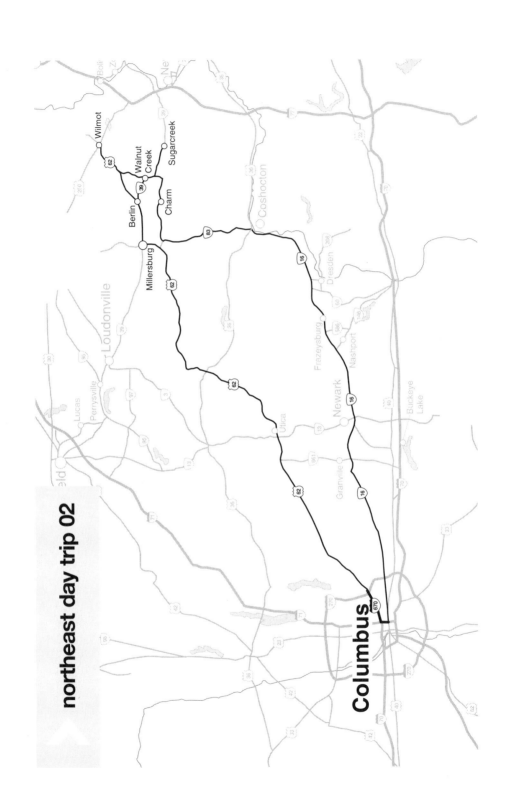

northeast day trip 02

Wilmot

Walnut Creek

Sugarcreek

Berlin

Charm

Millersburg

Loudonville

Coshocton

Dresden

Frazeysburg

Nashport

Perrysville

Lucas

Newark

Buckeye Lake

Utica

Granville

Columbus

encounter of the vehicular kind. The buggies lack turn signals, and horses tend to back up when stopped, so leave tailgating and road rage in the big city, especially during dawn and dusk hours when visibility is poorest.

Also leave your navigation system and MapQuest printouts at home. They might work in the middle of nowhere, but not where the address says one thing but the actual location is several miles down the road. So when in doubt, man up and call the place for directions.

millersburg

There are a couple of ways to get to Millersburg, one of the larger towns in Holmes County. From downtown Columbus, go east on SR 16 (Broad Street), until you reach SR 83, then drive north to U.S. 62. Continue north to Millersburg, about an hour and fifteen minutes from Columbus. Or you can take the scenic, winding route of U.S. 62 north from I–270, which will take considerably longer because it's on a crowded, two-lane highway.

where to go

Amish Mennonite Heritage Center. 5798 CR 77, Millersburg, OH 44654. A thirty-minute interpretive tour includes Behalt, a striking and colorful 10-by-265-foot cyclorama depicting the heritage of the Amish and Mennonite people, from their beginnings in Zurich, Switzerland, in 1525, until today. Painted by German-born artist Heinz Gaugel, the mural covers the persecution of these groups by state churches, the migration to Russia and North America, and more. Gaugel continues to paint in a studio on the premises, and there's a large selection of Amish/Mennonite-related books, crafts, and other items for sale in the gift shop. Admission is charged. Open Monday through Saturday. (330) 893–3192; www.behalt.com.

Victorian House Museum. 434 Wooster Road, Millersburg, OH 44654. Home of the Holmes County Historical Society, this four-floor, twenty-eight-room mansion boasts Queen Anne architecture, a white oak staircase, a ballroom, and even a sauna and steam room in the basement. Many of the furnishings and antiques have been provided by local citizens, making it a true community effort. Open daily. Admission is charged. (330) 674–0022; www.victorianhouse.org.

Yoder's Amish Farm. 6050 SR 515, Millersburg, OH 44654. This 116-acre working farm features two homes for tours, a petting zoo, buggy and hay rides, and crafts. The friendly native staff will also answer any and all questions about the Amish. Open Monday through Saturday, April through October. Admission is charged. (330) 893–2541; www.yodersamishhome.com.

Rolling Ridge Ranch. 3961 County Road 168, Millersburg, OH, 44654. A safari in Amish Country; what a concept! The ranch features over 500 animals and birds from around the world and visitors can experience it through either a guided horse-drawn wagon tour or from the safety (their words) of your own car. Either way, the animals are so tame that some are relegated to a petting zoo where you can feed them as well. Open from April–Oct; closed Sundays and Ascension Day, which for the less-churched is May 1. Admission is charged. (330) 893–3777; www.visitrollingridge.com.

where to shop

Shopping in Amish country can involve more than browsing, buying, and bustling out the door. Visitors get a chance to watch items being manufactured or crafted through firsthand demonstrations, videos, even murals. Many of the enterprises have been in families for generations, which provides an added personal touch. So add some extra time to your itinerary so you can enjoy such pleasant diversions. Listed here are but a few of dozens of offerings (some are open only during the warmer months, so it's best to call ahead from November to March).

Heini's Cheese Chalet/Bunker Hill Cheese. 6005 CR 77, Millersburg, OH 44654. Few escape here without ingesting several thousand calories: Along with free samples of more than fifty cheeses, cheese fudge, and other goodies, visitors can choose from sixteen flavors of ice cream. A specialty of the house is yogurt cheese, which the company claims tastes no different than the regular stuff, yet aids digestion. Other offerings include popcorn, Amish potato chips, fudge, and chocolates, and nonedibles like collectibles, Amish throws, and country home accessories. (800) 253–6636, www.heinis.com.

Guggisberg Cheese. 5060 SR 557, Millersburg, OH 44654. Home of the original Baby Swiss, this operation also welcomes visitors to view cheese-making processes. The original owner, the late Alfred Guggisberg, was trained in Switzerland and brought his expertise to Holmes County in 1947. Along with forty varieties of cheese, you'll also find cuckoo clocks and Swiss chocolates for sale. (800) 262–2505; www.guggisberg.com.

Holmes County's Amish Flea Market. 4587 SR 39, Millersburg, OH 44654. With more than 100,000 square feet, 500 shopping areas, and hundreds of vendors, this is a universe of collectibles, crafts, and quilts, to mention a few items. A restaurant and elevators are especially useful for breaks (the former) and when loaded down with purchases (the latter). (330) 893–0900; www.holmesfleamarket.com.

where to eat

Chalet of the Valley. 5060 SR 577, Millersburg, OH 44654. Dine in an authentic Swiss chalet while enjoying members of the Schnitzel family: wiener (veal cutlet prepared a traditional German style), rahm (veal with creamy wine sauce), jaeger (veal marinated in wine and served with mushroom sauce), and swine, er, schwein, specially seasoned tenderized pork. More American-style dishes include chef and chicken salads, roast beef, ham steak, and spaghetti. The Black Forest cake is layered with chocolate mousse, butter icing, and marinated cherries. $$. (330) 893–2550; www.chaletinthevalley.com.

Bags Sports Pub. 88 E. Jackson Street, Millersburg, OH, 44654. Old world meets new in this refurbished historic building turned sports pub. Daily specials, homemade burgers, ribs, and steaks wash down nicely with a wide selection of beer and wine. A refreshing change of pace from Amish home cookin' and you can catch the game, too. $$. (330) 674–0279.

where to stay

The Barn Inn. 6838 CR 203, Millersburg, OH 44654. Sleeping in a barn has never been so comfy. The site of a dairy in the early 1900s, this building, which retains its original beams, has been restored in Victorian style and has a spacious and elegant sitting room with a 33-foot-high fireplace. A full country breakfast consists of homemade bread, eggs, apple dumplings, and Belgian waffles with whipped cream. $$–$$$. (877) 674–7600; www .thebarninn.com.

Berlin Hotel & Suites. 5330 County Road 201, Millersburg, OH 44654. Arguably the Ritz-Carlton of Amish country, this property boasts a 26-seat movie theater; a 17,000 square-foot fitness facility with workout equipment, indoor pool, hot tub, sauna, and racquetball room; even spa services, like massages and manicures. Chose from a variety of accommodations from a no-frills economy room to luxurious executive and presidential suites with plasma TVs and fireplaces. $–$$$. (800)-935–5218, (330) 893–3000; www .berlinhotelandsuites.com.

berlin

From Millersburg, Berlin's about a 15-mile drive east on U.S. 62 until you reach SR 39.

where to go

Schrock's Amish Farm and Home. 4363 SR 39, Berlin, OH 44610. From Millersburg, go east on 62 about 15 miles until you reach SR 39. If Walt Disney had been Amish, this might have been his vision. Along with guided home tours, including the family's, which was built in 1847, there's animal petting and feeding; a slide presentation of "The Amish Way"; crafts like quilt making, wood and furniture building, and potting; and baking, canning, and cooking. A train ride, back-road tours, a health club and spa, a restaurant, and several shops make for more than one might expect from a "Plain" culture. Open Monday through Saturday, April through October. Admission is charged. (330) 893–3051; www.amishfarm marketing.com.

where to shop

Schrock's. 4363 SR 39, Berlin, OH 44610. With woodcrafts and Amish-made furniture, home and outdoor decor, snacks, antiques, pottery, and more, this is truly one-stop shopping. Bonuses: You can even purchase obscure toys and collectibles for men and boys and there's a year-round Christmas store. Shops are open year-round. (330) 893–3051; www .amish-r-us.com.

Wendell August Gift Shop and Forge. 7007 Dutch Country Lane, Berlin, OH 44610. These creators and merchants of distinctive hand-forged aluminum, bronze, and pewter items give new meaning to heavy metal. Selection ranges from plates and cups to bookmarks and more. Bonus: They also claim to have the world's largest buggy. (866) 354–5192; www.wendellaugust.com.

Stone Barn Furnishings. 8613 Township Road 635, Mt. Hope, OH 44660. Two floors of handmade Amish furniture and accessories contain home accents, gifts, upholstered and hardwood furniture, mattresses, and more. Nearly every room and function is covered, from free-standing sinks to coat trees to entertainment centers to computer desks. (330) 674–2064; www.stonebarnfurnishings.com.

where to eat

Boyd & Wurthman. 4819 East Main, Berlin, OH 44610. Since 1938, this institution has been dishing up Amish food and friendly service. Specialties include homemade pies, such as sour apple cream, way tastier than it sounds. And it's a true plain people experience; locals and tourists alike take their meals on no-frills tables with hard wood benches. $$. (330) 893–3287.

Cindy's Diner. 4774 US 62, Berlin, OH 44610. Home of the "Berlin Burger" and "Diner Dog," Cindy's has more home-cooked meals than you can shake a stick of butter at: hot roast beef, fish or turkey dinners, soups, homemade cream pies, Amish date pudding, cheesecake, ice cream milkshakes, and more. It's served up in a retro '50s atmosphere. $–$$. (330) 893–3400.

where to stay

Zinck's Inn. 4703 SR 39, Berlin, OH 44610. Options in the forty-six available rooms include nice views of farmlands, a king- or queen-size bed, refrigerator, Jacuzzi, and free continental breakfast. It's also within walking distance of many of the town's shops and restaurants. $–$$. (330) 893–6699; www.zincksinn.com.

A Day in the Country. 4744 SR 49, Berlin, OH 44610. Spend more than a day, if you'd like. Also close to town, this cozy B&B has rooms with private showers, a whirlpool suite, and a large front porch where you can sit on a rocker and watch the world go buy, uh, by.

The hosts will also ply you with hot cocoa and cookies, if you're game. $$. (888) 893–7017; www.bbonline.com/oh/country.

wilmot

From Berlin, continue northeast on U.S. 62 to U.S. 250 in Wilmot.

where to shop

Alpine-Alpa Cheese Co. 1504 U.S. 62, Wilmot, OH 44689. The home of the world's largest cuckoo clock, this enterprise also peddles many of its smaller cousins and has a large assortment of Black Forest timepieces. Given the decor, you might even think you've been beamed into Switzerland. And, of course, there's cheese and cheesemaking. (330) 359–5454; www.alpine-alpa.com.

1881 Antique Barn. 927 U.S. 62, Wilmot, OH 44689. Along with furniture, glass, tools, and pottery, you can purchase antique kitchen collectibles, Depression toys, advertising pieces, and more in a novel setting. (330) 359–7957; www.amishdoor.com.

Lehman's. Kidron Road, Kidron OH 44363. For a unique experience, hitch your buggy and trot on down SR250 to Lehman's, a few miles northwest of Wilmot. Rub shoulders with "real" Amish while they shop for hand-powered kitchen supplies like butter churns, homesteading tools, composting toilets, oil lamps—anything without a wire or plug. Many items date back to the 1800s; but in a huge instance of worlds colliding, there's an extensive online catalog that lists everything from scythes to salves. Directions are available on their Web site via Google Earth. (888) 438–5346 or (330) 674–7474; www.lehmans.com.

Gateway Place. 14875 Navarre Road, Wilmot, OH 44689. This mecca for Ohio wines has become a popular destination, providing respite from the unrelenting wholesomeness of the surrounding countryside. The 1890 home has been lovingly restored and retrofitted, with vinos from over fifty Ohio wineries housed on wooden shelves. The store carries local cheeses, trail bologna, Amish-made wooden toys, art, and local gifts, as well as antiques. Samples of the various vintages are available for a quarter, the best deal in town. (330) 359–5535.

where to eat

Alpine Homestead Restaurant. 1504 U.S. 62, Wilmot, OH 44689. The cuisine consists of Swiss, German, and Amish cooking, although there's a modern-style salad bar and large Sunday buffet. $$.(330) 359–5454; www.alpine-alpa.com.

Amish Door. 1210 Winesburg Street, Wilmot, OH 44689. Along with the traditional fried, breaded, and gravied items, this menu also features heart-healthy meals and salads.

You can also work off some calories at the adjacent shops. $$. (800) 891–6142; www
.amishdoor.com.

where to stay

Hasseman House. 925 U.S. 62, Wilmot, OH 44689. This Victorian home is loaded with
antiques, stained-glass windows, and intricate woodwork, and has a "honeymoon" attic
suite. All rooms come with private baths. Breakfast is at the nearby Amish Door restaurant.
$$–$$$. (330) 359–7904; www.amishdoor.com.

Simple Pleasures Bed and Breakfast. 1004 SR 62, Wilmot, OH 44689. Channel your
inner plain person, with postmodern amenities such as individual thermostat, microwave,
and TV and Internet access, of course. Choose from "Aunt Hallie's Room," "Aunt Marion
and Aunt Katie's Room," and a personal favorite, Great Grandpa and Grandma Culp's crib,
replete with simulated flickering oil lamps and their clothes still hanging on the wall. Creepy
or a turn-on, depending on your point of view. High tea and a full breakfast are included. $$.
(877) 722–3772, (330) 473–2084; www.simplepleasuresbedandbreakfast.com.

walnut creek

Back track on U.S. 62 to SR 515. Turn left and head south to reach Walnut Creek.

where to shop

Troyer's Trail Bologna. 6552 SR 515, Dundee, OH 44624. On your way from Wilmot
to Walnut Creek, stop and pick up a homemade favorite, made here since 1912. Troyer's
has added a slimmed-down version in the form of turkey bologna. Offerings are in an old-
fashioned general store, which also peddles an assortment of jams, jellies, noodles, and
more food and other stuff. (330) 893–2414.

Carlisle Gifts. 4962 Walnut Street, Walnut Creek, OH 44687. Owned by Dutchman
Hospitality Group, Amish Country's version of Darden Restaurants (including Der Dutchman, below, as well as several others) this shop wraps its offerings in a stately Victorian
home. Embroidered linens, fleece throws. teapots, wooden toys and more are artfully
arranged throughout. Goods are manufactured by the familiar names like Thomas Kinkade,
Republic of Tea, Crabtree & Evelyn, Vera Bradley, and many more. (330) 893–2535; www
.carlislegifts.com.

where to eat

Der Dutchman. 4967 Walnut Street, Walnut Creek, OH 44687. Here you can enjoy
home-style Amish cooking in a relaxing atmosphere. The restaurant and deck overlook
the Genza Bottom Valley, and there are plenty of rocking chairs on the front porch. Stop

by the bakery and take home fattening mementos of your trip. $$. (330) 893–2981; www .derdutchman.com.

sugarcreek

To get to Sugarcreek, take SR 39 southeast until you reach SR 93.

where to go

Alpine Hills Historical Museum. 106 West Main Street, Sugarcreek, OH 44681. This museum, which depicts the merging of the Swiss and Amish cultures, has a bit of everything: a reproduction of an early cheese factory, an Amish kitchen, turn-of-the-twentieth-century woodworking and printing shops, an 1895 Sugarcreek Fire Department display, and more. There are three floors of antiques and artifacts, plus videos about cheese making, area industry, and Amish life. Open April through October. Free. (888) 609–7592.

where to shop

Swiss Village Quilts and Crafts. 113 South Broadway, Sugarcreek, OH 44681. Here you'll find Amish quilts, wall hangings, pillows, and tablecloths, in addition to hand-fashioned dolls, pinewood crafts, and other farm toys. (330) 852–4855.

where to eat

Dutch Valley Restaurant. 1343 Old Route 39, Sugarcreek, OH 44681. Specialties of the newly expanded and renovated "house" include family-style dinners of panfried chicken, ham, or roast beef. Another favorite, the "Manhattan," is a hot beef or turkey gut-buster served with stuffing or mashed potatoes and covered with gravy. The latter sandwich undoubtedly harks back to the days when New York was owned by the Dutch, *waaay* before Jerry Seinfeld and the onset of thin, anxious people who always seem to be in a hurry. A country breakfast buffet is served daily. $$. (330) 852–4627; www.dhgroup.com.

charm

Charm can be reached by driving south on SR 93 from Sugarcreek, then west on SR 557.

where to shop

Keim Lumber. 4465 SR 557, Charm, OH 44617. This hardware-lover's heaven features a 30,000-square-foot tool display along with an amazing array of wallpaper, kitchen cabinets, vanities, lights, and more. If you want to build it, you will come. (800) 362–6682; www .keimlumber.com.

Ruthie's Gift Shop. P.O. Box 130, State Route 557, Charm, OH 44617. The shop lives up to its namesake town via a large selection of country curtains and table linens, lace, baking utensils, Amish dolls, candles, clocks pictures, and more. (330) 893–3369.

Old Blacksmith Shop Gifts. 4427 State Route 557, Charm, OH 44617. Where once the village smithy stood is yet another tschocke emporium. Here you'll find garden and home decor, including stepping stones, windchimes, kitchen gadgets, scrapbooking accessories and toys. (330) 893–4516.

where to stay

The Charm Countryview Inn. P.O. Box 100, Charm, OH 44617. With private baths, hand-made quilts, solid oak furniture, and evening snacks, charmed you might surely be. This lodging, which has fifteen rooms, serves full breakfasts Monday through Saturday and a continental offering on Sunday. $$–$$$. (330) 893–3003; www.charmcountryviewinn.com.

day trip 03

northeast

>>>

christians, indians, and presidents:
new philadelphia • zoar •bolivar • canton

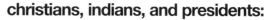

Despite being in the middle of America's heartland, Ohio has had its share of maver-
icks and do-gooders, many of whom settled here. Iconoclastic religious groups share geography with Revolutionary War ruins and a diverse assortment of museums and memorials.

new philadelphia

To get to New Philadelphia from Columbus, take I–70 east to I–77. Travel north to exit 81,
then go east on SR 39. It's a drive of less than 100 miles.

where to go

Schoenbrunn Village. 1984 East High Avenue, New Philadelphia, OH 44663. Founded
in 1772 as a Moravian mission to the Delaware Indians, this was the first Christian settlement in Ohio, which established the first civil code, Protestant church, and school in the
state. At its peak, Schoenbrunn had more than 300 residents, sixty structures, and eighty
fields, although pressures from encroaching settlers and British-aligned Indians forced its
abandonment in 1777. The original cemetery and eighteen reconstructed log structures are
maintained in the restored village, with men and women dressed in period clothing dem-
onstrating crafts and customs. There are also artifacts and an instructional film. Open daily
from Memorial Day through Labor Day; weekends only from Labor Day through October.
Admission is charged. (877) 278–8020; www.ohiohistory.org/places/schoenbr.

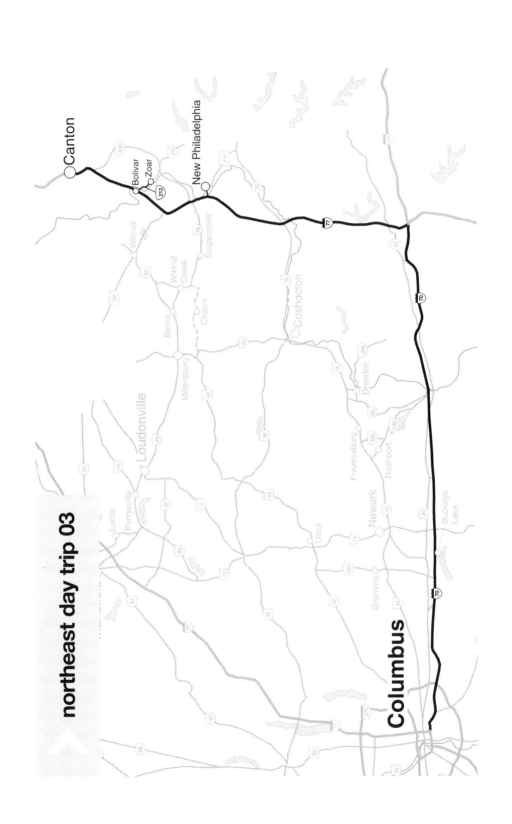

northeast day trip 03

Canton

Bolivar

Zoar

212

New Philadelphia

Wilmot

Walnut Creek

Sugarcreek

77

22

Berlin

Charm

Coshocton

70

Millersburg

Dresden

Loudonville

Frazeysburg

Nashport

146

70

Lucas

Perrysville

Newark

Buckeye Lake

Utica

Granville

Columbus

70

270

where to eat

Michael's Restaurant. 134 East High Avenue, New Philadelphia, OH 44663. Although it may sound like an upscale eatery, this diner serves unadorned breakfast and lunch with daily soup specials, along with salads, sandwiches, and burgers. $–$$. (330) 343–8670.

Hog Heaven. 1290 West High Avenue, New Philadelphia, OH 44663. Go "Hog Wild" with appetizers, sandwiches, salads, and (but of course) barbeque ribs, chicken, skewers, and combos. The adventuresome can go for the hog balls or prehistoric hog eggs. $–$$. (330) 308–8040; www.hogheaven-bbq.com.

Perfect Landing. 1816 E High Ave. New Philadelphia, OH 44663. Located at the region's airport, Harry Clover Field, this restaurant flies high with a wide selection of steaks, chicken, ribs, and chops. The budget-minded can taxi up to the pizza and pasta corner or extensive menu of starters, most of which are under $10. $–$$. (330) 308–9000.

where to stay

The Schoenbrunn Inn. 1186 West High Avenue, New Philadelphia, OH 44663. This sixty-six-room lodge boasts a variety of room choices; an indoor pool, hot tub, and sauna; a pub for sandwiches and beverages; a fitness room; and continental breakfast. With Amish-style decor, it's the best of the Old and New Worlds. $$. (800) 929–7799; www.christopherhotels .com.

zoar

In 1817 a small society of German Separatists who had their own mystical brand of worship and leader purchased 5,500 acres in the Tuscarawas River Valley. They named their settlement Zoar, after Lot's biblical town of refuge, and adopted a seven-pointed star of Bethlehem and a "Tree of Life," a huge Norway spruce representing Christ, as their emblems. Individual property and earnings became communal, and men and women possessed equal political rights, two unheard-of concepts back then. The commune thrived until the mid-1800s, when the leader died. By 1898 it was dissolved, and all assets reverted to the original families. Take I-77 12 miles north from New Philadelphia to exit 93. Zoar is located 3 miles east on SR 212.

where to go

Zoar Village. Box 404, Main Street, Zoar, OH 44697. This 12-block historic district consists of renovated private residences as well as small shops, restaurants, B&Bs, and museums populated by costumed interpreters. Listed here are some of the highlights. Unless otherwise noted, all are open daily in April and May; Wednesday through Sunday from Memorial

Day through Labor Day; Saturday and Sunday in September and October; other times by appointment. Admission is charged. (800) 874–4336; www.zca.org.

- **Zoar Store.** Constructed in 1833, this hotbed of village life—which was used as a community center by the locals and whose products attracted outside buyers as well—is still a post office, ticket center, and gift shop. You can also see an introductory video about the society.

- **Number One House, Magazine and Kitchen.** This two-story Georgian-style abode served as the home of leader Joseph Baumeler (who later changed his name to Bimeler) and two other families and is loaded with original furniture and crafts. Food for the entire commune was stored in the cellar; it was distributed via the magazine.

- **Garden and Greenhouse.** The biblically inspired design of the garden features a "Tree of Life" layout with twelve apostle trees that represent direct routes to Christ and eternal life. The warm months bring an awesome display of asters, larkspur, zinnias, petunias, and more.

- **Bimeler Museum.** This 1868 residence was remodeled after the society dissolved; however, it's been furnished to re-create the commune's last few years. Open Monday through Friday, March through May and September through December; Monday and Tuesday, June through August. Free.

- **Bakery.** Members of the commune came here to receive their daily bread, as much as they needed, for free. The brick ovens still work: Loaves, pretzels, and other comestibles are produced for demonstration purposes.

- **Tin/Wagon/Blacksmith Shops.** In one two-room structure, the tinsmith created cups, buckets, pitchers, and milk pails for sale in the main store. Down the street, the village smithy and wheelwright toiled next to each other so the buggies and farm tools could quickly and conveniently be fitted with iron parts.

where to eat

Firehouse Grill and Pub. 162 Main Street, Zoar, OH 44697. A full-service menu offers two squares (lunch and dinner), from bar munchies and salads to German cuisine and vegetarian entrees to good ol' American burgers and steaks. Specialties include salmon burger and beer-batter whitefish. Desserts, sandwiches, seafood, and pasta are also served. $$. (888) 874–2170.

where to stay and shop

Cobbler Shop Bed and Breakfast. 121 East Second Street, Zoar, OH 44697. Restored and furnished with period antiques, this accommodation offers five guest rooms, two with private baths and a screened porch that overlooks the gardens. Breakfast can be purchased, and you're within walking distance of attractions. They also sell period antiques, including furniture, pottery, pewter, and china. $$–$$$. (800) 287–1547; www .cobblershop.com.

The Cider Mill of Zoar Bed and Breakfast. 198 Second Street, P.O. Box 437, Zoar, OH, 44697. Yet another B&B/antique store combo, this one boasts three private rooms with baths, located on the upper level of what was originally a steam-operated mill built in 1863. The gift shop can be found on the ground floor and features antiques, original folk art and primitive reproductions. $$ (330) 874–3500; www.cidermillofzoar.com.

bolivar

From Zoar, go west on SR 212, crossing I–77 to the petite burg of Bolivar, about 15 miles away.

where to go

Fort Laurens State Memorial. 11067 Fort Laurens Road NW, Bolivar, OH 44612. Harking back to the days when Ohio was a remote outpost, this was the only American fort built during the Revolutionary War. Constructed with available timber, it featured corner bastions and a blockhouse and was the site of much suffering, including starvation and attacks by hostile Indians who supported the Brits. Abandoned in 1779, most of the original structure has decayed. However, a museum and Tomb of the Unknown Patriot, which holds the remains of an anonymous soldier who died on the grounds, were erected in the 1970s. The museum contains a crypt with the bodies of others who perished there as well as artifacts and weapons of the era. On a more cheerful note, the memorial is also a favorite site of Revolutionary War reenactments. The park is open daily from April through October. The museum is open daily from Memorial Day through Labor Day; weekends only in September and October. Admission is charged. (800) 283–8914; www.ohiohistory.org/places/ftlaurens.

Burfield Wiseman Farms. 605 Highway 212, Bolivar, OH 44612. The place to be "stalked," as in the Stalker Haunted Corn Maze around Halloween time. The rest of the season is somewhat tamer with fruits and vegetables for sale in spring and summer and, in the fall, pumpkins and gourds along with a Pumpkin Patch, Kiddie Hayride, and Great Animal Encounters. The farm is a family affair, owned and operated by second-generation Lori Burfield Wiseman and her husband and kids. Open seasonally; call for hours. Admission may be charged. (330) 874–2315; www.burfieldwisemanfarms.com

Wolf Timbers. P.O. Box 107, Bolivar, OH 44612. Run solely by volunteers, this unique facility highlights three pure North American Gray wolves—Nira, Keely, and Ingo—who reside in a natural setting. Round up your pack for educational, awareness, and howling programs, designed to help students, families, researchers, and others understand this much-maligned creature. Although they are open May–Oct., and other times by appointment, call before visiting and wait for the beep. Visit their Web site for directions. Admission is charged. (866) 874–9653, (330) 874–7022, (330) 323–0815; www.wolftimbers.org.

where to stay

Enchanted Pines Retreat. 1862 Old Trail Road NE, Bolivar, OH 44612. Gather up the Red Hat gang for a diva weekend and shop in your jammies. Along with a Victorian tea room, this bed-and-breakfast boasts a gift shop to delight grandma's darlings and hostesses alike. For the rest of us, the scenic, six-acre property features an outdoor pool, hot tub, deck, and more, along with a gourmet homemade breakfast. Each of the three uniquely designed suites has a private bath and Jacuzzi, refrigerator, microwave, television, and other amenities. Breakfast can be taken in the dining room with other guests or (yes!) on the decks outside or in your own room. $$$. (330) 874–3197, (877) 536–7508; www.enchantedpines .com.

where to eat

Canal Street Diner. 157 W Canal Street SE, Bolivar, OH 44612. This well-trod eatery has become a destination for some, despite the "diner" designation. Stop by for an ice cream cone or a full meal, amid retro decorations. And if you're a sucker for a good breadstick, this is the place. $–$$. (330) 874–4814.

Georgio's Grille. 10748 Wilkshire Blvd NE, Bolivar, OH 44612. Bolivar's bid for the fine dining arena includes a wide variety of specialty pastas, chicken, seafood, and steak as well as unpretentious soups, salads, and sandwiches. Not many places offer deep-fried homemade sauerkraut balls and butternut squash ravioli on the same menu. $$–$$$. (330) 874–3889; www.georgiosgrille.com.

canton

Any place founded by a man with the name of Bezaleel Wells is bound to be eclectic. So it's no surprise that this small city is the home of a sports hall of fame, a First Ladies' center, a vacuum cleaner museum, a presidential memorial, and some of the yummiest candy around. From Bolivar, go back north on I-77; Canton is about a fifteen-minute drive.

where to go

Pro Football Hall of Fame. 2121 George Halas Drive NW, Canton, OH 44708. From the moment you step inside until you walk out of the museum store, it's all football, all the time. In between, you'll learn about the origins of the game and various other leagues that challenged the NFL, test your skill in calling various plays, and get an up-close and personal view of training camps and the Super Bowl in an interactive stadium exhibit, among other diversions. A new Hall of Fame Gallery pours even more adulation on the 200-plus enshrinees via bronze portrait busts and includes a Game Day Stadium rotating theatre to relive not-so-instant replays. Open daily except Christmas. Admission is charged. (330) 456–8207; www.profootballhof.com.

Hoover Historical Center. Walsh University, 1875 Easton Street NW, North Canton, OH 44720. Devices, rather than humans, suck it up in this recently refurbished museum, a walk down memory lane of the boyhood home of vacuum cleaner magnate William "Boss" Hoover. Highlights include the first Hoover model made in 1908; a bowling-ball-shaped Constellation canister from the '50s that floats on an airstream above the carpet; and non-Hoover appliances such as a 1910 Kotten suction cleaner, which required the user to stand on a platform and rock, so as to activate the device. Open Tuesday through Sunday; closed major holidays. Free. (330) 499–0287; www.walsh.edu/hooverhistoricalcenter.htm.

Canton Classic Car Museum. 612 Market Avenue South at Sixth Street SW, Canton, OH 44702. More than forty vehicles from 1907–81 include Amelia Earhart's 1916 Pierce-Arrow, a 1939 Lincoln believed to have been used by England's Queen Mother, and a 1981 DeLorean driven by Johnny Carson, among others. The large selection of artifacts includes petroliana, toys, period clothing, and highway history displays. The museum is located in one of the country's earliest Ford dealerships. Open daily. Admission is charged. (330) 455–3603; www.cantonclassiccar.org.

National First Ladies' Library. Saxton McKinley House, 331 South Market Avenue, Canton, OH 44702. The home of former First Lady Ida McKinley, this structure has been restored with great attention to period detail and accuracy. It also contains a comprehensive bibliography of books, manuscripts, diaries, journals, and other materials related to First Ladies and is developing and expanding its education programs and holdings. Open Tuesday through Saturday for historical tours by advance reservation only; other times by appointment. Admission is charged. (330) 452–0876 ext. 320; www.firstladies.org.

MAPS Air Museum. 2260 International Parkway, North Canton, OH 44720. Located in a 16,000-square-foot facility next to (where else?) the airport, this accumulation's displays range from a Polish MiG–17 to a rare Martin B–26 Marauder to a Douglass Dauntless Dive Bomber. There are also documents, paintings, and memorabilia, along with more than 800 handbuilt aircraft. Open Monday, Wednesday, and Saturday. Admission is charged. (330) 896–6332; www.mapsairmuseum.org.

Harry London Candies. 5353 Lauby Road, North Canton, OH 44720. With more than 20,000 square feet, a state-of-the-art factory, and family recipes used since 1922, this establishment makes Willy Wonka look like a dilettante. The tour encompasses the Chocolate Hall of Fame, and there are lots of free samples. And few can resist the temptation of the gift shop. Open daily. Admission is charged. (800) 321–0444; www.harrylondon.com.

where to shop

Westfield Belden Village. 4230 Belden Village Mall NW, Canton, OH 44718. This is one of the more diverse shopping arenas around and includes more than one hundred retail stores. Dillard's, Kaufmann's, Sears, American Eagle, Victoria's Secret, the Disney Store, and many others can be found here. (330) 494–5490; www.westfield.com/beldenvillage.

Lazar's Art Gallery of American Craft. 2490 Woodlawn Avenue NW, Canton, OH 44708. Browsers can choose from the work of more than 700 craftspeople. There's handblown glass, pottery, Judaica, sculpture, jewelry, porcelain, and more. (800) 400–8351; www .lazarsartgallery.com.

J.M. Smucker Company Store and Café. 333 Wadsworth Road, Orrville, OH 44667. Although it's about a half-hour ride on 77S to Route 30W to 57N, a trip to the Smucker's mothership is tasty and fun for the whole gang. Besides you can't miss the building—it's that tall white barn with giant kissing strawberries in the middle of nowhere. Inside are hundreds of different jellies, jams, toppings, and more along with kitchen gewgaws, magnets, and clothing. It just *has* to be good. (330) 684–1500; www.smuckers.com.

where to eat

The Stables Restaurant and Hall of Fame Grille. 2317 Thirteenth Street, Canton, OH 44708. Those whose appetites for the gridiron have been whetted by the Pro Football Hall of Fame need only go a few blocks to this former horse barn, which continues the tradition with a statue and memorabilia. There's also a game and entertainment room as well as outdoor dining. Menu items include hickory grilled steaks, seafood, burgers, and salads. $$–$$$. (330) 452–1230.

356th Fighter Group Restaurant. 4919 Mt. Pleasant Road, North Canton, OH 44720. Ditto for folks visiting the MAPS Air Museum (wonder what a vacuum-cleaner-themed restaurant would be like?). Located at the airport, this restaurant serves American chow amid 1940s flier and other types of souvenirs, artifacts, and music. $$–$$$. (800) 994–2662; www.356fg.com.

Walther's Cafe. 1836 Maple Avenue NE, Canton, OH 44705. This reasonably priced eatery caters to families and large groups and even sells Ohio lottery tickets. Specialties include frog legs and broasted chicken (some might say the former tastes like the latter), and breakfast is served all day. $$. (330) 452–0785.

91 Wood Fired Oven. 5570 Fulton Drive, Canton, OH 44718. Pasta, grilled entrees, and pizzas blend well with the chic, upscale decor. Many offerings are prepared in wood-fired ovens, although patrons also give high marks to the steak, mixed drinks, and desserts. A good place to chill after a hard day of touring. $$. (330) 497–9111; www.91oven.com.

Benders Tavern. 137 Court Ave. SW, Canton, OH 44702. Since 1902, this Canton institution has been the locus for professionals, tourists, and natives, and according to local legend, the informal birthplace of the NFL. The building's old-school ambiance remains, despite the ravages of a 1988 fire and it's been family-owned for four generations. Specialties include steak, fish, and an extensive wine list. $$$. (330) 453–8424; www.benders restaurant.com.

where to stay

The Bertram Inn at Glenmoor. 4191 Glenmoor Road, Canton, OH 44718. With seventy-four luxuriously appointed rooms, each of which is decorated differently, a presidential suite, a Jack Nicklaus–designed golf course, and several gourmet dining options, this lodging should satisfy the most discriminating tastes. There's also a full-service spa for those who wish the pampering to continue. $$$. (888) 456–6667; www.glenmoorcc.com.

Heatherwood Farms. 9320 Kent Avenue NE, North Canton, OH 44721. This B&B's amenities include hot tub, airport shuttle, and full breakfast. However, the two rooms have a shared bath. No animals are allowed. $$. (888) 637–6763.

McKinley Grand Hotel. 320 Market Avenue South, Canton, OH 44702. Party like a president at this boutique hotel located in the middle of downtown close to many attractions. Along with an indoor heated pool, spa services, and a café, this property boasts rooms and suites with wireless Internet, ample space to work and relax, and this author's favorite toiletries from Bath & Body Works. Truly bipartisan, they offer free transportation to and from the airport, and may even give discounts to Ohio residents. $$. (330) 454–5000, (877) 454–5008; www.mckinleygrandhotel.com.

day trip 04

northeast

akron

One of the nation's first canal towns, which eventually became the home of Quaker Oats and a rubber hub (manufacturer B. F. Goodrich was drawn by the easy railroad access and the large water supply), Akron is an eclectic mix of old-time industrialism, nouveau culture, and high-tech innovation. On one hand are diverse manufacturing plants and their curious accoutrements and on the other are artistic draws such as Blossom Music Center (1145 West Steels Corners Road, Cuyahoga Falls, OH 44223; 330–920–8040, www.blossom music.com), which attracts top musical acts from around the world and is the summer home of the Cleveland Orchestra. Much of the city's economy revolves around the development of polymers; in fact, the University of Akron has an internationally noted program in that particular science.

From Columbus, Akron is a straight shot of about 125 miles: Take I–71 north to I–76 east, which leads directly to downtown.

where to go

Goodyear World of Rubber. 1144 East Market Street, Akron, OH 44316. Here you'll learn that vulcanization does not always relate to Mr. Spock and was, in fact, a process discovered by Charles Goodyear. Also on display are Goodyear's personal mementos, descriptions of how products are made with rubber components, and Indianapolis 500 race cars.

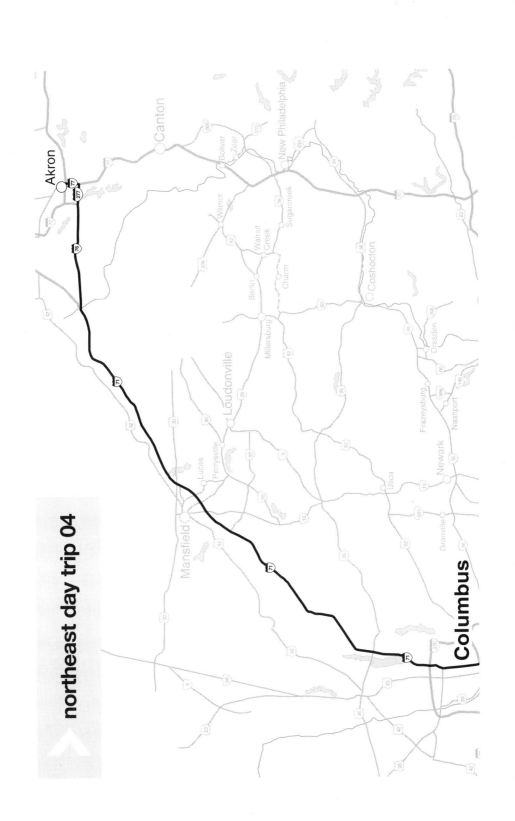

Of special interest is a discussion of the glory years of blimps, which peaked in the 1930s with elaborate and luxurious airships. Open Monday through Friday. Free. (330) 796–7117; www.goodyear.com.

Lockheed Martin Airdock (Blimp Hangar). Take I–76 east to I–277 east to U.S. 224; continue east past SR 8 to the Airdock on the left. Mailing address: Lockheed Martin Tactical Defense Systems, 1210 Massillon Road, Akron, OH 44306. At twenty-two stories high and as long as two Washington Monuments, this fascinating structure is the world's largest building without interior supports. It even has its own climate, occasionally creating a lightning system or fog. Built by Goodyear in 1929 to construct blimps, it's now used to manufacture aerospace products. Drive by only, unless you have security clearance to get inside. (330) 796–2800.

National Inventors Hall of Fame. 221 South Broadway, Akron, OH 44308. Want to get a handle on your inner genius? The Inventor's Workshop includes a laser area for creating mazes and sounds; fiber optics to experiment with color mixing, translucence, and composition; microscopics for an up close and personal view of objects; strobes and animation; and more. Learn and be inspired by the multitiered tribute to hundreds of men and women who helped shape life as we know it today. Open daily except Monday. Admission is charged. (800) 968–4332; www.invent.org.

Stan Hywet Hall. 714 North Portage Path, Akron, OH 44303. Eat your heart out, Martha Stewart. This exquisite sixty-five-room Tudor Revival manor boasts richly carved paneling, stained-glass windows, and sumptuous furnishings. Other opulent excesses include walls and fireplaces imported from England; hidden telephones, radiators, and closets; Persian rugs handwoven for the house; and various "theme" rooms (e.g., Chinese, music) furnished with authentic period pieces. Exterior touches include formal gardens, a lagoon, and a greenhouse. All this was patched together in 1898 by tire magnate Frank Seiberling, cofounder of Goodyear Tire and Rubber. Open daily, April through January; closed Monday in February and March. Admission is charged. (888) 836–5533; www.stanhywet.org.

Hower House. University of Akron, 60 Fir Hill, Akron, OH 44325. Before Stan Hywet, there was this Second Empire Italianate mansion constructed in 1871, some areas of which are, oddly, octagonal. Inhabited by industrialist John Hower and his descendants for 102 years, this twenty-eight-room structure has eight fireplaces, six chimneys, and many of the original furnishings and heirlooms set amid black walnut woodwork and oak parquet floors. Open Wednesday through Sunday; closed in January and on major holidays. Admission is charged. (330) 972–6909.

Perkins Stone Mansion/John Brown House. 550 Copley Road, Akron, OH 44320. Even farther back in time are these two abodes, which are across the street from each other. Built in the 1830s by Colonel Simon Perkins Jr., namesake son of Akron's founder, the former is a well-preserved example of Greek Revival architecture and contains period pieces and other displays depicting local history. The John Brown home was the abolitionist's residence from 1844 to 1846 and includes an exhibit tracing the insurrection at Harper's Ferry and the antislavery movement. Open Tuesday through Sunday; closed in January. Admission is charged. (330) 535–1120.

Dr. Bob's Home. 855 Ardmore Avenue, Akron, OH 44302. This is the spot where stockbroker William Wilson helped Akron resident Dr. Robert Smith sober up and began Alcoholics Anonymous in 1935. This "dynamic duo" then continued to hold meetings to help other alcoholics at this residence, which has many of the original furnishings. Open daily. Free. (330) 864–1935; www.drbobshome.com.

where to shop

Mustard Seed Market & Cafe. 3885 West Market Street, Akron, OH 44333. Aisles of organic produce, handcrafted breads, a supplement section with herb and homeopathic remedies, and a full line of cruelty-free body-care products help back up its claim as Ohio's largest natural-food store. A full-service cafe, extensive deli, and gourmet foods and wines section round out the offerings. (888) 476–2379; www.mustardseedmarket.com.

Summit Mall. 3265 West Market Street, Akron, OH 44333. Anchored by Dillard's and Kaufmann's and with more than 120 specialty stores, this shopping arena includes Ann Taylor, Banana Republic, The Disney Store, Eddie Bauer, Brookstone, Gymboree, Victoria's Secret, Williams-Sonoma, and Zany Brainy. (330) 867–1555; www.shopsimon.com.

Don Drumm Studio and Gallery. 437 Crouse Street, Akron, OH 44311. The largest showroom of contemporary crafts in the state, this two-building emporium offers up glass, jewelry, ceramics, sculpture, wood, and graphics from more than 500 artists. (330) 253–6268; www.dondrummstudios.com.

West Point Market. 1711 West Market Street, Akron, OH 44313. Even folks who dislike grocery shopping might want to stop by. You'll find an amazing selection of chocolates, cheese, prime meats, imported foods, fine wines, and more and may leave understanding why regular customers come from as far as 50 miles away. (800) 838–2156; www.west pointmarket.com.

where to eat

Bistro 532 at Tangier. 532 West Market Street, Akron, OH 44303. This unique Akron institution that fed and entertained presidents, celebrities, and even foreign heads of state has undergone a makeover in both its menu (from Moroccan to beef, seafood, and pasta) and decor (New York steakhouse). But reminders of its glory days remain in touches of exotica around the bar and in photos of famous patrons. $$$. (330) 376–7171; www .thetangier.com.

Trackside Grille. Quaker Square, 135 South Broadway, Akron, OH 44308. All aboard for a restaurant built around the 1930s-era Broadway Limited Railroad run from New York City to Chicago. Sit in an original Pullman car surrounded by antiques and memorabilia while enjoying sandwiches, entrees, and salads. There are also luncheon specials and a large and varied Sunday brunch. $$–$$$. (330) 253–4541.

Papa Joe's/Iancomini's. 1561 Akron Peninsula Road, Akron, OH 44313. Established in 1932, the family-owned enterprise specializes in Italian entrees, steaks, seafood, and salads. Although the founder passed away in 1998, his daughter and children continue the culinary tradition. $$–$$$. (330) 923–7999.

Crave. 57 E Market Street, Akron, OH 44308. This reasonably-priced eatery practically reinvents trendy. Meals are taken amid a black, orange, brick, and chrome decor with well-spaced booths and tables. The menu ranges from comfort foods made hip, like smoked-gouda mac and cheese with blackened chicken to inventions such as fried pumpkin and apple empanadas with five-spice whipped cream and caramel sauce. If you visit their Web site, however, turn the volume down; it's noisier than the restaurant itself. $$. (330) 253–1234; www.eatdrinkcrave.com.

where to stay

Crowne Plaza Quaker Square. 135 South Broadway, Akron, OH 44308. If you've ever wondered what it's like to sleep in a Quaker Oats box, albeit a luxurious one, this is the place for you. Not only are all the rooms round but the rest of the hotel is as well. Of particular interest is the lobby, a striking combination of modern art and company memorabilia. Make sure you remember your room number because it's easy to get confused. $$$. (330) 253–5970; www.quakersquareakron.com.

Portage House. 601 Copley Road, Akron, OH 44320. This large home was built in 1918 as part of the Perkins family farm and is near Simon Jr.'s home (see Perkins Stone Mansion). Located on the second floor, sleeping quarters consist of four bedrooms and two baths. Guests can also relax downstairs in the living room on the first floor. $–$$. (330) 535–1952.

O'Neil House. 1290 West Exchange Street, Akron, OH 44313. Built in the 1920s, this Tudor mansion offers an expansive living room, a well-stocked library, and four bedrooms, all with private baths. The home of William O'Neil, founder of General Tire, it can serve as a warm-up for a visit to Stan Hywet Hall. Gourmet breakfast, one dog, and two cats included. $$. (330) 867–2650; www.oneilhouse.com.

day trip 05

northeast

old stuff and new thrills:
bath • peninsula • aurora

This region has both the old and the new: Amish history, skiing, shopping (crafts and outlets), amusement parks, and more. Now reincarnated as Geauga Lake's Wildwater Kingdom, the former Six Flags amusement park is a H_2O-filled thrill from the folks that brought you Cedar Point.

bath

Far from being all washed up, this tiny town boasts the Hale Farm and Village, located in the picturesque Cuyahoga Valley. A drive of about an hour and a half, Bath can be reached by heading north from Columbus on I–71 to exit 218. Turn right (east) on SR 18 and continue approximately 5 miles to Cleveland-Massillon Road. Turn left on Cleveland-Massillon Road, heading north, and turn right on Ira Road to Oak Hill Road.

where to go

Hale Farm and Village. 2686 Oak Hill Road, Bath, OH 44210. This attraction allows you to experience the attitudes and beliefs of 1848 Amish culture without worrying about taking out a buggy with your vehicle or having your ringing cell phone or teenager's attire offend Old Order sensibilities. Populated with townspeople-cum-actors who discuss the struggles, triumphs, and rewards of pioneering the Western Reserve, the land was originally settled in 1810 by Jonathan Hale, who constructed a three-story redbrick house on the grounds. A

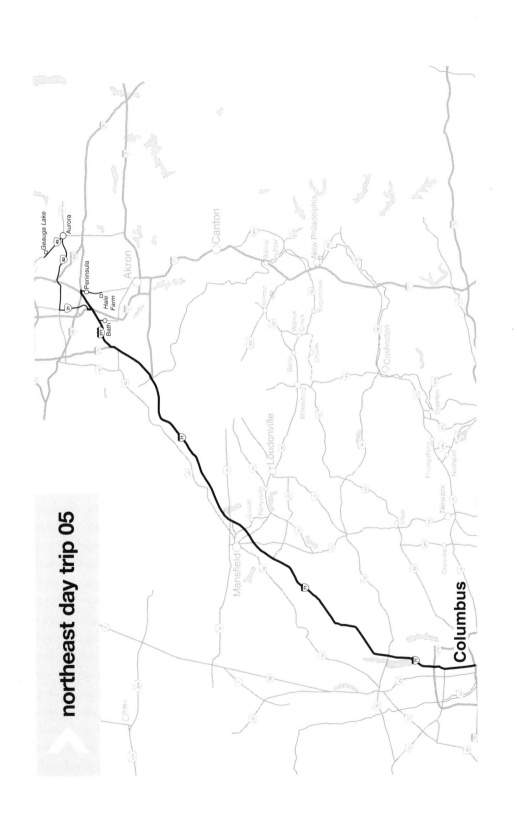

northeast day trip 05

glassblower, candle maker, potter, and blacksmith also demonstrate the early trades of the region. Open daily May through October. Admission is charged. (800) 589–9703.

peninsula

Situated in the heart of the Ohio Valley, the charming village of Peninsula is a short hop north of Bath on I–271. Get off at SR 303 and turn right (east).

where to go

Cuyahoga Valley Scenic Railroad. 1630 Mill Street, Peninsula, OH 44264. This ninety-minute round-trip excursion runs through 26 miles of the Cuyahoga Valley National Recreation Area. Relax in climate-controlled vintage coaches circa 1939–40; you can also take a guided tour with a park ranger through the area. Other round-trip destinations include Hale Farm and Village, Stan Hywet Hall, Quaker Square/Inventure Place, and others. Dates and times vary. Closed in January. Admission is charged. (800) 468–4070; www.cvsr.com.

Boston Mills/Brandywine Ski Resort. 7100 Riverview Road, Peninsula, OH 44264. With nineteen slopes and eighteen chairlifts, you can plow through a plethora of skiing, snowboarding, and tubing activities. When the weather fails to cooperate, there's snowmaking equipment, so you can still get the drift. Lessons are available, as are locker and equipment rental, shuttle bus service, and sale of apparel. Hours vary, depending on weather conditions. Fee varies. (800) 875–4241; www.bmbw.com.

where to shop

Fine Art Services. 1600 West Mill Street, Peninsula, OH 44264. This custom framing shop is also a full-service art gallery that features the works of internationally recognized photographer Luciano Duse. There's a continually changing selection of photography, paintings, sculpture, and gift items, as well as "Meet the Artist" receptions. (330) 657–2228; www .fineart-services.com.

Bures PotteryElements Gallery. 1619 West Mill Street, Peninsula, OH 44264. You can watch craftspeople at work, creating bowls and other pottery. The studios of Bures Pottery, this shop also showcases the work of other artists. (330) 657–2788; www.bures pottery.com.

The Ewe Tree. 61 Geoppert Road, Peninsula, OH 44264. Owned by two sisters, this enterprise creates fine woven clothing, rugs, and bags. Wool, yarns, spindles and other equipment, and books are available at the supply barn adjacent to the studio. Call before coming.(800) 219–8342; www.ewetree.com.

Heritage Farms. 6050 Riverview, Peninsula, OH 44264. Here you can find that perfect Christmas tree in December, pick out a pumpkin in October, or view more than 250 varieties of daylilies in the summer. The area's oldest family-run farm, it's been operational since 1848 and has covered bridges and a barn with a stone fireplace big enough to stand in. (330) 657–2330; www.heritagefarms.com.

Century Cycles Peninsula. 1621 Main Street, Peninsula, OH 44264. Talk about a prime location: This cycle shop is next to a 25-mile towpath. You can rent or buy a bike or get your bike repaired here. (330) 657–2209; www.centurycycles.com.

where to eat

Winking Lizard. 1615 Main Street, Peninsula, OH 44264. Come meet "Heisman," the restaurant's resident namesake and catch your favorite game while noshing on a menu of barbecue, sandwiches, wings, and pizza. Daily drink and meal specials round out a dining experience for all ages. There are over a dozen "lizards" throughout Ohio. $$. (330) 657–2770; www.winkinglizard.com.

Fisher's Café and Pub. 1607 Main Street, Peninsula, OH 44264. Practically next to the Lizard is this laid-back café, which serves sandwiches, salads, chicken, steaks, desserts, along with beers and wines, sans reptile. Breakfast as well as outdoor dining are also offered. $–$$. (330) 657–2651.

where to stay

Inn at Brandywine Falls. 8230 Brandywine Road, Sagamore Hills, OH 44067. Located a little less than halfway between Peninsula and Aurora, Sagamore Hills is off SR 82. Part of a recreational area that includes a waterfall, this 1848 restored Greek Revival home boasts six luxurious rooms, each with private bath. Other amenities include gourmet foods, exercise facilities, and Ohio historic decor. $$$. (888) 306–3381; www.innatbrandywinefalls.com.

aurora

Established nearly 200 years ago, this well-maintained New England–style town has enjoyed increased tourism along with a respectable growth in population and industry. Diversions range from amusement parks to shopping to getaways. There is also some good eatin', mostly in shopping areas and lodges. Aurora is accessible from major interstates such as I–271 and I–480. From Peninsula/Sagamore Hills, go east on SR 82 about 15 miles and turn left (north) on SR 306.

where to go

Geauga Lake's Wildwater Kingdom. 1100 Squires Road, Aurora, OH 44202. Here the surf is *really* up. Put the fun in funnel by racing down a 60' tall, 245' long tube with three screaming strangers and/or friends. Or drop a cool 10 stories down the state's tallest water slide. Frolic in a 390,000 gallon tsunami with rolling waves and erupting geysers, a lot gentler than it sounds. Or chill out on the Lazy River or children-themed Coral Cove. Private cabanas are available for day rental and there are a variety of fast-food options as well. A great place to get soaked on a hot summer day—with water, that is. Open daily end of May through end of August; weekends only in early May, September, and October. Admission is charged. (330) 562–8303; www.wildwaterfun.com.

Thorn Creek Winery and Gardens. 155 Treat Road, Aurora, OH 44202. Part living room, part French countryside chalet, and part art gallery, this winery's tasting area also specializes in seasonal appetizers and unique dessert selections. Oh, and there are the wines, too, including several reds, rosés, and whites. Open daily; hours vary according to season. Free (unless you buy wine, of course). (330) 562–9245; www.thorncreekwinery.com.

where to shop

Aurora Farms Premium Outlets. 549 South Chillicothe Road, Aurora, OH 44202. This is the place for close encounters of the bargain kind. More than seventy outlet stores are housed in an early American–style village and include Polo, Ralph Lauren, Off 5th–Saks Fifth Avenue, DKNY Jeans, Ann Taylor, Big Dog, and more. There are also shoes, children's things, luggage and leather goods, gift and specialty items, home accessories, and more, as well as restaurants and a food court. (330) 562–2000; www.premiumoutlets.com.

where to stay

Aurora Inn of Mario's International. 30 Shawnee Trail, Aurora, OH 44202. This nineteenth-century lodging resides in beautiful downtown Aurora and is an excellent example of Western Reserve architecture. Guests can indulge in indoor and outdoor pools, sauna, Jacuzzi, and tennis courts. Restaurant offerings range from country cooking to lighter fare. $$–$$$. (800) 444–6121; www.marios-spa.com.

Inn Walden. 1119 Aurora Hudson Road, Aurora, OH 44202. This exclusive getaway is located on 1,000 acres that would do Thoreau proud. Thirty-two Arabian horses graze the property, and riding is available. Suites come with cedar-paneled ceilings and a variety of fireplaces, and the beds boast fine Italian linens. Jacuzzis, full kitchens, and fine to casual dining options may tempt you not to leave the grounds. $$–$$$. (330) 562–5508; www .yourwalden.com.

Bertram Inn and Conference Center. 600 North Aurora Road, Aurora, OH 44202. With 156 rooms, an exercise facility, and several restaurants and bars, this lodging suits travelers from business to pleasure. High-speed Internet access, Play Station, and premium cable TV will satisfy the high-tech junkie. $$$. (877) 995–0200; www.thebertraminn.com.

Mario's International Spa and Hotel. 35 East Garfield Road, Aurora, OH 44202. This is the spot for reasonably priced pampering. The nationally recognized facility offers elegant accommodations, fine and casual dining with a variety of cuisine (low-cal and up), even limousine service. Most rooms have a private whirlpool; other public areas contain cozy fireplaces. There's a large menu of spa services as well: skin and beauty care; body and water therapies, scrubs, and masks; and hand and foot treatments. Spa days and retreats are also available. $$–$$$. (888) 464–7721; www.marios-spa.com.

day trip 06

northeast

>>>

comeback city:
cleveland

cleveland

Cleveland has come a long way. (Yes, you can, Detroit!). Once plagued by poverty and pollution, this venerable metropolis tapped into its inner city and pulled out a model of urban renewal, which includes hip ethnic neighborhoods, an emerald necklace of a park system, and a holy trinity of A-league sports teams—Cleveland Browns football, Cleveland Indians baseball, Cleveland Cavaliers basketball, not to mention numerous smaller entities like soccer and hockey. One of Ohio oldest settlements founded only twenty years after the Revolutionary War, Cleveland is part of Cuyahoga County, the most populous in the state. It's also the birthplace of Life Savers (the candy, not the rescue) rock 'n' roll, Superman, the electric streetcar, and the gas mask. Cleveland revels in its diversity and was the first city to have an African-American newspaper (1853, *The Aliened American*) and mayor (Carl Stokes, 1967).

Culture buffs can choose from Severance Hall (11001 Euclid Avenue; 216–231–1111; www.clevelandorchestra. com), home of the renowned Cleveland Orchestra; the Play-house Square Center (Euclid at East Seventeenth, 216–771–4444; www.playhousesquare .com) with five magnificently restored theaters and the largest venue of its kind outside of New York City; the Cleveland Opera (1422 Euclid Avenue; 216–575–0903; www.cleveland opera.org); the locally based Cleveland Playhouse (8500 Euclid Avenue; 216–795–7000; www.clevelandplayhouse.org), and more. With nightclubs, coffee shops, and jazz and

northeast day trip 06

Lake Erie

State Park
SOUTH BASS
ISLAND

Put-In-Bay

Kelleys
Island

Lakeside Marblehead

Port
Clinton

Cedar Point
Amusement Park

Sandusky

Milan

Bellevue

○ Cleveland

Peninsula

Bath

Hale
Farm

Akro

Mansfield

Lucas

Perrysville

Loudonville

Berlin

Walnut
Creek

Wilmot

Millersburg

Charm

Sugarcreek

Coshocton

Utica

Frazeysburg

Dresden

Granville

Newark

Nashport

Columbus

Buckeye
Lake

blues bars, as well as major performers who make Cleveland a regular gig, nightlife is ubiquitous.

When visiting Cleveland, it's always difficult to choose what to do. The only way around this is to return, again and again, because there's always something new and different. Although Cleveland's about 140 miles from Columbus, it's a straight shot up I-71 and you can make it in a little more than two hours without getting pulled over by those guys with sirens who frequent highway turnarounds.

where to go

Trolley Tours. 1790 Columbus Road, Cleveland, OH 44113. On rigs with names such as Lolly the Trolley and Gus the Bus, you're in for an entertaining ride. This is a good way to get oriented and learn about the city, its history, and landmarks. Reservations are required. Admission is charged. (800) 848–0173; www.lollytrolley.com.

Rock and Roll Hall of Fame. 751 Erieside Avenue, Cleveland, OH 44114. Not only is this 150,000-square-foot facility visually stunning with its cantilevered spaces and glass "tent," but the interactive exhibits, intimate performance spaces, and rotating costume and artifact displays make it a treat for other senses as well. Listening to songs and oral histories and seeing genuine objects that shaped so much popular culture can be awe-inspiring for any age. Where else can you view Buddy Holly's high school diploma, Jim Morrison's Cub Scout uniform, or diverse, rotating exhibitions on everything from U2 and Jimi Hendrix to the music of Ohio? Plus, there's a really cool gift shop. Open daily except Thanksgiving and Christmas. Admission is charged. (216) 781–7625; www.rockhall.com.

Great Lakes Science Center. 601 Erieside Avenue, North Coast Harbor, Cleveland, OH 44114. With more than 340 hands-on exhibits and an OMNIMAX cinema, this attraction, which focuses on science, environment, and technology, makes learning fun. There's an indoor tornado, a static-electricity generator that literally makes your hair stand on end, and a "Shadow Room" that just cries out for you to leap in the air for that special effect. You can pilot a blimp, experience virtual reality, and visit "sick Earth" in a hospital bed or a house "haunted" by toxic chemicals and pollutants. Open daily. Admission is charged. (216) 692–2000; www.greatscience.com.

Steamship *William G. Mather*. 305 Mather Way, Cleveland, OH 44114. In its previous life, this 1925 vessel was a Great Lakes freighter carrying millions of tons of ore and coal. Now a museum and completely restored, the *Mather* consists of cavernous cargo holds, a shipshape pilot house, and a four-story engine room. It also boasts classy guest and dining accommodations (and not-so upscale cribs for deckhands), as well as captain's quarters. An exhibit details the history of Great Lakes shipping; a video is also available. Open Friday through Sunday, May through October. Admission is charged. (216) 574–6262; www.wgmather.nhlink.net.

Goodtime III. 825 East Ninth Street Pier, North Coast Harbor, Cleveland, OH 44114. OK, so it's not sailing the Bahamas, but this quadruple-deck, 1,000-passenger luxury cruise ship offers two-hour narrated tours as well as fun and/or romantic luncheon and dinner options. The ship has an enclosed, heated/air-conditioned lower deck and a topside that allows for sunning. Snacks and drinks are available. Open daily from Memorial Day through Labor Day, limited hours in May and September. Admission is charged. (216) 861–5110; www.goodtimeiii.com.

Cleveland Browns Stadium Tours. 1083 West Third Street, Cleveland, OH 44113. See Cleveland's lakefront jewel, which opened in 1999, without the crowds. You'll visit the locker room, the Dawg Pound where the most rabid fans sit (think diehards in canine masks or painted faces and bodies), and the Browns Hall of Fame, among other spots. The Browns Team Shop offers the largest selection of team-related gear and souvenirs around, and there's a bar and grille and Hall of Fame as well. Tours at specified hours, April through December, except on game days. Admission is charged. Reservations required. (440) 824–3361; www.clevelandbrowns.com.

Cleveland Museum of Art. 11150 East Boulevard, Cleveland, OH 44106. Those searching for more highbrow endeavors will find cultural satisfaction at what the *New York Times* calls "one of the nation's premier collections." More than 30,000 works of art encompass 5,000 years, from Egyptian vase paintings (3500 b.c.–a.d. 300) to Medieval and Islamic Art (a.d. 300–1500) to Old Master paintings (thirteenth through eighteenth centuries), nineteenth-century European portraits, and contemporary art and photography. In between you'll find a collection of armor and other weapons of war; sculpture, decorative arts, and textiles; and Asian art, among other items. Open daily. Admission is charged. (877) 262–4748; www.clevelandart.org.

The Cleveland Museum of Natural History. 1 Wade Oval Drive, Cleveland OH 44106. Begun in the 1830s as a "Noah's Ark" of animal specimens, the CMNH has evolved into a sophisticated research, education, and conservation entity with more than 5 million artifacts. They recently merged with HealthSpace Cleveland, the first museum to ever focus on regional health and its attendant exhibits, including the circa 1950 icon Juno the Transparent Woman. They also combined forces with EcoCity Cleveland to create the GreenCity-BlueLake Institute, a center for regional sustainability. Still the CMNH has remained true to humble roots with exhibits such as Lucy, a skeletal cast of a 3.2-million-year-old human ancestor; Happy, a 70-foot-long, 14-foot-high dinosaur skeleton; and Dunk, a 360-million-year-old fish with a big bite, to mention a few. Open daily, except for major holidays. Admission is charged. (216) 231–4600, (800) 317–9155; www.cmnh.org.

Western Reserve Historical Society. 10825 East Boulevard, Cleveland, OH 44106. This complex houses the Crawford-Auto Aviation Museum and the History Museum and Library. The former highlights more than 200 autos and aircraft, with special focus on turn-of-the-twentieth-century and Cleveland-made cars. There's also an early 1900s Curtis Hydroplane flown by local aviator Al Engel. The History Museum features a mansion built in 1911 and is home to the Chisolm Halle Costume Wing, which has more than 30,000 items for rotating exhibitions. Open daily. Admission is charged. (216) 721–5722; www.wrhs.org.

NASA Glenn Research Center. 21000 Brookpark Road, Cleveland, OH 44135. Opened to the public in 1976, this facility had been conducting aerospace research since the early '40s. Its six galleries consist of displays on innovative engines and space communications and a tribute to local hero John Glenn. There's also an Apollo command module that was used on *Skylab 3,* a microgravity laboratory with a drop tower, and a launch center where you can conduct your own countdown sequence. Far out! Open daily except major holidays. Free. (216) 433–4000; www.nasa.gov/centers/glenn.

Cleveland Metroparks Zoo. 3900 Wildlife Way, Cleveland, OH 44109. Home to some 3,000 animals representing 600 species, many of which are endangered, Cleveland Metroparks Zoo boasts an indoor rain forest that re-creates that vital but dwindling atmosphere; an Australian adventure featuring koalas, kangaroos, kookaburras, and kowaris; and an African savanna with grassy plains, with, among others, lions, giraffes, and zebras, oh my! A waterfowl lake and the primate, cat and aquatics building make it a real jungle in here. The completion of the most recent addition, an African elephant crossing will more than quadruple the amount of indoor and outdoor space dedicated to pachyderms and will hopefully get them in the mood for love, er reproduction. Open daily except Christmas and New Year's. Admission is charged. (216) 661–6500; www.clemetzoo.com.

where to shop

Tower City Center. 230 West Huron Road, Cleveland, OH 44112. A former train depot, this complex boasts over 100 shopping, dining, and entertainment venues. Options range from the Cleveland Store to Jones New York and include a Hard Rock Cafe and a multiplex. Bonuses: a leapfrog fountain where water shoots up unexpectedly, an observation deck on the forty-second floor, and easy access to downtown attractions. A fitness center and amphitheater/performance space round out the offerings. (216) 623–4750; www.towercity center.com.

Westside Market. 1979 West 25th Street and Lorain Avenue, Cleveland, OH 44113. On Mondays, Wednesdays, Fridays, and Saturdays an outdoor arcade and a vintage grand hall fill with more than 115 vendors. Hailing from all over the world, they peddle meat and dairy products, baked goods, fruits and vegetables, ethnic foods, and more. The building also has lots of nifty stone carvings of foodstuffs in doorways and interior arches. (216) 664–3387; www.westsidemarket.com.

Shaker Square. Corner of Shaker and Van Aken Boulevards. Mailing address: 13110 Shaker Square #104, Cleveland, OH 44120. Constructed in 1927, this historic spot is

Ohio's first and the nation's second oldest shopping center and has been redeveloped, attracting purveyors such as Ann Taylor and upscale ethnic restaurants, all housed in classic Georgian-style architecture. Just 1 block north is Larchmere Boulevard, a mix of antiques shops, specialty boutiques, fine and folk art galleries, and more. (216) 991–8700; www .visitshakersquare.com.

Beachwood Place. 26300 Cedar Road, Beachwood, OH 44122. Located in a suburb on the east side of Cleveland, this is worth a few extra miles of driving, especially if you like upscale shopping. Saks Fifth Avenue, Nordstrom, the Galleries of Neiman Marcus, and Dillard's are but a few of the 150 options with which to max out your charge card. It's Beverly Hills with a change of seasons. (216) 464–9460; www.beachwoodplace.com.

Legacy Village. 25001 Cedar Road, Cleveland, OH 44122. Within spitting (well, almost) distance of Beachwood Place is this brand-new, self-proclaimed "lifestyle" center, which features many retailers and restaurants that will be breaking ground (and bread) in the area for the first time. Among the open-air fountain and bricked walkways you'll find Brio Tuscan Grille, Cheesecake Factory, California Pizza Kitchen, Flemming's Prime Steak House and Wine Bar, Expo Design Center, Crate & Barrel, Z Gallerie, Coldwater Creek, Anthropologie, and more. (216) 382–3871; www.legacy-village.com.

where to eat

Cleveland has an amazing restaurant scene, comparable in depth and scope to Chicago and New York. Each of the neighborhoods has popular dining staples that have been around for decades as well as innovative new places. The following is a very brief sampler.

***Nautica Queen* Cruise Dining Ship.** 1153 Main Avenue, Cleveland, OH 44113. Enjoy a lavish buffet in plush splendor while perusing Cleveland's ever-changing skyline. Afterward you can relax on the observation decks or see the sights from inside the ship. Cruises are from April through New Year's Eve. $$$. (800) 837–0604; www.nauticaqueen.com.

Lola Bistro. 2058 E 4th Street, Cleveland, OH 44115. Superstar chef Michael Symon of Food Network whips up a menu made from local ingredients amid trendy decor. Entrees change according to season but can range from Atlantic char with beets and potato puree to beef hangar steak with pickle sauce. The adventurous might want to try squab (aka pigeons or rats with wings) with foie gras, sweet potato, and cherries. A sister bistro, **Lolita** (900 Literary Road, 216–771–5652, $$) is also available for those wanting to spend less for a good thing. $$$, (216) 621–5652; www.lolabistro.com.

Momocho. 1835 Fulton Rd., Cleveland, OH 44113. This is the place for mad, er, mod Mex, including six kinds of guacamole (including one with goat cheese and poblano chiles); a sampler of mango, cucumber and hibiscus margaritas; and Mexican-style meatballs with smoked jalapeno-tomato salsita, among others. There are a few familiar items like chimichangas and quesadillas, but even these are no ordinary run for the border. $$–$$$. (216) 694–2122; www.momocho.com.

West Side Market. 1979 W 25th Street, Cleveland, OH 44113. Set amid Byzantine/Neoclassical architecture, this indoor/outdoor market has been feeding Clevelanders since 1912. Fresh items include seasonal produce straight from the farm, Amish chickens, Hungarian sausage, homemade pasta from Ohio City, as well as hundreds of kinds of cheeses. If all this makes you hungry, grab a to-go bratwurst, hot dogs, pretzels, and more. There's also a short-order sit-down restaurant and sampling is also good. $–$$. (216) 664–3386; www.westsidemarket.org.

Great Lakes Brewing Company. 2516 Market Avenue, Cleveland, OH 44113. Located in Ohio City, this eatery is Cleveland's first microbrewery and the first brewpub in the state since Prohibition ended. Solid food offerings range from beer-battered fish to pretzel chicken to pizza. A wide variety of salads and sandwiches, Stilton-cheddar cheese soup (also made with beer), and a gift shop and tours are other highlights. $$. (216) 771–4404; www.greatlakesbrewing.com.

Corky & Lenny's. 27091 Chagrin Boulevard, Cleveland, OH 44122. One of the few "real" (i.e., Kosher-style) delis in the state of Ohio, its menu items range from traditional Jewish favorites like towering corned beef sandwiches, matzo ball soup, lox and eggs, outrageous desserts, and, of course, bagels. $$. (877) 858–3838; www.corkyandlennys.com.

where to stay

The city offers a plethora of choices, from the Super 8 to the Ritz-Carlton and beyond. In general, however, hotel and motel accommodations are more expensive here than in the rest of the state, with even moderately priced rooms being in the $150 range. Below are some inns and bed-and-breakfasts that may be less costly.

The Brownstone Inn. 3649 Prospect Avenue East, Cleveland, OH 44115. This renovated and elegantly furnished Victorian Italianate town house is both an official Cleveland landmark and on the National Register of Historic Places. There's a choice of rooms (medium to large) and sherry or port in the evening. It's also centrally situated in midtown. $$–$$$. (216) 426–1753; www.brownstoneinndowntown.com.

The Glidden House. 1901 Ford Drive, Cleveland, OH 44106. This University Circle–based accommodation was originally constructed for the founder of the Glidden Paint Company in 1910; the family resided there until the early '50s. It's been restored to its original French Gothic grandeur and boasts a restaurant and light dining options. You can even chow down in the former library. Suites have a sitting room and wet bar. $$. (866) 812–4537; www.gliddenhouse.com.

Crest Bed & Breakfast. 1489 Crest Road, Cleveland, OH 44121. With antique-filled rooms and a shared bath, this lodging, on a residential tree-lined street, is ideal for families. Also included are a continental breakfast, a living room with a piano, and an afternoon glass of wine for those twenty-one and older. $$. (216) 382–5801.

Bourbon House. 6116 Franklin Boulevard, Cleveland, OH 44102. This Victorian-style home has retained much of its original ambience and includes an old-fashioned receiving room, a parlor with pump organ, and a large fireplace with window seats. Suites are available; the cost includes breakfast. There's a generous supply of books about Cleveland, and you can learn about the genealogy of European royal families from the innkeeper. $$–$$$. (877) 444–7279; www.bbhost.com/bourbon_house.

east

day trip 01

east

>>> **step back in time:**
granville • buckeye lake • utica

The village of Granville and surrounding area offer plenty of activities, from history to the outdoors. Along with shopping and dining, the friendliness of the natives and beautiful architecture make for a well-rounded excursion.

granville

Founded in 1805, the quiet New England–style village of Granville was named by the folks who settled there from Granville, Massachusetts. Although it harks back to a simpler, slower era, it's got the added torque of a prestigious college in the form of Denison University (100 West College Street, Granville 43023; 800–336–4766; www.denison.edu), which provides an upscale academic flavor thanks to professors, an ever-changing cast of students, and well-to-do alumni who love to visit.

About 30 miles from Columbus, Granville can be reached by going east on I–70 and getting off at exit 126, Granville-Lancaster (SR 37). Go north on SR 37 until you reach Broadway, then turn right into town.

where to go

Robbins Hunter Museum. 221 East Broadway, Granville, OH 43023. Can you say toga? This 1842 Greek Revival home was built by Alfred Avery, one of Granville's founders. It's been added to over the years and was a private residence for various branches of the Avery

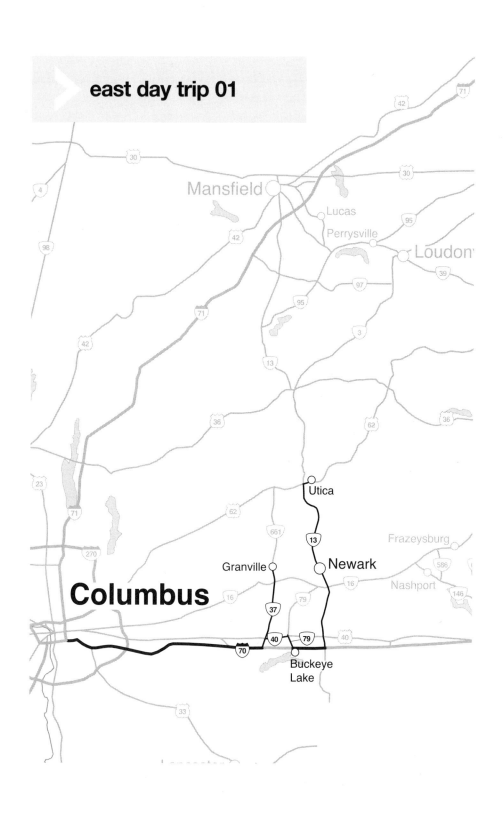

Mansfield

Lucas

Perrysville

Loudon

Utica

Newark

Granville

Frazeysburg

Nashport

Columbus

Buckeye
Lake

family until 1903, when it was turned over—perhaps *turned loose* might be a better term—to the Phi Gamma Delta and Kappa Sigma fraternities. This lasted until 1956, when local historian Robbins Hunter purchased the property as a combination domicile and antiques business. Upon his death in 1979, it was converted to a museum and opened two years later. Although there's plenty of eighteenth- and nineteenth-century American and European furniture, paintings and sculptures, oriental rugs, and more, perhaps the truly amazing thing is that the home survived in decent condition. Open Tuesday through Sunday and by appointment; closed January through March. Depending on the program, donations may be required. (740) 587–0430; www.robbinshunter.org.

Granville Historical Society. 115 East Broadway, Granville, OH 43023. Dedicated to preserving the town's heritage and genealogy, this building—the oldest structure in Granville—houses pioneer collections dating from 1805. These include hand tools and furniture from early settlers, as well as an exhibit chronicling local agriculture. Open Friday through Sunday, April through October; other times by appointment. Donations are welcome. (740) 587–3951; www.granvillehistory.org.

Alligator Mound. End of Bryn Du Drive, Granville, OH 43023. A gigantic sculpture of a four-footed creature made of mounded earth and small chunks of burned and broken rock, this structure was built by prehistoric Indians between 1200 and 800 b.c. Although it loosely resembles an alligator (hence its name), other guesses have ranged from opossum to panther to salamander. What it isn't is a burial ground. Open daily. Free. www.lchsohio .org/alligator_mound.htm.

The Granville Golf Course. 555 Newark-Granville Road, Granville, OH 43023. Designed in 1924 by course guru Donald Ross, this spot has been top-rated by *Golf Digest* and boasts fully irrigated tees, fairway, greens, and rough. You can hone your game with lessons or at the driving range and rent any necessary equipment. There's also a fully equipped pro shop for all those wild-looking pants and shirts, among many other items. Open year-round. Call for tee times and fees. (740) 587–4653; www.granvillegolf.com.

where to shop

Scrapbookery. 1189 River Road, Granville, OH 43023. It's to "die" for: a $20,000 cutting center that allows you to create unique mementoes from hundreds of designs. Cashing in on the major trend of scrapbooking, this store offers equipment, supplies, and accessories as well as a sewing center and classes for all levels of skill. (740) 587–1555; www.scrap bookery.com.

Kussmaul Gallery and Flower Market. 140 East Broadway, Granville, OH 43023. Known among locals as the "Koos," this shop not only sells all kinds of flowers but also provides frame jobs of the picture kind. There's also a continuously changing array of jewelry, paintings, prints, and other objets d'art. (740) 587–4640; www.kussmaulgallery.com.

Artiflora. 605 W. Broadway, Granville, OH 43023. During the summer, Artiflora operates a fresh flower open-air market in downtown Granville. Customers can select hand-tied bouquets in a variety of styles, all inspired by Dutch floral design. The rest of the year, you can get your flower fix by ordering from the Web site, although nothing quite equals being surrounded by the real thing. (740) 587–3515; www.artifloragranville.com.

where to eat

Granville Inn. 314 East Broadway, Granville, OH 43023. This restaurant is a destination in itself. It has fine oak paneling, a copper-hooded fireplace, and colorful stained-glass windows. Menu items vary from full-course meals to light snacks, and the Sunday brunch buffet serves up something to please every palate. $$–$$$. (740) 587–3333; www.granville inn.com.

Buxton Inn. 313 East Broadway, Granville, OH 43023. With nifty dining rooms, a more casual tavern, and a beautiful porch area filled with greenery, this eatery has atmosphere to spare. You can choose from appetizers, soups, and salads,   as well as gourmet and American offerings. $$–$$$. (740) 587–0001; www.buxtoninn.com.

Victoria's Parlour. 134 East Broadway, Granville, OH 43023. A favorite of locals, this eatery specializes in soups, sandwiches, and other quick snacks. $–$$. (740) 587–0322.

Short Story Restaurant. 923 River Road, Granville, OH 43023. Although it was inspired by the brevity of Hemingway, the online menu is some 13 pages long. However, it's mostly devoted to wine, beer and other spirits. But the plot is pretty concise, with only about a half dozen chilled and hot appetizers and main entrees. That leaves room for the "Dirty Little Secret" dessert . . . Shhh, don't tell! $$–$$$. (740) 587 0281; www.theshort-storyrestaurant.com.

Brew's Cafe. 116 East Broadway, Granville, OH 43023. Along with specialty beers and an upstairs that has free live music on weekends, big-screen TV, and a pool table, this restaurant offers a fun and diverse menu. You can choose from fried 'n' fattening starters, a wide assortment of salads and sandwiches, and pasta or pizza. $$. (740) 587–0249; www .brewscafe.com.

where to stay

Granville Inn. 314 East Broadway, Granville, OH 43023. Set amid tall, sheltering maples with a native sandstone exterior, this seems more like an English country house than a hotel. But the redecorated rooms have individual themes, along with modern amenities. Continental breakfast is included. (Note: If you try to book accommodations during Denison's fall Parents or Graduation Weekends, you're out of luck, unless you get picked by a lottery.) $$–$$$. (740) 587–3333; www.granvilleinn.com.

Buxton Inn. 313 East Broadway, Granville, OH 43023. Built in 1812 as a tavern to service a stagecoach crossing, the Buxton is Ohio's oldest operating lodging in an original building. Somewhere along the way, it also picked up a ghost or two. So, along with two-story porches, formal gardens, period antiques, and all the contemporary conveniences (including refrigerators and coffee/tea service) you might encounter a lost soul. Or not. $$. (740) 587–0001; www.buxtoninn.com.

Follett-Wright House. 403 East Broadway, Granville, OH 43023. This historic residence, constructed in 1860, offers two guest rooms with queen-size beds and private baths. Breakfast consists of Danish rolls, coffee cake, and other caloric comestibles. $$. (740) 587–0941; www.bbonline.com/oh/follett-wright.

Porch House. 241 East Maple Street, Granville, OH 43023. This turn-of-the-twentieth-century home with a large front porch provides quaint and charming guest rooms, each with private bath and air-conditioning. Breakfast is included; if you want an additional bed, you'll need to pay a nominal fee. $$. (800) 587–1995; www.porchhouse.com.

Fraley House. 257 Clouse Lane, Granville, OH 43023. This circa 1800s replica of a colonial home features four working fireplaces and many antiques as well as modern amenities like air-conditioning, swimming pool, and communal TV/VCR. A full breakfast is included, and there's a patio as well. $$. (800) 578–0611; www.fraleyhouse.com.

buckeye lake

From Granville, take 37S to I-70E and get off at SR 79S to reach Ohio's oldest state park.

where to go

Buckeye Lake State Park. Mailing address: 2095 Liebs Island Road, Millersport, OH 43046. This natural pond started out as a salt spring that attracted deer and bison, making it popular among Native Americans in search of fast food. It later underwent an enlargement procedure by palefaces, who made it part of the Ohio-Erie Canal System. Today it offers a 32-mile shoreline and 3,800 surface acres for water-related recreational opportunities. Boating, swimming, fishing and hunting (in season only, and designated areas), and picnicking can be enjoyed here, but there are no overnight facilities. You can also visit Cranberry Marsh, an ancient bog, a remnant of Ohio's glacial period from more than 17,000 years ago. Free. Open daily. (740) 467–2690; www.buckeyelakestatepark.com.

Greater Buckeye Lake Historical Society. 4729 Walnut Road, Buckeye Lake, OH 43008. Since opening its doors in 1998, this minute museum has seen nearly 20,000 visitors. Hark back to Buckeye Lake Amusement Park's glory days in the early to mid-1900s, when it was the place to be for family gatherings, big band dances, and summer vacation.

Exhibits include the Rocket Ride, Skee Ball, and hundreds of photos and artifacts. Those of a certain age may rediscover childhood memories here. Admission is charged. Open Tues through Sun; closed Mon. (740) 929–1998; www.buckeyelakehistory.org.

The Queen of the Lake II. Mailing address: 4729 Walnut Road, Buckeye Lake, OH 43008. Okay, so it's not the Pacific Ocean or even Lake Erie, but this 40-passenger pontoon boat offers a local's eye view of the region, as well as providing a sense of its history. Tours depart from Buckeye Lake North Shore Boat Launch and Park, located off SR 79 in the village. Admission is charged. Tours start in May on Saturdays and Sundays. (740) 929–1998; www.buckeyelakehistory.org/queen.html.

where to eat

Papa Boo's. 11356 Avondale Road, Thornville, OH 43076. This self-proclaimed "Lake Place" serves up a sense of humor along with bar food, sandwiches, sides, and pricier entrees. There's trivia, karaoke, and other regular entertainment, and the daily specials are a good deal. $$. (740) 928–2667; www.papaboos.com.

Smittys On The Lake. 3545 Sellers Drive, Millersport, OH 43046. Originally the Sellars Hotel where rooms went for a dollar and meals were a mere two bits and dime (35 cents), this restaurant has long been a local favorite, especially of the late Dave Thomas, founder of Wendy's. Offerings range from pub pickles to the chef's salad to the catch of the day, as well as a variety of burgers and dinners, including maple baked salmon. Closed in winter. $–$$. (888) 490–0641.

where to stay

Buckeye Lake/Columbus East KOA. P.O. Box 972, 4460 Walnut Road SE, Buckeye Lake, OH 43008. Take your pick: stay in your own camper, pitch a tent, or opt for one of fifteen "Kamping Kabins" equipped with beds, electricity, heat, and air-conditioning but no linens (bring your own). More than forty acres offers plenty of trees and open space along with access to three bathroom/shower facilities. $. (800) 562–0792.

utica

Although it's about 20 miles from Buckeye Lake, Utica is a straight shot north on SR 13.

where to go

Ye Old Mill. 11324 Mount Vernon Road, Utica, OH 43080. This is one sweet historic site. Built in 1817, the mill was a traditional gathering place and is now the home of a museum, ice cream parlor and restaurant, and picnic area owned by the Velvet Ice Cream

Company. Originally one of the largest of its kind in the Ohio frontier, it was utilized as a gristmill and has been reconstructed, the last version being completed after the Civil War. The wide selection of flavors is also complemented by special events, such as an ice-cream festival and crafts. Open daily, May through October. Free. (800) 589–5000; www.velveticecream.com.

day trip 02

longaberger basket country:
newark • nashport • frazeysburg • dresden • coshocton

At the turn of the last century, factory worker J. W. Longaberger, who created baskets in his spare time while supporting a wife and twelve children, found his handiwork replaced by paper bags and plastic containers. In the early 1970s his fifth son, Dave, became convinced that consumers desired well-crafted items from a bygone era. He started hawking the hampers at $10 a pop, marketing them via direct sales associates. Soon Dave, who passed away in 1999, and his two grown daughters had woven themselves the largest manufacturer of handmade baskets in the United States.

The venture pumped prosperity into Dave's economically depressed hometown of Dresden. The Longaberger family also played a key role in developing the village and surrounding area, funding schools, social services, and businesses. Dresden and environs have not only become a basket-lover's mecca but a major tourist draw, which includes the Longaberger Homestead in Frazeysburg.

The region itself is loaded with golf courses, recreational areas, and some of the best paths in Ohio. Walkers, bikers, joggers, and birders can go for miles and enjoy the topography, no matter what the season.

newark

About an hour from downtown Columbus, Longaberger country is reached via I–270 to SR 161 east, which eventually turns into SR 16 about 6 miles west of Newark.

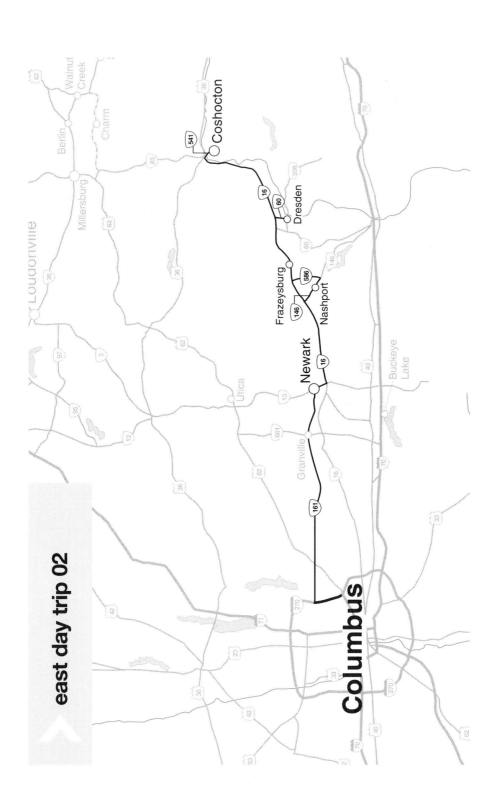

east day trip 02

Coshocton

541

16

60

Dresden

Frazeysburg

586

146

Nashport

Newark

16

Granville

161

Columbus

Walnut
Creek

62

Charm

Berlin

83

208

60

146

Millersburg

62

Loudonville

39

36

97

3

62

95

13

Utica

13

661

36

40

Buckeye
Lake

70

62

16

33

36

42

71

270

23

33

36

42

270

40

70

33

2

where to go

Longaberger Home Office. 1500 East Main Street, Newark, OH 43055. You'll see this one coming and going: It's a seven-story basket that, rather than being the purveyor of a gargantuan picnic, contains employees who work in the corporate office. Along with receiving local and national media attention, the vast vessel boasts a 30,000-square-foot atrium, which provides a light, airy feel, and two 75-ton handles on the roof with heated humidity sensors to prevent the formation of ice. Much of the big basket's woodwork and trim was harvested and milled from Longaberger properties, keeping the construction within the family, so to speak. Inside are offices as well as educational tours and displays of company offerings. Ants are optional. Open daily except major holidays. Free. (740) 322–5000; www .longaberger.com.

Blackhand Gorge. 5213 Rock Haven Road SE, Newark, OH 43055. With 970 acres and an awesome, huge abyss cut by the Licking River, this is a *gorge*-ous experience, especially in the spring when wildflowers abound. Along with old locks of the Ohio and Erie River Canal and a tunnel of the Interurban railway, there's a 4.3–mile bike trail to explore, plus hiking, canoeing, and bird-watching. Open daily. Free. (740) 763–4411.

Dawes Arboretum. 7770 Jacksontown Road , Newark, OH 43056. Founded in 1929, this 9.5-mile stretch of greenery traverses accumulations of hollies, crab apples, rare trees, and horticulture. There's a Japanese garden, a nature center, and the Daweswood House museum, summer home of the family that donated the land, plus a variety of educational programs. A bonsai collection and bird-watching garden are other highlights. Should you forget the name of the place, it's spelled out in one of the world's largest lettered hedges. Open daily except Thanksgiving, Christmas, and New Year's. Free. (800) 443–2937; www .dawesarb.org.

The Great Circle Earthworks. 99 Cooper Avenue, Newark, OH 43055. Built by the Hopewell culture nearly 2,000 years ago, this earthwork is nearly 1,200 feet in diameter. Used as a ceremonial center and part of a larger system of such mounds, this is one of the few remaining remnants of prehistoric Ohio. Open Sunday through Wednesday, Memorial Day through Labor Day; weekends, Labor Day through October. Admission is charged. (800) 600–7178.

where to stay

The Place Off the Square. 50 North Second Street, Newark, OH 43055. With 117 guest rooms, on-site shopping featuring Longaberger products, and an indoor swimming pool, this property mixes big-city luxury with small-town amenities. Full-service restaurant; continental breakfast included. $$–$$$. (740) 322–6455; www.longaberger.com.

Cherry Valley Lodge. 2299 Cherry Valley Road, Newark, OH 43055. This relaxing and elegant retreat offers 200 rooms, some with Jacuzzis; exercise and gaming areas; restaurant; and more. Two recent additions—CoCo Key Water Resorts indoor water park with slides, activity pools, and a Key West theme and the Banyon Leaf Spa, 1500 square feet of pampering including massages, waxing, hair care, manicures, etc.—cover just about every age and demographic. Set on eighteen wooded acres, this is the only hotel in North America to claim its own arboretum. $$–$$$. (800) 788–8008; www.cherryvalleylodge.com.

nashport

Down the road a ways is Nashport. Turn south on SR 146 from SR 16, about 10 miles east of Newark.

where to go

Longaberger Golf Club. One Long Drive, Nashport, OH 43830. An avid duffer, Dave Longaberger hired architect Arthur Hills (really!) to design an eighteen-hole, par 72 course set amid rolling inclines, heavily wooded areas, and ponds. Named one of the "top ten you can play" in *Golf* magazine, the facility also offers a full-service clubhouse with grill room, a pro shop, and lockers, in addition to space for banquets, business meetings, and bar mitzvahs. Open daily. Greens fees. Call (740) 763–1100 to arrange tee times; www.longa bergergolfclub.com.

frazeysburg

Get back on SR 16 and go east about 10 more miles to get to Frazeysburg, where you can learn everything there is to know about baskets.

where to go

Longaberger Homestead. 5563 Raiders Road, Frazeysburg, OH 43822. While Dad's out pretending to be Tiger Woods, the rest of the family can hang out at the thirty-four-acre Longaberger Homestead. Here you can shop, dine, and weave your own basket, personalizing it with a variety of stains, colors, and designs. A replica of Dave Longaberger's family home and the original workshop where J. W. created baskets for farmers and potters can be found here, as well as the Crawford Barn, which was built in the 1890s and is one of the largest structures of its kind. Open daily, except holidays. Free. (740) 322–5588; www .longaberger.com.

Manufacturing Campus. 5563 Raiders Road, Frazeysburg, OH 43822. During the self-guided tour, employees demonstrate how baskets are woven and show a video on the production process. Then it's on to the glassed-in mezzanine with its bird's-eye view of the creation of thousands of baskets, an impressive if somewhat noisy sight. The next stop is the staining, quality assurance, and shipping departments, and then the school of basket-making. There are plenty of photo and shopping opportunities, and you might even get a chance to help put together a basket of your own. Open daily, but it's best to come before 1 p.m. on weekdays, the usual hours of production. Free. (740) 322–5588.

where to eat

The Bakery. 5563 Raiders Road, Frazeysburg, OH 43822. Starbucks meets Longaberger with lattes, cappuccinos, white chocolate mochas, and caramel macchiatos. Oh, and there's fudge too (buy a pound get a half pound free), assorted "regular" and sugar-free chocolates, and baked goods. Located at the Homestead, in the Crawford Barn. $$. (740) 322–5588.

Longaberger Homestead Restaurant. 5563 Raiders Road, Frazeysburg, OH 43822. This is rapidly becoming a destination eatery for those searching for healthful, delicious, and reasonably priced home-cooked food. Along with the roasted chicken, salads, and a wide assortment of veggies, the fattening-but-worth-it category includes sweet country biscuits and homemade whipped potatoes. And then there's the apple basket: With warm apple slices, vanilla ice cream, and caramel sauce fenced in a waffle bowl, it's comfort food, Longaberger style. $$. (740) 322–5588.

The Barn. 5563 Raiders Road, Frazeysburg, OH 43822. Breakfast, sandwiches, salads, and more can be found on a BBQ-intensive menu. The Barn Loft offers snacks, drinks, and ice cream. Entrees can be enjoyed on the patio in nice weather, or you can eat inside. $. (740) 322–5588.

dresden

Now that you've bought your baskets, you'll need to accessorize, and Dresden is the place to do it. From Frazeysburg, take SR 16 east and go south on SR 60, a drive of approximately 15 minutes.

where to go

World's Largest Basket. Corner of Fifth and Main Streets, Dresden, OH 43821. Now a misnomer, thanks to the behemoth bin in Newark, this 48-foot-long, 11-foot-wide, 23-foot-high structure with two swinging handles is still quite the conversation piece. Made from ten hardwood maple trees and requiring 2,000 hours of work, it was carted around to the Ohio State Fair, Columbus Convention Center, and Longaberger corporate offices before being set down permanently in the center of town. It's always open and available for photos, no matter what the weather.

where to shop

With more than forty shops, this quasi-quaint village has everything from basket accessories and minutiae to crafts and collectibles. Most stores are within walking distance of each other.

Olive Oyl's. 511 Main Street, Dresden, OH 43821. More than 300 baskets, along with tie-ons, basket stands and hangers, basket-themed shirts, canisters, and dishes can make choices difficult (what would Popeye's girlfriend do?). Cheesecake, gourmet coffee, umbrellas, and more are thrown into the mix as well. (866) 928–6778; www.oliveoyls.com.

Dresden Pottery. 721 Main Street, Dresden, OH 43821. One of the first shops to open due to the influence of Dave Longaberger, it carries American- and European-made pottery, Stevens linens, and all manners of collectibles. There's also basket jewelry in 14-karat gold, sterling, and pewter. (740) 754–3000; www.thedresdenpottery.com.

The Patio Shops. 606 Main Street, Dresden, OH 43821. This basket-accessory mother ship not only offers products highlighted at the Longaberger Homestead but also peddles pewter items, apparel, collectible bears, and scented candles. (740) 754–2518.

Dresden Country Cupboard. 515 Main Street, Dresden, OH 43821. In addition to the usual lineup of basket accessories, this emporium peddles the handmade stylings of over 150 area crafters and family-based businesses. So you're unlikely find the same accessory in a friend's home. (740) 754–2340, (800) 754–5159; www.dresdencountrycupboard.com.

Charm of Dresden. 517 Main Street, Dresden, OH 43821. Along with colorful Zulugrass Jewelry made by the Maasai women of Kenya, this unique shop has the largest selection of Pandora and Trollbeads in the area. Shoppers will also find much to delight in one-of-a-kind practical offerings such as Switchflop changeable strap shoes and Pouchee carry-all bags. (740) 754–1525; www.charmofdresden.com.

where to eat

Popeye's Soda Shop. 416 Main Street, Dresden, OH 43821. Oddly enough, this restaurant bears Dave Longaberger's childhood nickname, something most people might want to forget. But when he was alive, Dave loved the place and visited there often. And with good reason: Sandwiches, salads, and dinner entrees are served up in a spotless, fun '50s decor. Favorite menu items include onion rings, milk shakes, and red velvet cake. $$. (740) 754–5730.

Depot Restaurant and Pub. 18 E. 9th Street, Dresden, OH 43821. Its claim to fame is the longest bar in Dresden, which can't be much since there are only a few. However, what this whistle stop lacks in competition it makes up for in versatility, offering a large selection of breakfast and BBQ items as well as varied lunch and dinner menus. And after a day of looking at all things basket, alcohol in any form sounds awfully tempting. $$. (740) 754–1873; www.depotpub.com.

where to stay

The Pines of Dresden. 42 Dave Longaberger Avenue, Dresden, OH 43821. Constructed in 1820, this former farm is one of the oldest homes in the area. It boasts large rooms with queen-size beds, private baths, and a quiet country setting that's a few blocks from shops and restaurants. The hosts, Jean and Tom Elliott, will regale you during breakfast with tales of and information about the town. $$. (740) 754–4422; www.thepinesofdresden.com.

The Inn at Dresden. 209 Ames Drive, Dresden, OH 43821. With only ten spaces, this lodging reinvents the concept of intimate (it had originally been designed for corporate guests of Longaberger). Each room has its own theme, from "City Lights" to "Hideaway." Extras include kitchenettes, hot tubs, fireplaces, and private deck, plus a full breakfast with evening snacks and desserts. $$–$$$. (740) 754–1122; www.theinnatdresden.com.

Sarah's House on Main. 1015 Main Sreet, Dresden, OH 43821. Located within walking distance of beautiful downtown Dresden, this four-bedroom house was built circa 1860. Today it boasts four rooms with private baths, air-conditioning, and a full breakfast. $$. (740) 754–2097; www.sarahshouse.com.

The Ivy Bed and Breakfast. 719 Main Street, Dresden OH 43821. This sedate B&B offers a secluded entrance in addition to four rooms, each with private baths and cable TV. Choose from the obviously yellow and cheerful Sunshine Room, the small but heavenly Angel Room, or the Rose Trellis Room, less than rosy because the bath/shower is located across the hall. And but of course there's a Wicker Room in honor of all things basket. $$. (740) 754–2231, (800) 798–0229; www.dresdenbedandbreakfast.com.

Whispering Hills Bed and Breakfast. 10001 N Morrison Road, Dresden, OH 43821. The budget-minded might appreciate this property. Rooms are located in a separate guest house; each room has a queen-size bed, air-conditioning, TV, refrigerator, and private bath. A covered deck overlooks a large expanse of woods and well-stocked pond. Peacocks roam freely and breakfast is in the hosts' home. $. (740) 754–1512, (888) 772–8377; www.dresdenbed.com.

coshocton

Just 15 minutes northeast of Dresden, Coshocton can be reached by taking SR 16 north (which turns into SR 83) and going east on SR 541.

where to go

Roscoe Village. 381 Hill Street, Coshocton, OH 43812. Feeling buried in baskets? Near the junction of U.S. 36 east and SR 83 is a bit of living history. The storied and lovingly restored streets and buildings of this former canal town provide a taste of nineteenth-century Ohio. Costumed interpreters, a village smithy, an 1800s printing press, and a one-room schoolhouse add to the authenticity. Hours vary; check Web site. Admission is charged. (800) 877–1830; www.roscoevillage.com.

day trip 03

east

it's a gamble:
wheeling, west virginia •
moundsville, west virginia

wheeling

Wheeling, West Virginia, has a little bit of everything: gambling, culture, sports activities, shopping, and more. It calls itself the Friendly City—as opposed to Rude Town, which could be any number of places—and is manageable to navigate, despite the plethora of activities. If you go during the holiday season (Thanksgiving to New Year's), you are treated to a Christmas light show of dazzling proportions put on by both the city and Oglebay Resort and Conference Center. A candy cane wreath, dinosaur den, polyhedron star, and more brilliant works of art should bring a smile to even the most insurgent Scrooges.

Settled in 1769, Wheeling was established as a city in 1836 and, with its abundance of coal and natural gas, developed into a manufacturing and commercial center producing steel, chemicals, ceramics, glass, and textiles. Located on the site of a 1774 fort, it also became the western terminus for the National Road.

From Columbus, Wheeling is about 125 miles, a straight shot east on I–70. Cross the Ohio River and you're there. You can also explore a 150-year-old suspension bridge off Tenth Street, (1 block south of the I–70 overpass) that for many years was Wheeling's link to the rest of the world.

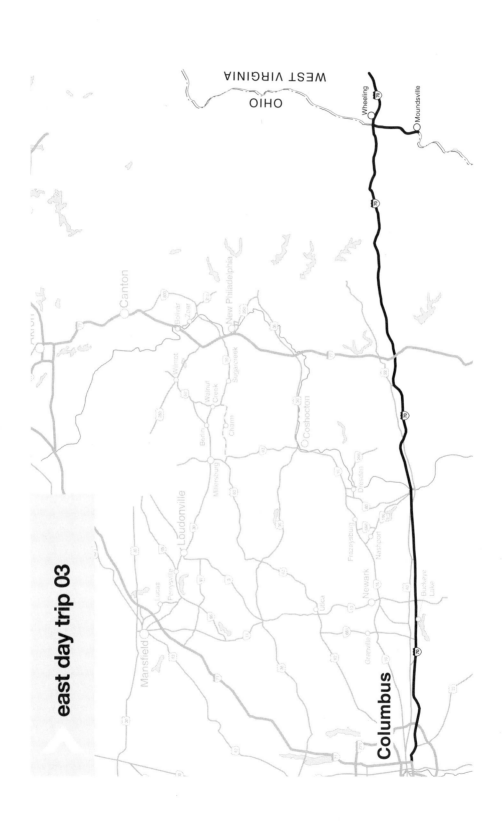

east day trip 03

where to go

Wheeling Island Race Track and Gaming Center. 1 South Stone Street, Wheeling, WV 26003. Those looking for some "reel" (aka slot machine) excitement need search no further. "Drop in a coin, pull the handle, and wait for the sound of coins dropping," states the brochure. Well, at least the first two will happen. Keno, video blackjack, and poker are also offered, and the facility recently added 30,000 square feet of gaming space and a hotel, among other amenities. Along with a simulcast parlor that allows participants to wager on various televised racing events, there's also live greyhound racing six days a week. Call ahead or check the Web site for the schedule. Open daily. Free, if you resist putting in that first quarter. (877) 943–3546; www.wheelingdowns.com.

Oglebay Resort and Conference Center. Route 88 North, Wheeling, WV 26003. This is one massive resort/park. Its 1,650 acres encompass tennis, fishing, and swimming; three golf courses, including one designed by Robert Trent Jones and another from Arnold Palmer; full formal gardens; a science lab and theater; horse stables and riding; even a zoo. There's a mansion and glass museum (see below), along with a train ride. And that's in addition to the usual accommodations and cottages (see Where to Stay), shopping, and dining. Open daily. Admission is charged. (800) 624–6988; www.oglebay-resort.com.

Mansion & Glass Museums. Oglebay Resort, Route 88 North, Wheeling, WV 26003. Originally built in 1846, this was a farmhouse that grew up into a mansion. It went through seven owners before being purchased by the Oglebay family, who made it their summer estate. Inside it's furnished with antiques as well as early pioneer furniture and Wheeling artifacts. The Glass Museum contains arguably the world's largest collection of glass manufactured in Wheeling, including pieces by such artisans and manufacturers as Sweeney, Hobbs-Brockunier, Central, and Northwood. A standout is a mammoth Sweeney punch bowl. There are also glassblowing and decorating demonstrations. Open daily. Admission is charged. (304) 242–7272; www.oionline.com.

Henry Stifel Schrader Environmental Education Center. Oglebay Resort, 1330 National Road, Wheeling, WV 26003. This entity focuses on environmental education. The building itself is a lesson in ecology, as it was constructed using earth-friendly products and processes. An EarthTrek exhibit hall, nature art gallery, bird observation area, children's awareness room, and forest canopy walkway round out the offerings. You can also explore 3-mile or 5-mile trail systems, observing waterfalls, birds, and other wildlife; and visit gardens consisting of butterfly-attracting landscaping, plants, and herbs. Open daily. Depending on activity, admission may be charged. (304) 242–6855; www.oionline.com.

West Virginia Independence Hall. 1528 Market Street, Wheeling, WV 26003. The completion of this structure coincided with the start of the Civil War, which presented a real pickle for local leaders, who were hotly divided on the issue of slavery. What resulted was the independent state of West Virginia (seceded from Virginia), which sided with the Union.

Displays, restored architecture and furnishings, and costumed guides provide insight into America's most divisive war. Open daily, except state holidays; closed Sunday in January and February. Admission is charged. (304) 238–1300; www.wvculture.org/sites/wvih.html.

Eckhart House Tours. 810 Main Street, Wheeling, WV 26003. Before the Civil War, Wheeling was the second largest city in Virginia, and it continued to prosper for nearly three decades afterward. Thus it became a draw for the wealthy and successful, who built stately Victorian abodes. You can tour four of these, three owned by the Victorian Wheeling Landmarks Foundation, and the Eckhart House, which, with its hand-painted florals, pocket doors, Queen Anne windows, ornate chandeliers, and more, was built to impress. Open Saturday and Sunday, May through December, other times by appointment. Admission is charged. (888) 700–0118; www.eckharthouse.com.

Kruger Street Toy & Train Museum. 144 Kruger Street, Wheeling, WV 26003. What a combo: More than 100,000 toys 'n' trains housed in a restored Victorian school. Standouts include the circa 1963 "Big Loo" Robot, with battery-powered eyes, a crank-operated voice, and Ping-Pong ball firing capability; a Disney Carry-All Dollhouse from 1972; and an amazing collection of trucks. And those are only the playthings manufactured by the Marx company, which had a plant near Wheeling from the 1930s until the '70s. Hours vary. Admission is charged. (877) 242–8133; www.toyandtrain.com.

where to shop

Eckhart House Victorian Gift Shoppe. 810 Main Street, Wheeling, WV 26003. This is the place to go for Victorian memorabilia. You'll find dolls, florals, candles, stained glass, prints, and lamps, to mention but a few. (888) 700–0118.

Wheeling Artisan Center. 1400 Main Street, Wheeling, WV 26003. Handcrafted creations by West Virginia and regional artists encompass pottery, jewelry, fabric arts, woodworking, and more. Plus there's a great selection of West Virginia glass and food products and historic souvenirs in a restored building. (304) 232–3087; www.artisancenter.com.

Antiques on the Market. 2265 Market Street, Wheeling, WV 26003. This three-story multidealer antiques mall is located in Historic Centre Market. Antiques from the nineteenth and twentieth centuries include glassware, art pottery, furniture, jewelry, quilts, linens, and accessories. (304) 232–1665.

Hughes Gift Gallery. 600 National Road, Wheeling, WV 26003. Along with design services and even gift wrapping, this store proffers baby items, dinnerware, jewelry, lamps, furniture, stationary, floral arrangements, and accessories. Displays of The Thymes, Crane's Fine Papers, and Vera Bradley share space with products from Chelsea House, Faith Walk Designs, GuildMaster, Mariposa, Mesa International, and more. (304) 232–2424; hughesdsgn.com.

Nini's Treasures. 8 Hyde Park Drive, Wheeling, WV 26003. This is definitely a "chic(k)" store: They claim to have the largest selection of Brighton products in the state, along with clothing by designers from California, New York, and Miami; unique jewelry and watches; and hats, purses, wallets, scarves, sunglasses, belts, and more. (304) 232–6464.

where to eat

Ye Olde Alpha. 50 Carmel Road, Wheeling, WV 26003. PETA might have issues with a place whose motto is "we pride ourselves on our dead animals, cold beer, and classic American food." However, this popular casual dining establishment serves up a crowd-pleasing variety of starters, soups, salads, and entrees along with all legal beverages (so there, tree huggers!). $$. (304) 242–1090; www.yeoldealpha.com.

Generations Pub at the Swing Club. 338 National Road, Wheeling, WV 26003. Owned and operated since 1914 by four generations of the Duplaga family, this eatery offers three meals, seven days a week. Appetizers, sandwiches, salads, burgers, ribs, chops, and other items are on the menu. Plus, there are eight TVs if conversation ever becomes a problem, along with a game room, outdoor deck, and entertainment. $$. (304) 232–7917; www.generationswhg.com.

Uncle Pete's. 753 Main Street, Wheeling, WV 26003. Ideal for those who like casual dining with a view of the river. What's cooking is wings, hoagies, and other daily specials as well as the three S's: soups, salads, and sandwiches. $–$$. (304) 234–6701.

River City Ale Works. 1400 Main Street, Wheeling, WV 26003. Located in the Wheeling Artisan Center, the state's largest brewpub features a wide variety of handcrafted beers along with a varied menu. $$. (304) 233–4555, www.rivercitybanquets.com.

Coleman's Fish Market. 2226 Market Street, Wheeling, WV 26003. Described as a "living legend of American gastronomy" by food reviewer Michael Stern, Coleman's fish sandwich is a destination in itself, and inexpensive to boot. Other offerings include shrimp boats and baskets, fried clams, and more. A family-owned fish purveyor for three generations, they obviously know how to hook 'em and reel 'em in. $. (304) 232–8510; www.centremarket.net.

where to stay

Wilson Lodge (Oglebay). Route 88 North, Wheeling, WV 26003. With 212 rooms and suites, an indoor pool, Jacuzzi, sauna, fitness facility, and even a tanning bed and in-room massage, this is the area's most popular accommodation. So if you want to stay here, be sure to make reservations early. $$–$$$. (800) 624–6988; www.oglebay-resort.com.

Cottages at Oglebay Resort. Route 88 North, Wheeling, WV 26003. Ideal for families or larger groups, these cottages have all the usual amenities from color TV to air-conditioning, yet provide additional privacy. You're expected to keep the place clean, as daily maid service is not included. $$–$$$. (800) 624–6988.

McLure City Center Hotel. 1200 Market Street, Wheeling, WV 26003. Before its present incarnation as a Ramada, this was the area's oldest functioning hotel. It contained a watering trough and hitching post for horses, and registration was on the second floor because the first was a muddy mess due to travelers. Today, it has all the goodies you'd expect from a full-service hotel: central location, restaurants, free parking, gift shops, room service, and more. $$–$$$. (304) 232–0300; www.mclurehotel.com.

Stratford Springs. 100 Kensington Drive, Wheeling, WV 26003. Situated on thirty acres of rolling, wooded hills, this bed-and-breakfast is listed on the National Register of Historic Places. It offers tennis, swimming, and more, in addition to a restaurant that's a heavy local and tourist draw. $$–$$$. (304) 233–5100; www.stratfordspringsrestaurant.com.

Bonnie Dwaine Bed & Breakfast. 505 Wheeling Avenue, Glen Dale, WV 26038. Located 7 miles south of Wheeling in Glen Dale (junction of State Routes 2 and 86), this lodging has amenities ranging from a fireplace to a whirlpool tub/shower in each room to a candlelight gourmet breakfast in the formal dining room. Decor-wise, you can choose from romantic Victorian, cozy country, classic charm, or a honeymoon suite. $$–$$$. (888) 507–4569; www.Bonnie-Dwaine.com.

moundsville

About 12 miles from Wheeling, Moundsville can be reached by taking SR 2 south from I-70 or I-470.

where to go

The Official Marx Toy Museum. 915 Second Street, Moundsville, WV 26041. Among some age groups, these toys were more popular than the movie brothers by the same name. From 1919 to 1980, Louis Marx & Co. was one of the largest toy manufacturers in the world. A short distance from the original factory, this museum provides blasts from the past for several generations—metal toys and trains, dollhouses, Army figures, Johnny West figures, Big Wheels, and more. Original footage of a factory tour and a series of black-and-white commercials from the 1950s may trigger memories. Open Thursday through Saturday, April through December. Admission is charged. (304) 845–6022; www.marxtoymuseum.com.

Grave Creek Mound Historic Site. 801 Jefferson Avenue, Moundsville, WV 26041. The creation of the largest of the Adena burial mounds required the movement of more than 60,000 tons of earth. The mound was constructed from about 250 to 150 b.c. Artifacts and exhibits interpreting the lifestyle of the Adena people are displayed at the adjacent Delf

Norona Museum. The museum also features a gift shop, theater, and a gallery with fine art. Open daily. Admission is charged. (304) 843–4128.

Prabhupada's Palace of Gold. RD 1 NBU# 24, Moundsville, WV 26041. OK, so it's not really gold, but it's close enough: An ornate exterior with thirty-one stained-glass windows, crystal chandeliers, and mirrored ceilings is set amid lush gardens, sculptures, and water fountains. Fifty-two varieties of marble and onyx were imported for floors and walls, and furniture is carved teakwood from India. You can stay one day or several and hang out with the members of the religious order who built the palace as a tribute to Srila Prabhupada, a prolific proponent of Eastern arts and culture. Open year-round. Admission is charged. (304) 843–1812; www.palaceofgold.com.

West Virginia Penitentiary Tours. 818 Jefferson Avenue, Moundsville, WV 26041. Here's a chance to "do time" without actually breaking the law. Options include a ninety-minute tour and monthly "ghost hunts," which involve spending the night (a perhaps ideal deterrent for criminals-in-training). With towering walls and an imposing brick exterior, this ten-acre Civil War–era facility served as a maximum security prison for more than 120 years. Open daily, except Monday, April through November; other times by appointment. Admission is charged. (304) 845–6200; www.wvpentours.com.

southeast

day trip 01

southeast

>>> **the hocking hills:**
logan • rockbridge

Few locales can claim beauty year-round, but the Hocking Hills are such a place. Winding roads reveal frozen waterfalls and pristine snow in the winter; verdant, leafy coolness and gushing gorges in the summer; a riotous palette in fall so dazzling that one hardly knows where to look first; and dewily abundant flowers, trees, and wildlife in spring. Although quaint and casually structured towns such as Logan seem out of step with today's frantic pace, they fit in with the Hills' slower tempo. So turn off the cell phone, computer, pager, and electronic organizer and explore what nature had in mind during Earth's early years.

logan

Located about 60 miles from downtown Columbus, Logan and the Hocking Hills can be reached in about an hour and fifteen minutes, depending on traffic, by going east and south on SR 33 from I–270. Many of the local roads are winding and narrow, however, so allow extra time for travel when visiting various sites.

where to go

Hocking Hills State Park. 19852 SR 664 South, Logan, OH 43138. This mother of all parks boasts several main attractions (see below) and was forged from sandstone and shales deposited more than 350 million years ago. Terrain ranges from the soft, loosely cemented grainlike dirt found in Ash Cave to razor-sharp hard layers at Cantwell Cliffs.

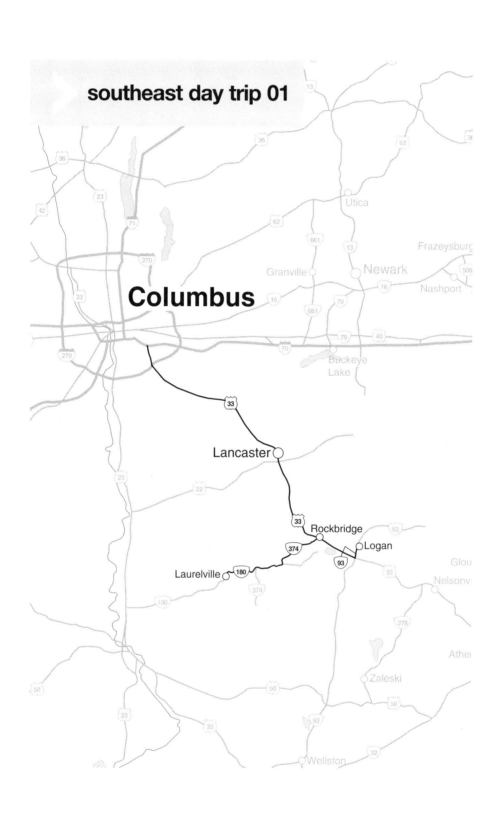

southeast day trip 01

The effect of the glaciers can still be felt in certain regions of the park that have retained a moist, cool environment. Hours vary; some portions may be open seasonally. Free. (740) 385–6841; www.friendsofhockinghills.org.

- **Old Man's Cave.** The most well-trodden of all the Hocking sites, this area has deep-cut gorges, impressive waterfalls, and in one section, a 150-foot-thick slice of rock that allows visitors to look into the earth's subsurface. In the late 1700s and early 1800s, it was also inhabited by two brothers, then by an elderly hermit, all of whom are buried there. Although recently renovated, the trails still require climbing and are a honeycomb of rocks and carved steps.

- **Ash Cave.** The largest recess of its kind in the state—700 feet from end to end and 100 feet deep—this cave is surrounded by hemlocks, beech trees, and hardwoods, as well as wildflowers. Named after the ashes found by the original settlers, it remains in use today for various gatherings, thanks to excellent acoustics and handicapped accessibility. Pulpit Rock, at the entrance, was once used for Sunday worship, and there's a spectacular water geyser toward the back.

- **Rock House.** The only "true" cave in the park, this natural phenomenon consists of a 200-foot-long, 25-foot-wide tunnel-like passage with a 25-foot-high "ceiling." Man-made additions like water troughs and nooks for cooking can also be found. Native Americans, explorers, and even horse thieves and bootleggers camped here; at one point it had the nickname "Robber's Roost."

- **Cantwell Cliffs.** Located in the more remote northern area of the park, these cliffs have narrow passages (one of which is called the politically incorrect "Fat Woman's Squeeze"), deep valleys, and a rock shelter underneath. The varied and colorful terrain is accented by reddish brown sandstone and commanding views.

- **Cedar Falls.** What a misnomer: Early settlers mistook the surrounding hemlock trees for cedars. The most voluminous waterfall in the Hocking Region, it was once harnessed for power by a mill to produce grain. Cedar Falls remains one of the park's most picturesque sites and boasts a well-tended picnic area.

- **Conkles.** Hollow. This rugged, rocky gorge is considered the steepest around. Ferns and wildflowers carpet the floor of the valley, while birch, hemlock, and other hardwoods dominate the top portion.

Lake Logan State Park. 30443 Lake Logan Road, Logan, OH 43138. This prime fishing hole offers pike, bass, bluegill, crappie, catfish, and more. Swimming and boating are other options; those who prefer dry land will find scenic picnic areas, secluded walking paths, and lots of plant and animal wildlife. Open daytime only. Free. (740) 385–6842; www.ohiostateparks.org.

Hocking Canoe Liveries. Both of the following offer canoe, kayak, and raft rentals in addition to organized trips, from a few hours to overnight, depending on skill level and preference. Specialized excursions can be tailored toward various spots in the Hocking Hills.

- **Hocking Hills Canoe Livery.** 12789 SR 664 South, Logan, OH 43138. Open April through October. Fee is charged. (800) 634–6820 and (740) 385–0523; www.hocking river.com.

- **Hocking Valley Canoe Livery.** 31251 Chieftain Drive, Logan, OH 43138. Open during the season; call for dates and times. Fee is charged. (800) 686–0386; www .hockinghillscanoeing.com.

where to shop

Artisan Mall. 703 West Hunter Street, Logan, OH 43138. The first floor offers hand-made crafts; homemade jellies, candy, and other foodstuffs; and gift items and souvenirs. Antiques, Amish-made oak furniture, and other collectibles can be found on the lower level. (740) 385–1118; www.artisanmall.com.

Logan Antique Mall. 12795 SR 664 South, Logan, OH 43138. This spot has everything from advertising memorabilia to cookie jars, from military items to Victorian collectibles. More than eighty dealers can be found in a 10,000-square-foot retail space; a reference library and black light are available for verification of authenticity. (740) 385–2061.

Great Expectations. 26776 US Hwy 33, Rockbridge, OH 43149. A bookstore with an old-fashioned flair, this enterprise offers a wide variety of current and children's literature as well as used books. Individual selections are displayed on tables and shelves, rather than being arranged in piles on large racks. Jewelry, handblown glass, pottery, and other crafts are also for sale. (740) 380–9177; www.hockinghills.com/greatexpectations.

Wind Chime Shop. 29205 Ilesboro Road, Logan, OH 43138. This array, arguably the largest in the state, should ring a bell with anyone who likes tinklers. Offerings include forty-five different lines of chimes, with an running inventory of almost 2,000. (740) 385–9537, (877) 385–9537; www.windchimeshopsales.com.

where to eat

Those willing to wander a bit more might do well to check out the diverse and excellent cuisine in Athens, 2.5 miles southeast via U.S. 33 (see Southeast Day Trip 2).

Great Expectations Cafe. 26776 US Hwy 33, Rockbridge, OH 43149. Here you'll find panini sandwiches and an espresso bar in a casual atmosphere. Other selections include salads, smoothies, and desserts with such enticing names as Lively Lemon Berry Bash and Milkyway Cheesecake. $. (740) 380–9177; www.hockinghills.com/greatexpectations.

Olde Dutch Restaurant. 12819 SR 664 South, Logan, OH 43138. This eatery offers something for everyone: Amish-style dinners, full dinner menu, sandwiches, a weekend breakfast buffet, and children's and seniors' selections. Specialties include broasted chicken as well as variations of same, along with turkey, pork, ham, and your basic spaghetti and meatballs. $$. (740) 785–1000; www.oldedutch.com.

Sandstone Restaurant. 117 W Main Street, Logan, OH 43138. Along with build-your-own pasta bowl or pizza option, this eatery offers a selection of meat to seafood entrees ranging from New York strip to scallop and shrimp sambuca, although it is somewhat chicken-impaired. Fresh bread is baked daily on premises, and there's an outside patio and bar with weekend live entertainment. $$–$$$. (740) 385–9479; www.sandstonerestaurant.com.

where to stay

Dozens of bed-and-breakfast, cabin, lodge, and camping options abound. The Hocking Hills Tourism Association (13178 SR 664 South, Logan, OH 43138; 800–462–5464) can provide a complete listing, which is also found at www.1800hocking.com.

Ravenwood Castle. 65666 Bethel Road, New Plymouth, OH 45654. From Logan and U.S. 33, take SR 93 south about 14 miles. Travel back in time to medieval England at this one-of-a-kind lodging that has all the comforts of the twenty-first century. You can opt for a room or suite in the main castle (the Sherwood Forest complete with "trees," a "dungeon" with a chain-link lighting fixture, and so forth) or motif cottages. Full breakfast included; special English-themed programs and weekend packages available. $$–$$$. (800) 477–1541; www.ravenwoodcastle.com.

The Inn and Spa at Cedar Falls. 21190 SR 374, Logan, OH 43138. Choose from antique-laden rooms or secluded 1840s cabins, all refurbished with modern amenities but lacking telephones and televisions. Gourmet meals are served in a nineteenth-century double log house or outside on the patio during clement weather, with many ingredients grown on-site. A cookbook and cooking classes are also available. $$–$$$. (800) 653–2557; www.innatcedarfalls.com.

Bear Run Inn—Cabins and Cottages. 8260 Bear Run Road, Logan, OH 43138. This B&B/cabin combo has a five-person hot tub, private fishing ponds, and 500 acres where deer, rabbit, and turkey—but no bear—roam. Continental breakfast included. $$–$$$. (800) 369–2937; www.bearrun.com.

rockbridge

Rockbridge is actually closer to Columbus and can be reached from Logan by going north on U.S. 33 about 10 miles. It's a nice place to tarry on the way back.

where to go

Clear Creek Metro Park. 185 Clear Creek Road, Rockbridge, OH 43139. Located at U.S. 33 and CR 114 (Clear Creek Road), this park offers 5,000 acres of hickory, oak, mesophytic, and bottomland forests mixed with rugged valleys, ridges, and sandstone cliffs. More than 800 flowering plants have been identified, including many that are rare or endangered in Ohio, and some forty species of ferns. Other unnatural habitats are a nesting trail for prairie warblers, which are typically indigenous to Canada, and fly- (in more ways than one) fishing for trout in steep, cold-water gorges. Open daily. Free. (740) 385–1834; www.metroparks.net.

Hocking State Forest. 19275 SR 374, Rockbridge, OH 43149. These 9,000 acres consist of sandstone cliffs, waterfalls, birch, and hemlock in addition to abandoned homesites and fallow corn, wheat, and hay fields, all of which date from the 1800s. Although the park is managed for plant and animal habitat, forestry research, and nursery seed and soil protection, certain areas are available for rock climbing, rappelling, hunting, fishing, hiking, and horseback riding. Open daily. Free. (740) 385–4402; www.ohiodnr.com.

Happy Trails Horseback Rides. 25851 Big Pine Road, Rockbridge, OH 43149. Along with exploring many sites at Hocking Hills State Park, visitors will get an up close and personal view of lesser-known caves, waterfalls, and rock formations. Trails are available for beginners, intermediates, and experts. Open Monday, Tuesday, Thursday, Saturday, and other times by arrangement. Fee is charged. (740) 380–6372; www.hthorsebackrides.com.

Spotted Horse Ranch. 17325 Deffenbaugh Road, Laurelville, OH 43135. Located off SR 180, this facility is BYOH (bring your own horse), or one can be supplied. Along with trail treks and cattle drives, supervised corral rides for young children are also available. There's a lighted outdoor arena as well as campgrounds and cabin. Call for reservations. Fee is charged. (877) 992–7433; www.thespottedhorse ranch.com.

where to eat

Shaw's Restaurant and Inn. 123 North Broad Street, Lancaster, OH 43130. This destination eatery is located about 20 miles north on U.S. 33 in Lancaster. A great place to dine on your way home, it has been recommended by the Zagat Survey, Mobil Guide, Wine Spectator, and AAA. The menu changes daily, but specialties include ribs, steaks, fresh fish flown in from Boston, chicken, pasta, and more. $$–$$$. (800) 654–2477; www.shawsinn.com.

Grouse Nest Restaurant. 25780 Liberty Hill Road, South Bloomingville, OH 43152. The menu changes seasonally with gourmet selections ranging from barbecue chicken quesadillas to white bean chili to peach-glazed pork. Pasta, seafood, and vegetarian items are also offered, and in nice weather, you can eat on the patio outside. $$–$$$. (740) 332–4501; www.ashcave.com.

where to stay

Thunder Ridge Cabins Bed & Breakfast. 11309 Starner Road, Rockbridge, OH 43149. Visitors can relax in luxurious one-room cabins with gourmet breakfasts served in the main house. Each accommodation has a kitchen with microwave and table for those wishing to prepare their own meals; there's also a communal fire pit for star gazing and marshmallow roasts. $$–$$$. (800) 600–0584; www.thunderridgecabins.com.

Hocking Hills Resort. 25780 Liberty Hill Road, South Bloomingville, OH 43152. Located between Rockbridge and Logan, off SR 664. Guests can choose from cozy "love bug" cabins with TV/VCR, charcoal grills, balconies, and gas fireplaces, or larger, secluded vacation homes that are ideal for groups or families. Special programs, such as photography weekends, are also offered. Breakfast is available and there's a full gourmet restaurant on-site. $$$. (800) 222–4655; www.ashcave.com.

Glenlaurel Inn. 14940 Mt. Olive Road, Hocking Hills, OH 43149. This could go under the classification "expensive, but worth it," especially for those looking to rekindle or ignite a relationship. Set on 140 acres that more closely resemble Scotland than mid-Ohio, this accommodation offers several choices of rooms, cottages, hot tubs, and fine dining packages. Wooded walking trails, rock cliffs and waterfalls, and the Inn's old-world elegance are designed to restore whatever sanity might have been lost in everyday living. $$$. (800) 809–7378; www.glenlaurel.com.

day trip 02

southeast

a little cosmopolitan:
nelsonville • athens • glouster

Okay, so it's not New York City or even Dayton, but Athens County has a lot going on for an area of its size and population. Along with a truly diverse array of restaurants and some interesting shopping, there's Ohio University (no street address, just Athens, OH 45701; 740–593–1000; www.ohiou.edu), a highly rated academic institution with a reputation for partying hearty. Several beautiful parks can also be found amid the green, gently rolling Appalachian foothills.

nelsonville

Nelsonville is a straight shot southeast on U.S. 33, about 67 miles from Columbus, halfway between Logan and Athens.

where to go

Hocking Valley Scenic Railway. 33 East Canal Street, Nelsonville, OH 45764. This train, made from bits and pieces of historic locomotives, runs round-trip from Nelsonville to Haydenville or East Logan. The Haydenville excursion takes around an hour and a half and is 14 miles long; the East Logan circuit is longer (22 miles, two and a half hours). At specific times, they include a stop at Robbins Crossing (see below). Open Saturday and Sunday, Memorial Day through mid-November. Admission is charged. (800) 967–7834; www.hvsry.com.

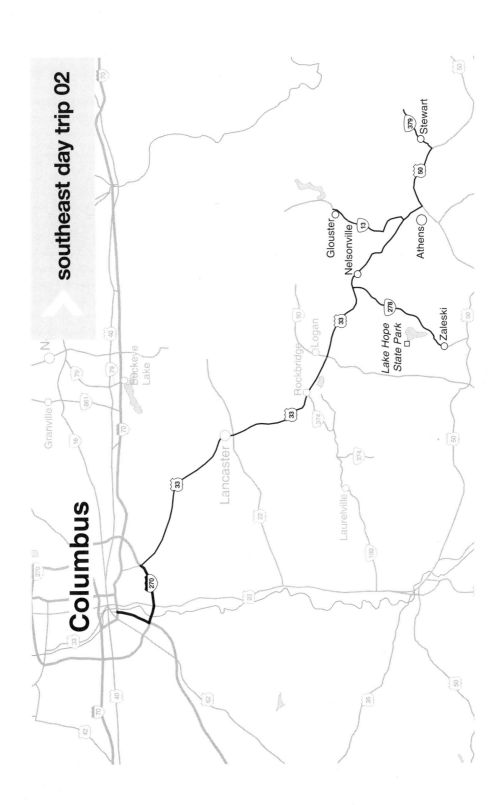

Columbus

N

Granville

Buckeye
Lake

Lancaster

Rockbridge

Logan

Laurelville

Nelsonville

Glouster

Lake Hope
State Park

Zaleski

Athens

Stewart

70
79
861
16
40
79
70
70
40
42
33
270
270
270
33
33
33
22
23
62
35
180
374
374
93
13
278
50
50
50
50
50
379

Robbins Crossing. 3301 Hocking Parkway, Nelsonville, OH 45764. Located on the campus of Hocking College, this restored 1840s-era Ohio village consists of a one-room schoolhouse, a general store, and several authentic-looking dwellings, including a cooper shop, blacksmith shop, and pottery station. Here you'll find people cooking on a wood-burning stove, making barrels and candles, as well as spinning yarn, both literally and figuratively. No, they aren't extremely well-preserved, but instead are Hocking College students being trained as historical interpreters. Arrive by car or for the full Monty, take the Hocking Valley Scenic Railway. Admission may be charged. Open Memorial Day through October. (877) 462–5464, (740) 753–6344.

Stuart's Opera House. 52 Public Square, Nelsonville, OH 45764. This second-story theater—storerooms are at street level—was constructed in 1879 with handmade bricks from local surface clay. Originally home to melodrama, vaudeville, medicine shows, comedies, and assorted musicals, it has been renovated recently. Hours and performances vary. Admission is charged. (740) 753–1924; www.stuartsoperahouse.org.

Lake Hope State Park. 27331 SR 278, McArthur, OH 45651. Take SR 278 south from U.S. 33 in Nelsonville. This rugged, heavily forested region offers steep gorges, constricted ridges, and unique sights such as ancient Indian burial mounds and abandoned mines. Formerly the site of an iron-smelting industry, much of the land has reclaimed its original topography. Reminders of the Civil War–era endeavor can be found in the few standing remains of the Hope Furnace. Hiking, horseback riding, nature programs, camping, swimming, and boating are also available. Open daily. Free. (740) 596–5253; www.lakehope statepark.com.

Zaleski State Forest. P.O. Box 330, SR 278, Zaleski, OH 45698. Just west and directly adjoining Lake Hope is the Zaleski State Forest, 28,000 acres of untouched land ideal for the serious sportsperson. The main trail loops around 23.5 miles; there's also a 10.5-mile option. Other highlights include a horse campground (and one for riders), 50 miles of bridle trails, a hunter's campground, a shooting range, a grouse-management area (the animals, not human complaints), and a sawmill. Open daily. Free. (740) 596–5781;www .ohiodnr.com.

where to shop

Rocky Outdoor Gear and Outlet Store. 45 East Canal Street, Nelsonville, OH 45764. Established in 1932, this factory-outlet store features a complete selection of boots and waders along with casual and rugged outdoor and occupational footwear. There's also a clearance center for the serious (bargain) hunter. (740) 753–3130; www.rockyboots.com.

where to stay

Because of its proximity to Hocking Hills, hundreds of cabins and bed-and-breakfasts are just a short drive away (see Southeast Day Trip 1). Contact (800) HOCKING or Web sites such as BBonline.com or Ohioparks.net for a complete listing and recommendations.

athens

Athens is around 13 miles farther on U.S. 33, a quick drive when students aren't moving into or out of dorms and apartments. Traffic and overcrowding are also an issue during special university events such as Mom's, Dad's, or Siblings Weekend or graduation as well as during unauthorized gatherings around Halloween and, in the spring, Daylight Savings weekend. The latter two honor a long-standing tradition of wandering around with or without costumes or clothes and protesting the bars closing an hour early, respectively. Then you might wish you were stuck on the subway in the Big Apple.

where to go

Hockhocking Adena Bikeway. 667 East State Street, Athens, OH 45701. This 17-mile route, formerly the Columbus and Hocking Valley Railroad bed, winds through Ohio University, Hocking College, abandoned "company" towns from mining endeavors, historic buildings, and Wayne National Forest. High cliffs, rock outcroppings, birds, wildlife, spring flowers, and fall foliage add to the "peak" experience. Open daily. Free. (800) 878–9767.

The Dairy Barn Arts Center. 8000 Dairy Lane, Athens, OH 45701. Rather than being dedicated to the preservation of cows, this venerated arts center milks exhibitions and cultural events from all disciplines and geographical areas. Emphasis is on arts, crafts, and cultural heritage in Southeastern Ohio. Highlights include the summer Quilt National (odd years) and Bead International (even years), with a variety of media during other months. Closed Monday. Admission is charged. (740) 592–4981; www.dairybarn.org.

Kennedy Museum of Art. Lin Hall, Ohio University, Athens, OH 45701. Located in what was once the administrative building of the former Athens Mental Health Center, this renovated venue has extensive Southwest Native American and contemporary print collections on permanent display. Rotating/traveling exhibitions range from Remington bronzes and contemporary Chinese American artists to the work of Western artist Walt Kuhn and a display of fifth-grade weaving projects. Closed Monday. Free. (740) 593–1304; www.ohiou.edu/museum.

Athens County Historical Society and Museum. 65 N. Court Street, Athens, OH 45701. With over 40,000 items, this museum offers up a wealth of local history and well as an extensive genealogical library. Interactive exhibits include a log cabin replica, memorabilia from veterans, and other artifacts. Educational programs and special events round out the offerings. Open Tues.–Sat. Admission is charged. 740–592–2280; www.athenshistory.org.

where to shop

Companion Plants. 7247 North Coolville Ridge Road, Athens, OH 45701. More than 600 varieties of herb plants and seeds from all over the world are on display from the end of March through November. People wanting to learn about or purchase offerings can check out the Web site or request information via mail. (740) 592–4643; www.companionplants .com.

Import House. 68 North Court Street, Athens, OH 45701. Those who think the '60s are over should stop at this place, which carries a full line of, uh, paraphernalia (called "tobacco accessories") as well as shoes, clothing, candles, and incense. In tune with the times, the selection of jewelry also includes piercing items. (740) 593–5155.

Beads and Things. 8 North Shafer Street, Athens, OH 45701. Located in a red house under a shade tree, this unique emporium peddles beads, from antique to new, as well as other doodads with which to create great wearables. You can purchase ready-made items or take lessons in doing it yourself. (740) 592–6453.

Glasshouse Works Greenhouse. 8950 SR 144, Stewart, OH 45778. From U.S. 33 in Athens, take U.S. 50 east to SR 329 north, a drive of about 12 miles. With 10,000 species, cultivars, and hybrids, this is flora nirvana. You can see tropical specimens in a small conservatory or perennials in a garden. Offerings are displayed in ponds, bamboo stands, rockeries, bog areas, and containers.(740) 662–2142; www.glasshouseworks.com.

Mountain Laurel Gifts. 25 S. Court Street, Athens, OH 45701. The work of local artisans shares space with leather goods, jewelry, candles, gourmet foods, household items, garden and home décor, and more. And with a mix of classic to trendy, arty to funky, the customers are almost as varied as the merchandise. (740) 592–5478; www.mountainlaurelathens .com.

where to eat

Because so many patrons are college students, entree prices are generally lower here than in other places (servers light up when they see an over-twenty-one, because they know they'll get a reasonable tip). Still, the quality of food in Athens is high, and although there's a fair amount of caloric stuff, always good for late-night study sessions, fine dining is available as well.

Bagel Street Deli. 27 South Court Street, Athens, OH 45701. Enjoy a variety of sandwiches on bagels, focaccia, pretzel bread, and kaiser rolls. The menu also includes omelettes and vegetarian entrees served in a brick-and-wood modern decor. $. (740) 593–3838.

Red BrickSports Pub. 14 North Court Street, Athens, OH 45701. Yeah, most of the entrees are fried, but with Athens memorabilia, old photos, and upside-down (fake) cows, this clubby bar is a fun place. Specialties include buffalo wings, french fries prepared with garlic, with chili and cheese, and with skins on, and plenty of sandwiches. Soups and salads are also available. $–$$. (740) 594–2077; www.redbricksportspub.com.

Burrito Buggy. Corner of Court and Union Streets, Athens. Those wanting to recapture campus memories should opt for this truly unique experience, which consists of ordering items from a camperlike trailer and then eating them wherever. Along with the usual Mexican fare, there are some low-fat items and during the warm months, even caffeine-free iced tea. Open for lunch and dinner. $. (740) 517–1102; www.45701.com/burritobuggy.

Casa Nueva. 4 West State Street, Athens, OH 45701. Along with daily specials, combo platters, and vegan items, this worker-owned Mexican restaurant offers a full bar (including Ohio brews), organic coffee, and live entertainment, from poetry readings to bands. $–$$. (740) 592–2016; www.casanueva.com.

Goodfella's. 35 Court Street, Athens, OH 45701. Pizza toppings range from the usual pepperoni and Italian sausage to pineapple, artichoke hearts, capicolla ham, and roasted red peppers. You can purchase it by the slice; subs and salads are also available. The atmosphere may be basic campus, but it's a favorite of students and alumni. $–$$. (740) 592–9000.

Lui Lui. 8 Station Street, Athens, OH 45701. This eatery offers seafood, pasta, and chicken with an Oriental flair. During fall and winter, personal pizzas are baked in wood-burning ovens. Menu items change throughout the year. $$. (740) 594–8905; www.luiluirestaurant .com.

Oak Room. 14 Station Street, Athens, OH 45701. The place for steaks and ribs, this restaurant offers a vast array of foodstuffs, from inexpensive sandwiches to pricier salads, chicken, and fish. $–$$$. (740) 593–8386; www.oakroom.net.

The Pub. 39 North Court Street, Athens, OH 45710. With a bar/restaurant that opens at 10:30 a.m., seven days a week, it's no surprise this establishment has been voted as having the most popular burger in town. Daily specials, soups, salads, sandwiches, and friendly service make this a local favorite. $–$$. (740) 592–2699.

Purple Chopstix. 371 1/2 Richland Avenue, Athens, OH 45701. This fine-dining experience is located off the beaten path and overlooks a creek and wooded area. It's also somewhat of a misnomer. Rather than Chinese grub, several different international cuisines are used to prepare inventive dishes. $$$. (740) 592–4798.

Seven Sauces. 66 North Court Street, Athens, OH 45701. Entrees run the gamut from Thai-style trout, prime rib, and shrimp and artichoke linguine to manicotti and West Indian

the bridges of 88 counties

Ohio has hundreds of covered bridges. Many are in excellent shape, while others are in various states of disrepair. No matter where you visit in the state, two excellent Web sites, www.ohiobarns.com/covbri/oh/ohio_cb_.html; and www2.dot.state.oh.us/se/coveredbridges (that's correct, www2) will help you locate nearby covered bridges. They provide details about the bridge, photos, addresses, cross streets and, in some cases, directions and maps. And they're free; photographer not included. Trust us, you won't want to miss some of the following:

- ***Marietta/Washington County.*** *This area boasts nine scenic covered bridges. A driving tour encompasses the Mill Branch Covered Bridge (circa 1832) to the Henry Covered Bridge (circa 1892). Many, such as the Bell, Shinn, Root, and Hildren Hills bridges, were constructed in the 1880s. Most are in excellent condition and look to be recently refurbished and painted.*

- ***Adams County.*** *This includes the Harshaville Covered Bridge, which was built circa 1855 and the last one still in use. Confederate General John Morgan and his raiders passed through it during the Civil War. Others include 1890 Kirker Bridge, a somewhat falling-apart dinosaur that leads to nowhere; the itty-bitty Bennington covered bridge which runs parallel to SR-348 (it's sooo cute!); the Arnold Covered Bridge, decorated with a bull skull (perhaps to deter cattle from crossing and making it collapse?); and others.*

- ***Ashtabula County.*** *With sixteen original, restored, and replicas from the nineteenth century, Ashtabula is covered bridge central, although there are actually more according to the ohiobarns.com Web site. The 1867 Mechanicsville Rd. bridge—at 156 feet, the longest single-span in the county—was recently renovated and opened to traffic; built a year later, the Harpersfield bridge, a 228-foot two-spanner, is the longest covered bridge in Ohio. There's also an annual October Covered Bridge Festival and year-round guided or self-driving tours (www.coveredbridgefestival.org; 440–576–3769). And if that isn't enough, Olin's Museum of Covered Bridges (1918 Dewey Road, Ashtabula, 440–992–7401, www.coveredbridgemuseum.org) located within walking distance of the museum's namesake covered bridge, offers a variety of art, artifacts, and educational displays in addition to memorabilia of the late Naomi Olin Bottorf. Eat your heart out, James Waller.*

vegetable curry. With elegant decor and an extensive wine list, it's a favorite spot to take parents, so reservations are recommended. $$. (740) 592–5555; www.sevensauces.com.

Union Street Cafe. 70 West Union Street, Athens, OH 45701. Here you can get breakfast anytime, which is just about 24/7. Sandwiches, salads, dinner entrees, and appetizers are also served. Those who are feeling especially adventuresome can go into the biker bar down the street (Smiling Skull Saloon, 108 West Union Street, 740–592–9688) for an aperitif. $–$$. (740) 594–6007.

where to stay

The Ohio University Inn. 331 Richland Avenue, Athens, OH 45701. Athens's only full-service hotel, it offers an outdoor swimming pool, fitness center, two restaurants, and complete facilities for business travelers. All rooms have been renovated. It's the most proximate lodging to the college and within mooing distance of the Dairy Barn. $$–$$$. (740) 593–6661; www.ouinn.com.

glouster

Glouster is 17 miles north of Athens. Take U.S. 33 northwest to SR 13, then drive north to SR 78 in Glouster.

where to go

Burr Oak State Park. 10220 Burr Oak Lodge Road, Glouster, OH 45732. This remote and rustic location boasts miles of forested ridge and hollows; wildlife such as white-tailed deer, grouse, and beaver; and plenty of woodland wildflowers, hardwoods, and majestic oaks and hickories. Recreational opportunities include hiking, backpacking, and picnicking, as well as swimming and boating at 664-acre Burr Oak Lake. Open daily. Free. (740) 767–3570; www.burroaksresort.com.

where to stay

Burr Oak State Park Lodge. 10660 Burr Oak Lodge Road, Glouster, OH 45732. Although it has only sixty rooms, the lodge offers a full dining room and lounge, boat launch, beach, tennis courts, indoor pool, and more. Or you can opt for an amenity-filled family cottage with cable TV, air-conditioning, complete kitchen, eating area, and screened-in porch overlooking the lake. Camping is also available and much less expensive. $$–$$$. (800) 282–7275; www.burroakresort.com.

day trip 03

southeast

>>> ### of stern-wheelers and museums:
marietta • belpre

Founded in 1788, Marietta was the first organized settlement in the Northwest Territory. With its redbrick streets and cobblestone levee, this small but elegant city boasts Victorian architecture with leaded glass windows and doors, a lively downtown, and thirteen museums. The area also has plenty of riverboat action for Twainees and shopping for aficionados of art glass, dolls, and pasta.

marietta

With an average temperature of 39.9 degrees in January and 75.2 in July, Marietta is in one of Ohio's balmier regions. Located at the confluence of the Ohio and Muskingham Rivers, the city is about 125 miles east from Columbus. Take I–70 east to I–77 south.

where to go

Trolley Tours. 127 Ohio Street, Marietta, OH 45750. This tour hits all the high points: downtown, churches, museums, and historic homes. Custom packages are also offered. The trolley originates and ends at the Levee House Cafe. Hours of operation and times vary seasonally. Admission is charged. (740) 374–2233.

***Valley Gem* Sternwheeler.** 601 Front Street, Marietta, OH 45750. Except for the air-conditioning and glass-enclosed lower deck, the largest stern-wheeler between Pittsburgh

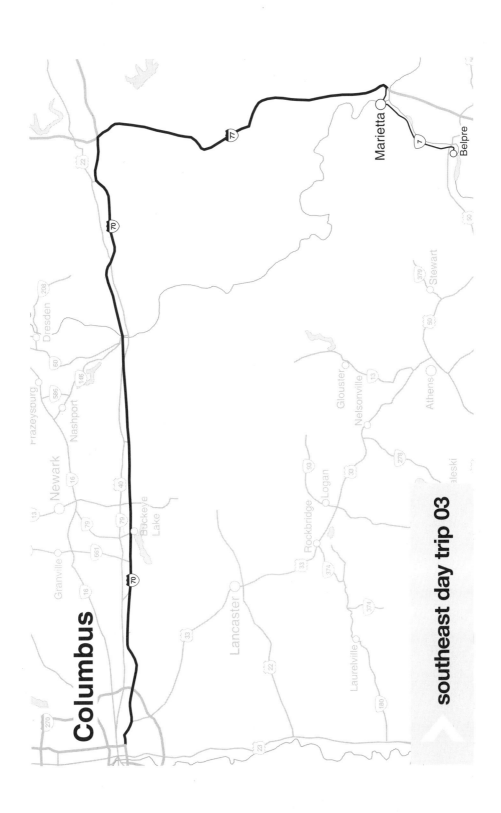

Columbus

Marietta

Belpre

southeast day trip 03

and Cincinnati is reminiscent of those from the height of the riverboat era. Touring options abound and range from educational one-hour trips and dinner cruises to overnight and specialized excursions. For instance, you can spend a delightful three hours floating down the Muskingham River to Lock #2 at Devol's Dam, America's last hand-operated lock system. Call for times and schedule. Admission is charged. (740) 373–7862; www.valleygemstern wheeler.com.

Harmar Village. 100 Block of Maple Street, Marietta, OH 45750. Originally a fort, this area on the west side of Marietta was physically linked to the town in 1859 via a railroad bridge, which is now a walkway to shops, museums, restaurants, and historic sites. You can visit a Civil War–era post office (222 Gilman Avenue), a French historic marker (corner of Gilman Avenue and Virginia Street), and several museums, including the two listed below. Open daily, although many businesses are closed Monday. Admission may be charged. (800) 288–2577.

- **Marietta Soda Museum.** 109 Maple Street. This collection dispenses tin signs, coolers, clothing, paper items, vintage machines, and more. A '50s and '60s-style soda fountain features hot dogs, milk shakes, and 10-cent Cokes. And there's stuff for sale, such as the counter stools so popular during those "happy" days. (740) 376–2653.

- **The Henry Fearing House.** 131 Gilman Avenue. This example of Federal-style architecture was built in 1847 for businessman Henry Fearing. An 1870 Italianate addition and several Victorian artifacts and antiques re-create middle-class Marietta during that era. Fearing supported the temperance movement, and donated the land for what today would be called a shelter for women. (740) 373–3226.

Campus Martius Museum. 601 Second Street, Marietta, OH 45750. Spanning almost two centuries, this comprehensive collection covers the three waves of migration essential to the development of Ohio. The first floor focuses on the settling of the Marietta area, which was originally called Fort Campus Martius in the late 1700s. The display includes the home of General Rufus Putnam, one of the original leaders, among other artifacts. The lower level concentrates on the emigration from farms into the cities between 1850 and 1910 and the exodus from Appalachia to Ohio from 1910 to 1970. Other highlights are the Ohio Company Land Office, created by Revolutionary War veterans, and hands-on activities of weaving, candle dipping, and more. Open daily, May through September; closed Monday and Tuesday other months and during holidays. Admission is charged. (800) 860–0145.

Ohio River Museum. 601 Second Street, Marietta, OH 45750. Also operated by the Ohio Historical Society, this collection of riverboat-era memorabilia includes the *W. P. Synder Jr.,* a real mouthful as America's sole surviving steam-powered stern-wheel tugboat (whew!). There's also a full-scale reproduction of a flatboat and one of the oldest steamboat pilothouses around, circa 1885. Boat building tools, cabin furnishings, models, and art round out the offerings. Open daily, May through September; closed Monday and Tuesday other months and during holidays. Admission is charged. (800) 860–0145.

The Castle. 418 Fourth Street, Marietta, OH 45750. One of the best examples of Gothic Revival architecture in the state, this nineteenth-century abode boasts an octagonal tower, trefoil attic window, and stone-capped spires. Inside you'll find ornate fireplaces and moldings, floor-to-ceiling shutters, and furnishings appropriate to the era. The Castle is also home to classes in tatting and herbs, as well as Victorian teas and tours. Hours vary; call for programs. Admission is charged. (740) 373–4180; www.mariettacastle.org.

Broughton Nature and Wildlife Education Area. 3177 Cambridge Road, Marietta, OH 45750. This 500-acre retreat has trails, ponds, a natural stream, and waterfall, as well as abundant wildlife. Bird-watching, nature studies of flora and fauna, and hiking can be enjoyed here. Call for hours. Free. (740) 376–0831.

Wayne National Forest. 27750 SR 7, Marietta, OH 45750. SR 26 runs into the forest a few miles east of I–77. The Marietta unit, part of this sprawling national forest system, offers primitive camping, hiking, fishing, and hunting. You can also do an informal circuit of historic sites, such as the Walter Ring House and mill, abandoned oil rigs, several covered bridges, and more. Call for hours. Free. (740) 373–9055.

where to shop

Rossi Pasta Retail Family Outlet. 106 Front Street, Marietta, OH 45750. With nearly twenty flavors of pasta as well as accompanying sauces, this establishment has plenty of twists and turns. Gourmet food items, pasta-making accessories, cookbooks, cutting boards, even dining music make for a tasty (and even low-fat) exploration. (800) 227–6774; www.rossipasta.com.

American Flags and Poles. 276 Front Street, Marietta, OH 45750. For the patriot in the family, this store specializes in—guess what—flags and accessories as well as specialty banners, wind socks, yard sculptures, chimes, and more. (800) 262–3524; www.american flagsandmore.com.

Hartel Shipyard. 116 Maple Street, Marietta, OH 45750. Huck himself might be right at home in this eclectic emporium, which has stern-wheeler folk art, slates, railroad ties, hand-painted rowing shells, and more. (740) 374–7447; www.hartelshipyard.com.

Rinky Dinks. 404 Fort Harmar, Marietta, OH 45750. Named after an old Rinks Department store, this flea market is the largest in the area and has bargains galore, although only on weekends (Friday through Sunday). (740) 373–4797.

Salem Candles. 112 Putnam Street, Marietta, OH 45750. With 120-plus scents and dozens of colors and fifty candlemakers represented, this can be an illuminating experience. They also carry candle accessories, wreaths, and oils. (740) 376–0611; www.salem candles.com.

Schafer Leather Store. 140 Front Street, Marietta, OH 45750. This fifth-generation family-owned enterprise carries such varied manufacturers as Swiss Army, Brighton, Montana Silversmith, and Tilley as well as manicure sets, wallets, belts, and portfolios. Their extensive luggage and travel accessories selection ranges from briefcases to Healthy Back Bags, and they have more than 2,500 pairs of boots in stock. (740) 373–5101; www .schaferleather.com.

Antiques and Needful Things. 177 Front Street, Marietta, OH 45750. Although items such as oak curved-glass china closets, pedestal tables with four leaves, barrister bookcases, and drop front secretaries hardly seem essential for survival, they are lovingly refurbished and for sale here. Plantation desks, clocks, quilts, glassware, and more are also available, and the proprietors purchase entire estates or single pieces. (740) 374–6206.

Fenton Art Glass Company. 700 Elizabeth Street, Williamstown, WV 26187. Located off I–77, just over the bridge that links Marietta to West Virginia. Along with a fine selection of discounted handblown "preferred seconds" and "retired firsts," you can tour the factory for free, watching artisans in action, and visit the Fenton Museum. Oh, and there's a large selection of Fenton Glass as well. (304) 375–6122; www.fenton-glass.com.

where to eat

Gun Room/Riverview Lounge. Lafayette Hotel, 101 Front Street, Marietta, OH 45750. Although its name might be more appropriate in Texas, the Gun Room is decorated in nineteenth-century steamboat and offers up quite a collection of long rifles along with three squares of American cuisine. Those twenty-one or older can enjoy cordials at the Riverview Lounge, which overlooks the Ohio. $$–$$$. (800) 331–9336; www.lafayettehotel.com.

Marietta Brewing Company. 167 Front Street, Marietta, OH 45750. Along with a wide range of fresh brews, this eatery provides a varied menu, ranging from creole chicken to burgers to create-your-own pastas, and more. $$. (740) 373–2739; www.mariettabrewing company.com.

House of Wines. SR 60 North, Marietta, OH 45750. Dine in a European-style bistro with wooden tables, fresh flowers, and a patio during the warm months. Specialties include Swiss cheese onion soup, Reuben sandwiches, and cheese boards served with hot mustard. Also available: a large selection of wines, microbrewed beers, and specialty gourmet products. $$–$$$. (740) 373–0996; www.houseofwines.com.

where to stay

Lafayette Hotel. 101 Front Street, Marietta, OH 45750. Constructed in the early 1900s, the Lafayette is one of the last riverboat-era hotels standing. Many rooms come with a river view, and the lobby boasts an 11-foot pilot wheel from the steamboat *J. D. Ayres.* Includes seventy-eight rooms, cable, and free airport shuttle service. $$–$$$. (800) 331–9336; www .lafayettehotel.com.

The Buckley House. 332 Front Street, Marietta, OH 45750. Built in 1879 and less than a block from downtown, this bed-and-breakfast faces the Muskingham River. Each of the three rooms has its own bath; a continental breakfast is included. $$. (740) 373–3080; www .bhrestaurant.com.

The House on Harmar Hill. 300 Bellevue Street, Marietta, OH 45750. With three full floors and a panoramic view of the confluence and the city, this Queen Anne Victorian also has a ballroom, grand staircase, and elegantly decorated guest rooms. Children under fourteen by prior arrangement only. $$–$$$. (740) 374–5451; (877) 914–5151.

Marietta Wine Cellars. 170 Front Street, Marietta, OH 45750. Bed, breakfast, and a wine tasting—what a combo! Along with regular tours as well as wines from Chambourcins to Reislings, the winery also offers accommodations at a private loft. Everything and the kitchen sink—a queen size bed, living room with fold-out couch, and full kitchen as well as vino straight from the winery, a cheese appetizer, and a Continental breakfast. Bonus: No annoying chit-chat from the other guests. $$$. (740) 373–9463; www.marietta winecellars.net.

belpre

Doll collectors in particular will want to visit Belpre, about 12 miles away. From Marietta, take SR 7 south.

where to shop

Lee Middleton Doll Home Store and Legacy Dollhouse Museum. 1301 Washington Boulevard, Belpre, OH 45714. These life-size tiny tots are molded, hand-painted, and assembled in a 50,000-square-foot factory on-site; tours are available. There's even a "newborn" nursery and plenty of new additions to choose from, including "My Own Baby" and others, which are almost as realistic as the genuine article. (800) 233–7479; www .leemiddleton.com.

where to stay

Bramble Creek Bed and Breakfast. 257 Old River Road, Little Hocking, OH 45742. From Belpre, take SR 32W about eight miles then turn left on SR 124. Built by a Revolutionary War soldier and his family, this historic home has been lovingly restored with modern amenities added. Choose from the nautical but nice Ebenezer's Room or the Cummings Suite, where the ethereal presence of former resident Lydia Cummings Porter is said to stop by from time to time. For an extra fee, families can opt for a farm weekend with some meals including a cookout; lessons on bygone crafts; guided studies on ecology, preservation, survival skills, and more. Or you can just go to the coop and gather your own eggs for breakfast. $$-$$$. (740) 989–0334; www.ohioriverinn.com.

day trip 04

southeast

salt of the earth:
jackson • wellston • oak hill •
bidwell/rio grande • gallipolis

Centuries before Columbus sailed the ocean blue, Native Americans used the "licks" on the creek near what is now Jackson for salt. According to legend, they forced Daniel Boone to collect the stuff when they captured him in the late 1700s. When Ohio became a state in 1803, the area was kept as a reserve.

But not for long. By 1815 salt resources had been depleted and settlers began to move in. One was John Wesley Powell, who spent his childhood in Jackson and was tormented because of his parents' abolitionist leanings. He went on to become the first white man to navigate the Grand Canyon. Another famous paleface, Bob Evans, carved out his own niche by creating a restaurant empire, the locus of which can be found near Rio Grande, in Bidwell.

jackson

With lots of greenery, lakes, and historical sites, the Jackson area draws visitors the way its salt used to attract deer. From Columbus, it can be reached by taking SR 23 south to U.S. 35 south and east, a drive of around an hour and a half.

where to go

Lillian E. Jones Museum. 75 Broadway, Jackson, OH 45640. This unique house museum is furnished circa 1920s and was the home of Lillian E. Jones, whose family was prominent

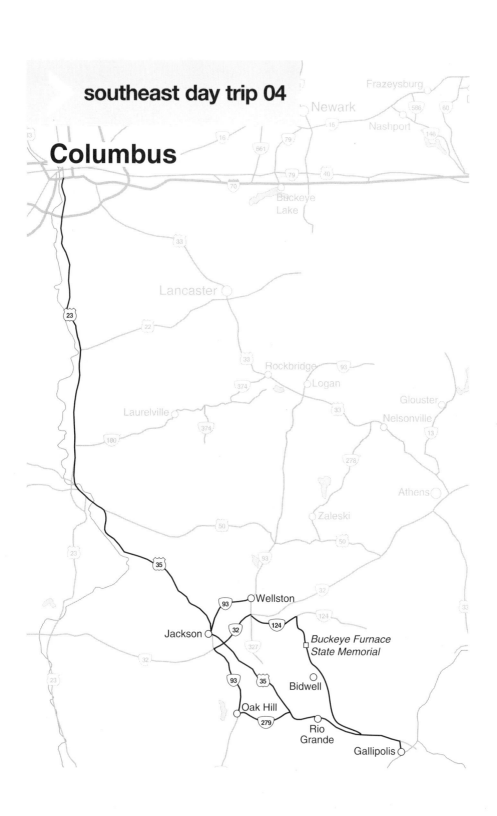

southeast day trip 04

Columbus

in the area. Along with changing exhibits and various seasonal events, it also features a genealogy research center. Open Tuesday, Wednesday, and Saturday, May through December. Free. (740) 286–2556; www.lillianjonesmuseum.com.

Lake Katharine. 1703 Lake Katharine Road, Jackson, OH 45640. Along with nearby Hammertown Lake (see below), this body of water contains some of the finest fishing in the area as well as picturesque views. Located in a rugged area noted for its excellent foliage and rare plants, Katharine offers scenic hiking trails.

Hammertown Lake. (Also known as Jackson City Reservoir). From Jackson take U.S. 35 south to SR 93 south to Beaver Pike and go west, then turn left on Reservoir Road. Hammertown, a 220-acre, U-shaped reservoir, is a popular recreation locale, especially for picnicking and outdoor sports. (614) 286–2201.

Leo Petroglyph. Township Road 224, Marietta. Mailing address: The Ohio Historical Society, 1982 Velma Avenue, Columbus, OH 43211. Take U.S. 35 north to CR 28 east; turn left on Township Road 224. This is the spot for prehistoric Indian inscriptions, particularly if you think you can figure them out (no one has yet). The thirty-seven primitive drawings include humans, hawks, bear, snakes, and more, and are attributed to the Fort Ancient Indians. Created between a.d. 1000 and 1650, the petroglyph is protected by a roof and can be viewed from a platform. Hiking and picnicking in this scenic region are also available. Open daily. Free. (800) 686–1535; www.ohiohistory.org.

where to stay

Jackson Motor Inn. 346 East Broadway, Jackson, OH 45640. Recently remodeled, this accommodation offers single or double beds, microwaves, refrigerators, and access to downtown. $. (740) 286–3258.

Camp Resorts. 1527 McGiffins Road, Jackson, OH 45640. This site has about eighty lots for campers, ten cabins, a pay lake (rate is based on hours fished rather than actual catch), restaurant, camp supply store, swimming pool, and recreation area. Public phones and bathhouse are also available, and kiddies of all ages can keep busy with miniature golf, a playground, and sports activities. $$. (740) 384–3060.

wellston

From Jackson, take SR 93 northeast to the town of Wellston, about 8 miles away.

where to go

Buckeye Furnace. 123 Buckeye Park Road, Wellston, OH 45692. This blast from the past, a reconstructed charcoal-fired iron furnace, is typical of those operating in the region more than one hundred years ago. As the second largest producer of iron ore in the nation, Ohio had several such enterprises, many of which created either wealth or bankruptcy. Built in 1852, its fire went out for the last time in 1894. Along with a charging loft used to load materials into the furnace and steam-powered engine compressor, there's a replica company store and office. Open Wednesday through Sunday, Memorial Day weekend through Labor Day. Donations accepted. (800) 860–0144; www.buckeyefurnace.com.

Lake Alma State Park. Lake Alma Road, Wellston, OH 45692. This 219-acre state park boasts 4 miles of hiking trails, a paved bicycle path, two beaches, and campgrounds. Originally developed in 1903 as an amusement park by a coal miner, it is now the host to excellent bass fishing. Open daily. Free. (740) 384–4474; www.ohiodnr.com.

oak hill

Backtrack on SR 93 to Jackson, and continue south about 12 miles to Oak Hill.

where to go

Welsh-American Heritage Museum. 412 East Main Street, Oak Hill, OH 45656. Located in the Old Welsh Congregational Church, this collection chronicles the life and times of six Welsh families who migrated to the area. They stayed because it reminded them of their native Cilcennin. Along with possible family ties, you'll find heirlooms, books, photographs, and more. Open Tuesday, Thursday, Saturday, and Sunday, May through October. Donations are welcome. (740) 682–7057.

Jackson Lake State Park. 35 Tommy Been Road, Oak Hill, OH 45656. This small but picturesque park offers hunting, fishing, swimming, boating, camping, and picnicking. It was also hot stuff during the mid-1800s, the key production period for iron ore. Remnants can be found in the moss-covered remains of the Jefferson Iron Furnace, which was used to forge the battleship Monitor during the Civil War. Open daily. Free. (740) 682–6197; www .ohiostateparks.org.

bidwell/rio grande

About 14 miles east of Oak Hill, Bidwell is the locus for all things Bob Evans, as personified in his namesake farm. Along with a museum, a restaurant, a festival, and camping, this 1,100-acre spread includes a log cabin village, small animal barnyard, and craft barn. Visitors can enjoy horseback riding, hayrides, trails, and more. Don't be confused by the different addresses and ZIP codes of the Homestead and the restaurant; they're right across the street from each other. Take SR 279 to U.S. 35 and turn right.

where to go

The Homestead Museum. 791 Farmview Drive, Bidwell, OH 45614. Some people feel like they're living in a museum; after raising their six kids there, Bob and Jewell Evans actually turned their house into one. Built in the early 1820s, the Homestead served as a stagecoach stop and an inn during its early years. Today, among other things, visitors can see life-size models of Bob and Jewell filming television commercials in the original kitchen, and then view said commercials through an old television console or the lens of an gen-u-ine camera of the era. No HD or digital here. Open daily, April through December. Free. (800) 994–3276, (740) 245–5305; www.bobevans.com.

where to eat

Bob Evans Restaurant and General Store. 10845 SR 588, Rio Grande, OH 45674. The mother ship of what eventually became a huge restaurant chain, this eatery retains the ambience of an old-time emporium. Along with "down on the farm" home cooking, you can purchase Bob Evans brand products and country kitsch. And you might even encounter the late founder's family, some of who still reside in the area. $$. (740) 245–5324.

gallipolis

In 1790 the Scioto Company had the Gaul—er, gall—to sell worthless property to middle-class French investors who were lured by its proximity to the Ohio River and potential for commerce. One can only imagine the reaction of doctors, merchants, dancing masters, and minor royalty when they arrived to take possession of a 16-by-20-foot dirt-floor hut complete with neighboring hostile natives, disease, and untamed wilderness. Yet they persevered, and the town retains an aristocratic touch.

Continue on U.S. 35 south to Gallipolis, which is about 10 miles from Rio Grande.

where to go

Gallipolis City Park. 300 Block of First Avenue, Gallipolis, OH 45631. This six-acre tract in the middle of town was the locale of the original settlement and now boasts a beautifully restored circa 1878 bandstand. How American: It's also the spot for July 4 festivities, war memorials, and a marker denoting various floods. Open daily. Free. (740) 441–6021.

Our House State Memorial. 432 First Avenue, Gallipolis, OH 45631. Built in 1819, this was formerly a tavern housing travelers and a local gathering spot. Founder Henry Cushing met visitors just off the boat, including Marquis de Lafayette, who visited in 1825. Now restored, the three-story, Federal-style brick structure has been refurbished to reflect the tenor of those times and includes an antique walnut bar in the taproom. Some pieces date back to the original French artisans who settled in 1790. Closed Monday. Admission is charged. (800) 752–2618.

French Art Colony. 530 First Avenue, Gallipolis, OH 45631. The multipurpose arts center curates up to twelve gallery exhibits a year, in a variety of media. Located in a historic Greek Revival home, it also offers arts classes, theater, recitals, and literary workshops. Open Tuesday through Friday, Sunday, and by appointment. Free. (740) 446–3834; www .frenchartcolony.org.

Ariel Theatre. 428 Second Avenue, Gallipolis, OH 45631. Established in 1895, this venue was the pride of the city and saw the likes of Will Rogers, the Ziegfeld Follies, and early "moving pictures" during its heyday. Closed during the early 1960s, it was rescued from disrepair by civic volunteers. Highlights include a luxe crimson drapery, Victorian-style seating, elaborate stenciling, and touches of oak and gold. Excellent acoustics make it a draw for the local symphony as well as regional and traveling performers. Admission may be charged for performances. Call for hours. (740) 446–2787; www.arieltheatre.org.

Fortification Hill. Portsmouth Road/SR 141, Gallipolis, OH 45631. Along with being the location of Mound Hill Cemetery, final resting place of many prominent residents, this historic site bristled with cannons during the Civil War. Today the bluff mostly calls tourists, as it overlooks Gallipolis, the Ohio River Valley, and the hills of West Virginia. Open daily. Free. (800) 765–6482.

where to shop

Aunt Clara's. 4001 SR 141, Gallipolis, OH 45631. Amish arts and crafts can be found here, along with a chance to relax with a cup of coffee and a treat. (704) 446–0205.

French City Mall. 31 Ohio River Plaza, Gallipolis, OH 45631. All manner of antiques, crafts, and collectibles are located on 12,000 square feet of floor space. The diverse selection includes flower arrangements, candles, lawn-goose outfits, hand-painted firescreens, religious artifacts, and old sheet music. Depression glass, mantels, and clothes are but a few more offerings. (740) 446–9038; www.frenchcitymall.com.

where to stay

Raccoon Falls Guest Cottage. 1094 Lincoln Pike, Gallipolis, OH 45631. Situated on a wooded hillside overlooking the falls, only one family, group, or couple at a time have access to the fully equipped but cozy three-bedroom cottage. Explore the peaceful fifteen-acre woods on foot or bicycle or simply kick back, Thoreau-style. Guests are responsible for their own food, but there's a little place a few miles down the road in Bidwell/Rio Grande if you don't feel like cooking. $$. (740) 446–7417; www.raccoonfalls.com.

State Street Manor. 68 State Street, Gallipolis, OH 45631. Built in 1936 and with much of the original mahogany woodwork intact, this rather unoriginally named B&B offers four bedrooms, full breakfast included. Although most rooms have private baths, some lack showers and are located down the hall (which can be a looong walk in the middle of the night when you're half asleep). Still the home is well-maintained and offers a wide choice of amenities. $$–$$$. (740) 441–9394, (740) 446–7999; www.statestreetmanor.com.

William Ann Motel. 918 Second Avenue, Gallipolis, OH 45631. Knotty pine paneling, refrigerators, and larger rooms are some options in this inexpensive accommodation. Clean and spacious with cable and wireless Internet, it's a favorite with families and business travelers alike, offering numerous discounts for veterans, power plant employees and others. $. (740) 446–3373.

south

day trip 01

south

>>> **down on the farm—adams county:**
peebles • seaman • manchester •
west union • lynx

Adams County is the kind of place where someone can tell you to turn left at a certain hill and go right at a stand of trees, and you'll locate your destination. The region consists of several small towns and rural areas amid mostly untouched, gently rolling land. Some might call it Amish Lite: Only a few dozen Old Order families can be found in the villages of Unity and Harshaville, which are so minute they fail to appear on a conventional map (they're in the Wheat Ridge area near West Union). So you'll need to watch for buggies and cap the camera, unless permission is obtained.

The locale also offers a bounty of outdoor options, including sacred Indian grounds, preserves, prairies, wildlife refuges, and state forests. Quality shopping, dining, and bed-and-breakfasts can also be found. No bright lights, big city, but a great place to commune with nature and recharge.

peebles

The first town we'll visit is Peebles, about 95 miles from Columbus. Take U.S. 23 south to SR 32 west and you'll run right into this charming village. Many of the roads are winding, so pay careful attention to signs and allow extra driving time.

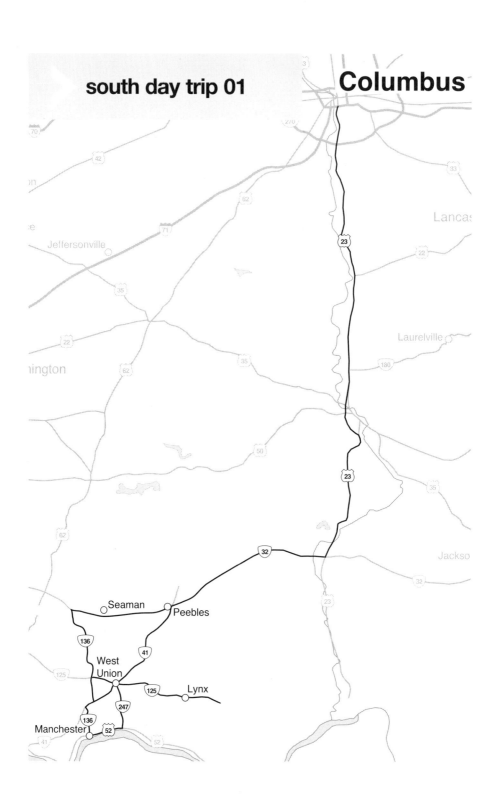

south day trip 01

Columbus

where to go

Serpent Mound. 3850 SR 73, Peebles, OH 45660. With an oval embankment at the end that looks like it's about to strike, this effigy is a real rattler. Nearly a quarter-mile long and an average of 3 feet high, it is the largest of its kind in North America. Yet who built it and why remain a mystery, although the prehistoric Adena people constructed nearby conical mounds for burials and implements around 800 b.c.–a.d. 100. A museum contains exhibits relating to the mound and local geology; hours vary. Mound open daily. Admission is charged. (800) 752–2757; www.ohiohistory.org.

Brush Creek State Forest. Route 3, Box 156, Peebles, OH 45660. These 12,000 acres of predominantly hardwood land comprise craggy hillsides, deep hollows, and narrow ridges. Although it's mostly uninhabited, there are 3 miles of hiking trails and 12 miles of bridle trails to explore. Open daily. Free. (740) 372–3194.

Davis Memorial State Nature Preserve. 2715 Davis Memorial Road, Peebles, OH 45660. Consisting of diverse plant groups and unusual geological formations, this eighty-eight-acre preserve bisects the boundary of two of Ohio's five landform regions. Two richly forested hiking trails provide for an interesting contrast in flora, fauna, and topography, and there's even a sinkhole. Open daily. Free. (614) 265–6453.

where to shop

Raber's Shoes and Saddlery. 5252 Unity Road, Peebles, OH 45660. This is the place for Red Wing footwear, shoe repair, chaps, and holsters. Accessorize your horse with saddles, bridles, and halters; custom items are also available. (937) 544–4545.

House of Phacops. 29894 State Route 41 Peebles, OH 45660. Rock on with this unusual emporium which has provided fossils to museums throughout the world. Or you can get your own rocks, from local to carved stones to gems. (937) 558–2766.

where to stay

Woodland Altars. 33200 SR 41, Peebles, OH 45660. This camp/retreat, run by the Church of the Brethren, offers chalets for individuals and families, along with hiking trails, swimming pools, a lake, and recreational campsites. Lodges are available for large groups only. $–$$$. (800) 213–1161; www.woodlandaltars.com.

seaman

A couple of interesting shopping venues make this town worth a visit. From Peebles, take SR 32 west about 8 miles, then go north on SR 247 for 2 miles to Seaman.

where to shop

Hilltop Designs. 4776 Graces Run Road, Seaman, OH 45679. With a selection that includes dried florals, old-time candy in a barrel, homemade soaps, vintage clothing, hummingbird feeders, grapevine trees, and more, this is the ideal browse. The proprietress, Jo Hall, also offers tours of the area as well as workshops on making an everlasting wreath or topiary. (937) 386–3258.

Keim Family Market. 2621 Burnt Cabin Road, Seaman, OH 45679. In addition to homemade goods, cheese, crafts, and indoor and outdoor furniture, you'll get lots of information about the Amish community and businesses. Along with free brochures and maps, you can purchase cabins, barns, gazebos, cereals, cookies, pies, and noodles (no yolk). (937) 386–2811.

manchester

From Seaman, take SR 136 south about 20 miles to Manchester, situated on the Ohio River.

where to shop

Lewis Mountain Herbs. 2345 State Route 247, Manchester, OH 45144. Dozens of herbs and everlasting flowers are cultivated in greenhouses and gardens that are carpeted with flowers in summer. After perusing the excellent selection of plants (including more than sixty varieties of scented geraniums), herbal products, wreaths, arrangements, and books, you can relax in a living gazebo consisting of Ohio apple trees.(937) 549–2484; www.lmherbs .com.

where to eat

Moyer Vineyards, Winery, and Restaurant. 3859 U.S. 52, Manchester, OH 45144. Constructed in the 1920s as a dance hall that sold bootleg beer, this eatery was a private gambling club during the World War II era, further evolving into a truck stop in the '50s and '60s. Today it's a much classier joint and serves such delectables as fillet of cod with tomato sweet pepper sauce accompanied by fine site-processed—and legal—wines. During the warm months, you can dine on the deck and watch boats and barges float by on the Ohio River. Moyer wines are also for sale. $$–$$$. (937) 549–2957.

where to stay

Hickory Ridge Bed and Breakfast. 1418 Germany Hill Road, Manchester, OH 45144. This cozy cabin is located within view of the Ohio River on a 180-acre estate with walking trails. Amenities include luxe linens, heirloom china, and unique furnishings coupled with modern conveniences. Guests are treated to an arrival gift, bedside desserts, and fresh flowers. $$. (800) 686–3563.

west union

About 2 miles from Manchester, West Union can be reached by driving east on U.S. 52 and north on SR 247.

where to go

William Lafferty Memorial Funeral and Carriage Collection. 205 South Cherry Street, West Union, OH 45693. Hearse looking at you: This accumulation includes motorized and horse-drawn vehicles from 1848 to 1967. Highlights are an 1860 "Dead Wagon" used to carry family members to their final resting place, an 1899 Brewster Omnibus for pallbearers and other attendees, and the area's first motorized ambulance, circa 1923. Caskets, mourning clothing, embalming equipment, and more round out this grave display, which is located next to the Ohio's oldest continuously operating funeral business. Open Saturdays; call for appointment. Donations welcome. (937) 544–2121.

Chapparal Prairie State Nature Preserve. Hawk Hill Road, West Union, OH 45693. Home to more than twenty rare or endangered species of plants, this sixty-six-acre habitat mimics prairie areas more commonly found in the Western states. Visitors can explore the ecosystem via a three-quarter-mile loop trail, and there are plenty of wildflowers and butterflies during warm months. Optimal viewing times for plants are late July and early August. Open daily. Free. (937) 544–9750.

Adams Lake State Park. 14633 SR 41, West Union, OH 45693. Located in what's known as Ohio's bluegrass region, this park is noted for its abundance of unique plant and animal species. Colorful prairie flowers, greenery normally found in northern regions, and a variety of birds and mammals can be found here. Along with a forty-seven-acre lake for boating and fishing, hiking and picnicking are available. Because of the area's rare ecology, visitors must stay on established trails. Open daily. Free. Contact: Shawnee State Park, Portsmouth, OH 45663. (740) 858–6652; www.ohiodnr.com.

where to shop

Miller's Bakery, Bulk Foods, and Furniture. 954 Wheat Ridge Road, West Union, OH 45693. It's three stores in one. Along with tables, chairs, hutches, stools, desks, and more, there is a section for bulk foods. No-sugar food items share shelf space with high-calorie pies, rolls, cakes, cheese, and trail bologna. Wind chimes, cookbooks, Minnetonka moccasins, and quilts round out the diffuse (to say the least) selections. (937) 544–8524, (937) 544–4520, or (937) 544–8449.

abc's of antiquing in adams

The region also has a number of antique shops, where one person's trash might end up being your retirement hedge fund. Many are open "by chance" so call before heading out.

- **As It Was in the Beginning.** *4192 Unity Road. West Union, OH 45693. Primitive collectibles and toys. (937) 544–2867.*

- **Barn Sale Antiques & Fall Pumpkins.** *817 Tater Ridge. West Union, OH 45693. Amish gear, such as grinding wheels, antique machinery, furniture, country collectibles, fixtures, pot belly stoves, etc. (937) 544–8252.*

- **Carriage Lane Antiques & More.** *180 Werline Lane, West Union, OH 45693. Along with antiques and primitives, this shop also features collectibles, glassware, A.I. Root candles and linens. (937) 549–4530.*

- **Land of the Singing Coyote Indian Center.** *17992 Hwy 249, Main St. Seaman, OH 45679. Native American arts and crafts, antiques, sports cards, and country crafts. (937) 386–0222.*

- **Maw's Chicken Coop.** *21123 State Route 125, Blue Creek, OH 45616. Which comes first—antiques, primitives, collectibles, rag dolls, candles, baskets, glassware, crafts, or soap? Maybe all of them; something for everyone. (937) 544–5353.*

- **Peebles Flower Shop & Antiques.** *25905 State Route 41, Peebles, OH 45660. Depression era—the one in the 1930s—glassware and country items. Small antiques to old furniture as well as cut flowers and planters. (937) 587–3044.*

Blake Pharmacy. 206 North Market Street, West Union, OH 45693. This has to be the only place in the known universe where a nickel will still buy a Coke. Decorated with cola memorabilia and with an old-fashioned soda fountain (and prices), you'll also find Hummel figurines, Fenton art glass, Lee Middleton dolls, and more. (937) 544–2451.

Hillside Bird's Nest. 35 Port Road, West Union, OH 45693. Birders can flock to this Amish-owned store. Along with window feeders, thistle sacks, hummingbird supplies, suet, and hooks, there is also a wide selection of pools for feathered friends. (937) 544–9983.

Montana Woodworks. 3645 Wheat Ridge Road, West Union, OH 45693. Although it's pretty far away from its namesake state, this emporium features redwood cedar products, rustic log furniture, tables, chairs, and more. An Amish woodworking shop specializes in carving out home accents. (937) 544–8004; www.montanawoodworks.com.

where to eat

Murphin Ridge Inn. 750 Murphin Ridge Road, West Union, OH 45693. Folks come from far and wide to partake of the Wheat Ridge pork chop, Kentucky bourbon-inflused chicken breast, surf 'n turf strip steak with crawfish-shallot béarnaise, and other regional specialties. Meals are served in an 1828 farmhouse, with many ingredients grown on-site or originating from local suppliers. Dinner reservations recommended. $$–$$$. (877) 687–7446; www.murphinridgeinn.com.

Olde Wayside Inn. 222 Main Street, West Union, OH 45693. Your search for comfort food is over: Home-cooked menu items can include chicken casserole, baked pork chops, meat loaf, whipped potatoes, old-fashioned dressing, candied sweet potatoes, and more. Desserts range from cheesecake and homemade apple dumplings to seasonal pumpkin confections. If you have room left, that is. $$. (937) 544–7103.

where to stay

Murphin Ridge Inn. 750 Murphin Ridge Road, West Union, OH 45693. This highly rated lodge is located on 140 acres with a view of Peach Mountain. Rooms are decorated with Shaker reproduction furniture, and there are some luxurious woodland cabins as well. Swimming pool, tennis courts, hiking trails, and other outdoor activities are available, along with an excellent restaurant and a gallery where local artists and crafters strut their stuff. And that's not even mentioning the fabulous breakfasts. $$–$$$. (877) 687–7446; www.murphinridgeinn.com.

Unity Woods. 1095 Marjorie Johnson Road, West Union, OH 45693. Those wanting to dip their toe into the Amish lifestyle might want to check out this 125-acre nature camp. Cottages have baths, fully equipped kitchens, and heat, but no electricity. Along with a well-stocked pond (bass, bluegill, catfish), there are 5 miles of nature trails, observation blinds, and bird-watching. $$. (937) 544–6908; www.unitywoods.org.

lynx

From West Union, take SR 125 East, about 8 miles to the largest privately owned group of nature preserves in Ohio.

where to go

Edge of Appalachia Preserve. 3223 Waggoner Riffle Road, West Union, OH 45693. This 12-mile stretch serves up rocky slopes, colorful meadows, cavernous ravines, and one hundred rare species of plants and animals. The Lynx Prairie section has more than 200 kinds of flora and fauna more commonly found west of the Mississippi, with such monikers as big and little bluestem, side-oats grama, purple coneflower, prairie dock, and rattlesnake master. The area containing Buzzardroost Rock bristles with scenic vistas, overlooking Ohio Brush Creek and the valley below. Should you fall, there are plenty of vultures (the "buzzards" that the rock is named after) soaring overhead, waiting for a handout. Open daily. Free. (937) 544–2880.

southwest

day trip 01

southwest

shopping marathon:
jeffersonville • wilmington

Clinton County has shopping for all inclinations and budgets: name brands, discounts, top-of-the-line products, and items of the one-person's-trash-is-another's-treasure kind. The county is named after George Clinton, the fourth vice-president of the United States (not the King of Funkadelic, and certainly not Citizen Bill).

jeffersonville

Jeffersonville is a shopper's Valhalla, as long as you bring plenty of charge cards and comfortable shoes. Serious shopaholics might also want to make hotel reservations—like potato chips, there's no stopping at just one store for an item or two. Located about forty minutes from Columbus, it's a straight shot south on I–71, off exits 65 and 69.

where to shop

Prime Outlets—Jeffersonville. 8000 Factory Shops Boulevard, Jeffersonville, OH 43128, off exit 65. Ohio's largest factory-outlet center has more than one hundred stores. Items are discounted up to 70 percent and include mostly first-quality, in-season factory overruns as well as some irregular and damaged merchandise, which is generally marked as such (check your purchases beforehand because returns may involve another day trip!). Shops include apparel for all ages and genders (Talbot's, Tommy Hilfiger, Gap), activewear (Adidas, Nautica, The Jockey Store), health and beauty (Bath & Body Works, GNC), luggage

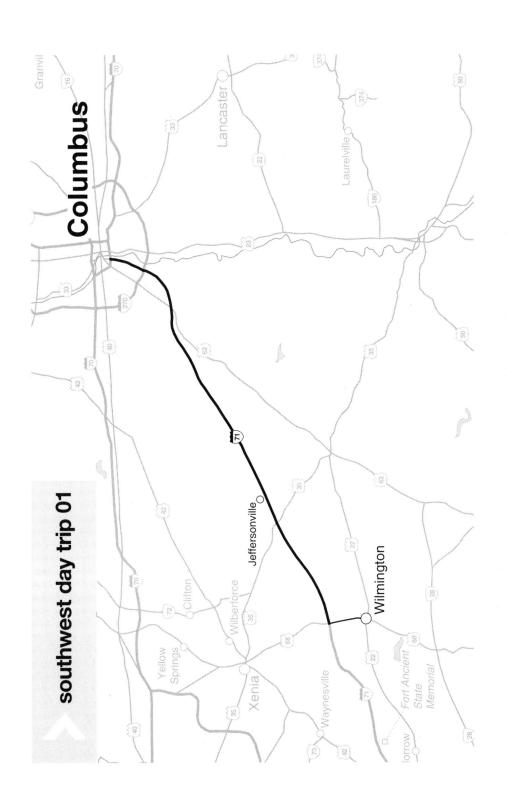

southwest day trip 01

Columbus

Granvil

Lancaster

Laurelville

Jeffersonville

Wilmington

Yellow Springs

Clifton

Wilberforce

Xenia

Waynesville

Fort Ancient
State
Memorial

Morrow

and accessories (Coach, Samsonite, and Zales), shoes (Easy Spirit, Bass, Nine West), and housewares (Corning,Williams Sonoma, Pottery Barn). You can even purchase books (Borders), kitchenware (Le Gourmet Chef), sound equipment (Bose), and edibles (Rocky Mountain Chocolate Factory, Harry and David), to mention a few. Although you may save in the long run, expect to spend more time (an average of two hours) and money (about $200) than you would in a regional mall. Don't forget to check the Web site or the office for various discounts and coupons. Open daily, but hours vary. (800) 746–7644; www .primeoutlets.com.

Home Works at Jeffersonville. 1100 McArthur Road, Jeffersonville, OH 43128, off exit 69. This "lite" open-air outlet cluster consists of more than a dozen stores, from Amish Heritage Furniture to Liz Claiborne/Liz Claiborne Woman to Reebok. It's neither as large or crowded as the megamall down the road. Free (as long as you don't buy anything). Open daily but hours vary. (740) 426–6991; www.homeworksjeffersonville.com.

where to stay

Periodically, several chain hotels offer "shop & stay" deals for consumers, with discounted rooms. The following options are located off the malls' exits.

- **Amerihost Inn.**11431 Allen Road NW, Washington Court House, OH 43128; **Amerihost Inn North.** Route 41, exit 69 off 1–71. Take your choice of lodging at either exit, although the South Amerihost has more fast-food restaurants and heavy-duty shopping than its neighbor to the north. Either way, you get amenities such as a pool and Internet connections, along with a complimentary continental breakfast and a coupon book for Jeffersonville. $$. (740) 948–2104 (South).

- **Hampton Inn.** 11484 Allen Road NW, Washington Court House, OH 43128, exit 65 off I–71. With an indoor heated pool, spa, elevator, exercise room, and in-room microwave and refrigerator, this already spiffy but recently renovated property was built in the late 1990s. And it gets better. Along with a complimentary continental breakfast and Laundromat, you can have all the rollaway beds and cribs you can handle in the room for no additional charge. $$. (740) 948–9499.

Deer Creek Resort and Conference Center. 22300 State Park Road 20, Mt. Sterling, OH 43143. From Jeffersonville, take 35E to 753N; check Web site for detailed directions. Although it's about a 30-minute drive from Jeffersonville, this 3100-acre property offers a respite from hectic consumerism. Choose from lodge rooms or cabins; other diversions include walking paths, marina, lake, and golf course. There's also a bistro-style restaurant featuring creative cuisine and traditional dishes, a relief from the fast-food options of Jeffersonville. $$–$$$. (740) 869–2020; www.visitdeercreek.com.

wilmington

Accolades for the charismatic burg of Wilmington include a listing in *The 100 Best Small Towns in America* and a designation as a "most livable" neighborhood by *Cincinnati* magazine. Visitors can enjoy the Victorian-era downtown with its historic homes, attractions, and, of course, shopping. Wilmington is another 20 miles from Jeffersonville. To get there, take I–71 south to U.S. 68 and continue south about 5 miles.

where to go

National Weather Service Forecast Office. 1901 South State Road 134, Wilmington, OH 45177. Open 24/7, rain or shine, this facility serves up forecasts for fifty-six counties in Ohio, Kentucky, and Indiana. It's also the home of the Ohio River Forecast Center, which provides flood guidance for thirteen states. Computer models, satellite, radar, and weather balloons provide insight into the combination of intuition and science that makes up weather prediction. Call for tour. Free. (937) 383–0031.

Clinton County Historical Society. 149 East Locust Street, Wilmington, OH 45177. Located in an 1885 Greek Revival mansion, this collection defines eclectic. Highlights include antique clothing, toys, and dolls; the Wilmington Tablet, an Adena Native American burial relic; an 1875 steam-powered engine; and paintings and sculpture by internationally recognized Quaker artist Eli Harvey. There is memorabilia of original resident General J. West Denver, who later helped Colorado achieve statehood; Southwestern Indian photography by local native Carl Moon; and last but certainly not least, an 1898 folding bathtub. Open Wednesday through Friday, March through December. Free. (937) 382–4684; www.clintoncountyhistory.org.

Clinton County Courthouse. 53 East Main Street, Wilmington, OH 45177. Built in 1918, this Second Renaissance Revival structure has been completely spiffed up and restored. Standouts are a colorful 36-foot mural dome, detailed plasterwork, and painted panels depicting agriculture, education, medicine, and industry. Open Monday through Friday. Free.(937) 383–1170; www.clinton countyohio.com.

Murphy Theatre. 50 West Main Street, Wilmington, OH 45177. With a thousand seats in a town of barely five times more than that, this venue was built in 1918 on the big dreams of native Charles Murphy, owner of the Chicago Cubs. Elegantly furnished and recently restored, with a flamboyant, old-fashioned marquee, this theater continues to draw such name acts as Glen Campbell, The Amazing Kreskin, and more. Hours and performance fees vary. Call (877) 274–3848 for schedule.

Cowan Lake State Park. 1750 Osborn Road, Wilmington, OH 45177. Swimming, fishing, sailing, and canoeing are popular pastimes in this peaceful setting. It's particularly picturesque during the warm months when the large, vivid American lotus water lily blooms on the lake. There are also 6 miles of hiking trails and hunting and fishing in season. Open daily. Free. (937) 382–1096;www.ohiodnr.com.

Cherrybend Pheasant Farms. 2326 Cherrybend Road, Wilmington, OH 45177. Get up close and personal with your food. This 386-acre grain farm has many large ring-necked pheasants that can be hunted from September through April. You can also flip the bird and dine on your catch or let someone else prepare it for you. Trap-shooting is also available. Call for times and rates. (937) 584–4269.

where to shop

Caesar Creek Flea Market. 7763 SR 73, Wilmington, OH 45177. Located on a large outdoor lot and with more than 110,000 square feet of space inside, this savings empire has everything from bizarre home furnishings and military memorabilia to bargain-basement socks and kitchen utensils to museum-quality antiques. Hundreds of vendors are on-site. Open Saturday and Sunday only. (937) 382–1660; www.caesarcreek.com.

Buffalo Trading Post. 280 West Curry Road, I–71 & SR 68, Wilmington, OH 45177. This 1880s-style emporium peddles cowboy memorabilia, antiques, and collectibles. There's also a full tack shop and historical displays. Don't take any wooden nickels, though. (937) 382–0141.

Grandpa's Pottery. 3558 SR 73 West, Wilmington, OH 45177. Come watch owner/potter Ray Storer turn raw materials into functional and attractive items. All wheel-thrown pottery and sculpture is created by the Storer family. (937) 382–6442.

Beehive Gallery & Browsers Cafe. 156 West Locust Street, Wilmington, OH 45177. Buzz around original works by southern Ohio artists in a late nineteenth-century Victorian-style home. Also featured: custom framing, antiques, collectibles, cards, prints, and a cafe with freshly brewed coffees, teas, cheesecakes, desserts, and other goodies. (937) 383–3938.

Shoppes at the Old Mill. 320 East Sugartree Street, Wilmington, OH 45177. This 100-year-old mill grinds out antiques and collectibles from several periods. Only in a manner of speaking, of course. (937) 655–8181.

Home Again II. 316 East Sugartree, Wilmington, OH 45177. Specialty foods, crafts, toys, Americana, candles, pottery, customized gift baskets, and more can be found in this emporium, which has been around for several years. (937) 383–1899.

where to eat

Beaugard's Southern BBQ. 975 South Street, Wilmington, OH 45177. A favorite as far away as Cincinnati (and possibly farther), this eatery recently moved to bigger quarters and serves barbecued ribs (but of course), brisket, pork, chicken, and more along with sides like macaroni and potato salad and beans. $–$$. (937) 655–8100; www.beaugardsbbq.com.

Werner's Pork House. 5356 U.S. Route 68 North, Wilmington, OH 45177. Although you can "pig" out on pork products here as well, this restaurant also offers chicken, shrimp, cod, and other food groups in a casual atmosphere. $$. (937) 382–1111.

Gibson's Goodies. 718 Ohio Avenue, Wilmington, OH 45177. This ice cream parlor not only has thirteen more flavors than that national chain, it makes a banana split that harks back to the good old days of 1907, when the treat was actually invented in Wilmington. $. (937) 383–2373.

68 Family Restaurant. 8295 North U.S. 68, Wilmington, OH 45177. This old-style road-side restaurant offers large portions accompanied by low prices. $–$$. (937) 486–2111.

where to stay

The Wilmington Inn. 909 Fife Avenue., Wilmington, OH 45177. Located near Wilmington College, this fifty-two-room hotel features a hospitality room, computer analog system, in-room voice mail, free cable and HBO, nonsmoking rooms, and a courtesy van. Guest rooms offer fine furnishings, comfortable beds, plush carpeting, and color television. Or you can go whole hog with the executive suite, which has a Jacuzzi tub. Continental breakfast included. $. (937) 382–6000; www.wilmingtoninn.com.

Cedar Hill B&B. 4003 SR 73, Wilmington, OH 45177. This lodging is set amid ten acres of woods and walking trails and has rooms with private entrances and baths, queen-size beds, TVs, refrigerators, great views, and more. Full breakfasts served on weekends, with continental other times. $$. (877) 722–2525 or (937) 383–2525.

The Lark's Nest. 619 Ward Road, Wilmington, OH 45177. Located near Caesar Creek State Park (see Southwest Day Trip 2), this log cabin home on eight acres provides a comfy getaway. All rooms have private baths and entrances. Kitchen is available for meals other than breakfast, which is served daily. $$. (937) 382–4788.

Cowan Lake State Park. 1750 Osborn Road, Wilmington, OH 45177. Two-bedroom cottages include full kitchen, private bathroom with shower, large living room, and a screened porch. The park also maintains more than 230 campsites that are set up for tents and RVs. Showers, flush toilets, laundry facilities, and a private beach/boat launch are nearby, making it such a deal. Campsites, $; cottages, $$$. (866) 644–6727.

day trip 02

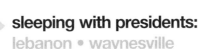

sleeping with presidents:
lebanon • waynesville

This region offers a bit of everything: history, indoor and outdoor recreation, and dining. And if nearby Jeffersonville/Caesar Creek aren't enough, Lebanon has plenty of antique and specialty shops.

lebanon

In 1803, the year Ohio achieved statehood, Lebanon resident Jonas Seaman was licensed to operate a "house of public entertainment" (as opposed to one of ill repute). Called the Golden Lamb Inn, the tavern hosted notables of the day, including a dozen American presidents and author Charles Dickens. One of the few communities in Ohio to attract a large number of settlers from the Shaker religious order, Lebanon has also won praise for its simple but architecturally significant downtown, with its nineteenth-century village green and lovingly restored neighborhoods.

A drive of about 75 miles, Lebanon can be reached from Columbus via I–71 south. Go north on SR 123 (exit 32), which will lead into town.

where to go

Warren County Historical Museum. 105 South Broadway, Lebanon, OH 45036. Lebanon's Shaker history is aptly churned up in this 1912 building. Drawn to the area's rich farmland, the Shakers formed nearby Union Village, the largest community of its kind in the

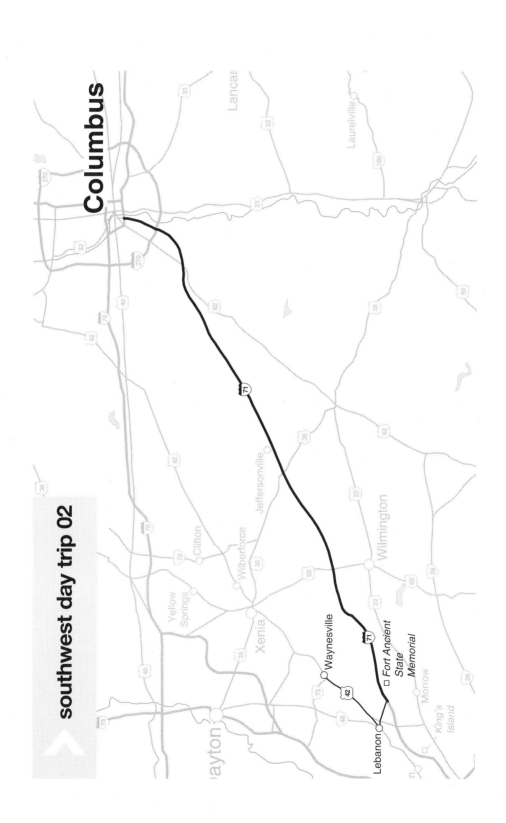

Columbus

71

71

Lancas

Laurelville

33

22

23

50

35

62

35

82

40

70

42

82

Jeffersonville

36

42

Clifton

70

72

Wilberforce

35

Yellow
Springs

Xenia

35

68

Wilmington

28

63

22

Morrow

King's
Island

Waynesville

73

42

48

Lebanon

Fort Ancient
State
Memorial

Dayton

75

40

270

270

region. This resulted in a rich legacy of furniture and artifacts, making this museum one of the Midwest's finest collections. Other exhibits focus on prehistoric times, the Victorian age, and genealogy. Open Tuesday through Sunday. Admission is charged. (513) 932–1817; www.wchsmuseum.com.

Glendower. 105 Cincinnati Avenue, Lebanon, OH 45036. Built between 1836 and 1840, this Greek Revival crib, the home of Civil War General Durbin Ward, boasts classic cornices and porticoes, columns of the fluted Ionic and unfluted Doric persuasion, and a hipped roof with a captain's walk. Furnished with period Empire- and Victorian-style pieces crafted by original settlers, the thirteen rooms reflect the gracious lifestyle of a bygone era and include a formal drawing room with two fireplaces. Open Wednesday through Sunday. Admission is charged. (800) 283–8927; www.ohio history.org.

Turtle Creek Valley Railway. 198 South Broadway, Lebanon, OH 45036. This one-hour train ride passes through farmland and nearby Turtle Creek, providing panoramic views. Running on track originally laid in 1880, it consists of four enclosed circa 1930 passenger coaches and an open gondola car. There's also a snack bar if you get hungry, and the conductor points out sites of historical interest. Call ahead for schedule. Admission is charged. (513) 398–8584; http://home.frognet.net/~mcfadden/wd8rif/tcvry.htm.

Lebanon Raceway. 655 North Broadway Street, Lebanon, OH 45036. And they're off! The Lebanon Raceway features the excitement of live harness races, which are simulcast with other racetracks and off-track betting parlors. You can also view and make wagers on races for other tracks. It's the "bet" of both worlds. Call for race days. Free (but only if you break even). (513) 932–4936; www.lebanonraceway.com.

Fort Ancient State Memorial. 6123 SR 350, Oregonia, OH 45054. From Lebanon take SR 123 south, then go east on SR 350, a total of about 5 miles. Two millennia ago, Native Americans utilized deer bones, elk antlers, clamshell hoes, and sticks to build this fortress, carrying nearly forty pounds of soil per basket to create 18,000 feet of earthen walls. Although mostly for defense and social and recreational gatherings, certain areas served as a calendar in conjunction with the sun and moon; no Palm Pilots for these guys. Hiking and interpretive trails, remains of prehistoric mounds, and scenic vistas are other highlights. The recently remodeled museum contains 9,000 square feet of exhibits focusing on 15,000 years of American Indian history in the Ohio Valley. An outdoor re-creation of a prehistoric Indian garden, a resource center, and a shop with Native American offerings round out the excursion. Hours vary according to season. Admission is charged. (800) 283–8904; www.ohiohistory.org.

where to shop

Miller's Antiques. 201 S. Broadway, Lebanon, OH 45036. Features antiques from selected exhibitors. Offerings range from jewelry to furniture and cover periods from primitive to Victorian and beyond. (513) 932–8710.

Blue Heron Studio. 25 West Mulberry Street, Lebanon, OH 45036. Get "framed" at this gallery, which represents local and regional artists. There's also custom framing, pre-framed pictures, and mirrors (but no smoke). (513) 934–9905.

Oh Suzanna. 16 South Broadway Lebanon, OH 45036. This is the place for quilts and custom bed groupings, including shams, dust skirts, duvets, tapestries, pieced pillows, and needlework. Vera Bradley, tummy tuck jeans and other brand-name clothing and nightwear add to the eclectic collection . (513) 932–8246; www.ohsuzannaoh.com.

Exotic Art & Antiques. 34 South Broadway Street, Lebanon, OH 45036. This appropriately monikered assortment ranges from watercolors by the resident artist to custom jewelry to Native American decorative arts to antique Chinese furniture and more. (513) 932–1317; www.exoticartandantiques.com.

The Garden Gate. 36 South Broadway, Lebanon, OH 45036. For the gardener in your life, the selection consists of antiques, collectibles, and gifts and includes books, home decor, ornaments, tools, apparel, and even bath and body-care products. A greenhouse displays seasonal plants and topiaries. (513) 932–8620; www.the gardengate.net.

Broadway Antique Mall. 15–17 South Broadway, Lebanon, OH 45036. Over 60 dealers are represented in this large assortment of antiques and collectibles. (513) 932–1410.

Golden Turtle Chocolate Factory. 120 South Broadway Street, Lebanon, OH 45036. No relation to the "Lamb," over 150 varieties of locally made chocolates, including premium toffee, dreamy creams, and its namesake concoction, Texas pecans covered in buttery caramel and drenched in chocolate. (513) 932–1990, (800) 345–1994; www.goldenturtle chocolatefactory.com.

where to eat

Golden Lamb. 27 South Broadway, Lebanon, OH 45036. No baa-d meals here: specialties of the house include sauerkraut balls, the namesake roast leg of leg of lamb with mint jelly, and turkey with dressing and mashed potatoes. For dessert ewe, er, you—can't go wrong with a toasted pecan ball with hot fudge sauce, the lemon stack pie, or "Sister Lizzy's" Shaker sugar pie for a teeth-rattling glucose buzz. $$–$$$. (513) 932–9065; www .goldenlamb.com.

Village Ice Cream Parlor. 22 South Broadway, Lebanon, OH 45036. Eat dessert first: There's an ice-cream and soda fountain, along with luncheon specials, sandwiches, salad bar, soups, and dinner. $–$$. (513) 932–6918.

where to stay

Golden Lamb Inn. 27 South Broadway, Lebanon, OH 45036. Ohio's oldest inn and restaurant has a museum-quality collection of gen-u-ine Shaker antiques, many of which are scattered throughout the property. What began as a two-story log building now has four floors, a lobby, several large public and private dining rooms, and guest rooms with all the modern amenities. A colonial porch and second- and third-floor balconies serve as a reminder of its early American origins. Reservations should be made well in advance, particularly during tourist season. $$–$$$. (513) 932–5065; www.goldenlamb.com.

Shaker Inn. 600 Cincinnati Avenue, U.S. 42 South, Lebanon, OH 45036. This family-owned, AAA-rated lodging boasts clean rooms in a variety of sizes. There's also an outside swimming pool and suites for families. $. (800) 752–6151; www.shakerinnmotel.com.

Hatfield Inn. 2563 Hatfield Road, Lebanon, OH 45036. This nineteenth-century farmhouse is the real McCoy. Completely modernized and located on fifty-five acres, it offers a front porch overlooking two ponds and large shade trees. All rooms have private baths, great views, and use of an outdoor hot tub. Full breakfast included. $$. (513) 932–3193.

Hardy's Haven. 212 Wright Avenue, Lebanon, OH 45036. Each suite has a private bath, living room, dining room/office, and fully equipped kitchen. You can choose from country, traditional, or Victorian decor, all of which are spiffed up by antiques, lace, and fresh flowers. Breakfast is served in the adjacent March Manor, which was built in 1900. $$–$$$. (877) 932–3266; www.hardysproperties.com.

waynesville

Waynesville's profusion of curio/relic emporiums earned it the title "Antique Capital of the Midwest" from *USA Today.* Most are located along Main and High Streets. Waynesville is about 10 miles from Lebanon, straight up U.S. 42.

where to go

Caesar Creek State Park. 8570 East SR 73, Waynesville, OH 45068. With pristine blue waters, generously abundant woodlands, and plentiful meadows and deep ravines, Caesar Creek is ideal for all types of recreation and has several shelter houses for family reunions and other gatherings. Forty-three miles of hiking trails, 31 miles of horseback riding trails, and a 2,800-acre lake for swimming, boating, and fishing are but some of the highlights. Open daily. Free. (513) 897–3055; www.ohiostateparks.org.

- **Caesar Creek Lake Visitor Center.** 4020 North Clarksville Road, Waynesville, OH 45068. Along with interpretive galleries and a theater, this center provides information regarding water resource management and the Corps of Engineers. Pictures, written material, rocks, and soil samples demonstrate the ecology of the Ohio River Basin, Caesar Creek Lake, and local natural history. Open daily. Free. (513) 897–1050.

- **Caesar Creek Lake Control Tower Tours.** 4020 North Clarksville Road, Waynesville, OH 45068. This tour provides insight into the creation of the dam that formed the lake. More than $2.5 million was saved in flood damages in one year alone. Appointments made by special request. Free. (513) 897–1050.

- **Caesar Creek Pioneer Village.** 3999 Pioneer Village Road, Waynesville, OH 45068. Consisting of nineteen restored log structures, this living museum focuses on Ohio pioneer life from 1793 to 1812. Settlers, militia, frontier explorers, and Native Americans come to life during reenactments, festivals, and other events. Buildings open Monday through Friday; call for schedule of performances. Free. (513) 897–1120; www.caesars creekpioneervillage.org.

Little Miami State Park. Mailing address: Caesar Creek State Park, 8570 East SR 73, Waynesville, OH 45068. Staging areas and entrances are located at Corwin (directly east of Waynesville, off SR 73), Morrow, and Loveland; call for directions. With nearly 70 miles of paved trails meandering through four counties, this is a hiker's and biker's dream. Cross-country skiing, in-line skating, backpacking, and horseback riding are other options. Rocky and steep cliffs, abundant wildlife such as great blue herons, and huge, ancient sycamores make for a big-time outdoor payoff. The Little Miami River also offers 86 miles of canoeing; smallmouth and rock-bass fishing is plentiful. Bike, skate, and canoe rentals are available at various staging areas. Open daily. Free. (513) 597–3055; www.ohiodnr.com.

La Comedia Dinner Theatre. 765 West Central Avenue, Springboro, OH 45066. To get to Springboro from U.S. 42/Waynesville, take SR 73 west about 8 miles. With seating for more than 600, La Comedia is the nation's fourth largest and the region's only professional dinner theater. Broadway performances and revues are accompanied by a buffet with meats, pastas, and fresh vegetables. Themed dishes are specially created for each show. Call for times and offerings. Admission is charged. (800) 677–9505; www.la comedia.com.

where to shop

Hour House Clock Repair. 97 South Main Street, Waynesville, OH 45068. With vintage tickers (including one built in 1798) and such names as Hentschel, Hermle, and Schneider, this store is timeless. They will also clean your clock in the sense that they provide parts and service. (513) 897–0805; www.hourhouseclocks.com.

Waynesville Gallery. 177 South Main Street, Waynesville, OH 45068. Those searching for Amish-crafted Shaker-style furniture will find tables, chairs, living and dining rooms, bedrooms, and office accessories as well as custom-made items. (513) 897–0888.

where to eat

Cobblestone Cafe. 10 North Main Street, Waynesville, OH 45068. Chef specials, gourmet sandwiches and desserts, homemade soups, and salads can be found at this attractively decorated eatery. Everything in the dining room is for sale (including the food, of course). $–$$. (513) 897–0021; www.cobblestonevillageonline.com.

Der Dutchman Restaurant. 230 North U.S. 42, Waynesville, OH 45068. This Amish-style eatery features panfried chicken, ham, and roast beef, "real" mashed potatoes with gravy, homemade dressing, and much, much more. There's dessert for those who have room: Dutch apple, peanut butter cream, and custard pies, date cake, bread pudding, and angel food cake. And that's not even mentioning lunch. $$. (513) 897–4716; www .dutchcorp.com.

where to stay

Sugar Camp Cottages. 711 Collett Road, Waynesville, OH 45068. Located on a work-ing farm, two fully refurbished cottages provide privacy, space, and luxury. A full country breakfast is served. $$. (937) 382–6075.

day trip 03

southwest

life's a beast:
morrow • mason

Those looking for thrills, cheap and otherwise, would do well to check out this region. Along with the profusion of heart-thumping and other rides at Kings Island, you can go on a canoe trip, float far above the earth in a balloon or helicopter, or immerse yourself in a watery sanctuary. There's golf as well, although excitement in that realm can be subject to interpretation. Additional shopping, restaurants, and lodging are only about a ten-minute drive to Lebanon (see Southwest Day Trip 2).

morrow

To get to Morrow from Columbus, take I–71 south to exit 32, then take SR 123 south, a drive of about an hour and twenty minutes.

where to go

Little Miami Scenic Trail. Mailing address: Warren County Convention and Visitors Bureau, Lebanon, OH 45036. Call for directions to Morrow staging area. From Morrow, you can pedal, skate, ride horseback, or walk to such attractions as the Valley Vineyards, Fort Ancient, and Lebanon. A 14.2-mile path between Morrow and Corwin leads north through the Ohio River Valley with its spectacular cliffs, rolling hills, lush vegetation, and plentiful wildlife. Stop for lunch at the town of Oregonia, an approximate midpoint. Or you

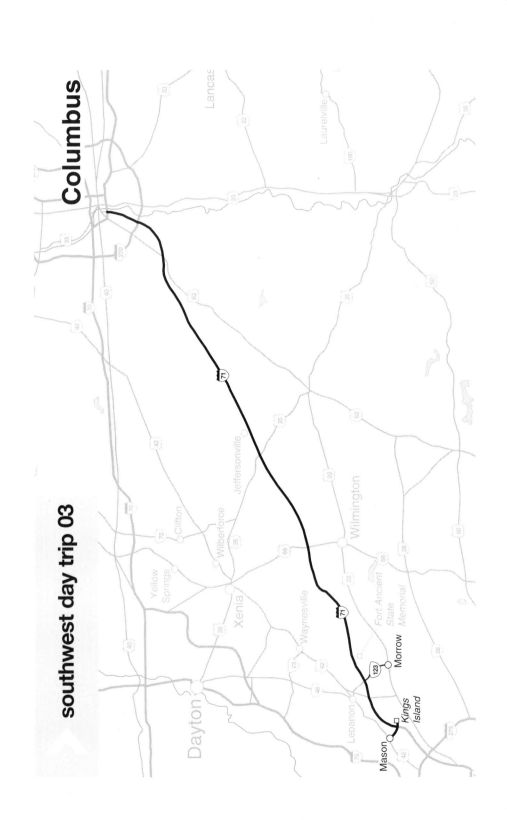

Columbus

southwest day trip 03

can take the southern Morrow-to-Loveland path (13.5 miles), with its secluded stretches of pristine natural wonders. Open daily. Free. (800) 791–4386; www.ohioslargestplay ground.com.

Little Miami Canoe Rental. 219 Mill Street (SR 123), Morrow, OH 45152. They provide the canoe, paddles, life vests, and shuttle (when needed), while you row, row, row down a National Scenic River to Fort Ancient, an old mill, or a covered bridge. Excursions can range from two to eight hours, depending on your destination. Weather permitting, open daily, May through September; weekends in April and October. Admission is charged. (800) 634–4277; www.littlemiamicanoe.com.

where to shop

Harrison Art Studio Santa Gallery. 100 East McKinley Street, South Lebanon, OH 45065. South Lebanon is a few miles west of Morrow on I–71. Located in a 1907 Colonial Revival building that was a town meeting hall, this shop offers mixed media sculptures of Santa and Father Christmas as well as Christmas ornaments. The General Store section peddles candles, quilts, incense, candies, antiques, and more. (513) 494–2244; www.santa gallery.com.

where to eat

Valley Vineyards Winery. 2276 U.S. 22-3, Morrow, OH 45152. Weekend steak cookouts include a wine tasting, fresh vegetables, homemade desserts, and a tour of the property. Saturday lunch only. Dinner on other days. Call for reservations. $$. (513) 899–2485; www .valley-vineyards.com.

mason

Mason and Kings Island are only a few miles farther south of Morrow on I–71, off exits 24 and 25.

where to go

Kings Island. 6300 Kings Island Drive, Kings Island, OH 45034. More than 80 rides, shows, and attractions, including 15 roller coasters, make these 364 acres literally tons of fun that can take up to two full days to see. The first inverted children's coaster in the world, the Rugrats Runaway Reptar suspends kids of all ages in midair in a frantic race to steer clear of a larger-than-life green dinosaur. At 230 feet at its highest point and with 10 vertical drops and two helixes, the Diamondback roller coaster strikes fear into grownups as it snakes through 5,282 feet of track at over 80 miles per hour. More relaxing are country

making tracks on the underground railroad

Before and during the Civil War, Ohio was a heavily traveled escape route for enslaved men and women seeking freedom. Several places around the state served as safe harbors, with stories and memorabilia being preserved today, both at the National Underground Railroad Freedom Center (see Southwest, Day Trip 4—Cincinnati) and through the Web site, www.passagetofreedomohio.org. Along with listing smaller museums and various points of interest, this site serves as a clearinghouse for all things Underground Railroad. Other points around the state offer tours as well.

- ***Underground Railroad Education Center.*** *Various sites, Sandusky. All aboard for a trolley tour that will provide a sense of the extraordinary courage and inventiveness of "conductors"—black and white citizens and leaders—moving the "cargo" (escaped slaves) from one "station" (safe place) to the next. Sites of interest in Sandusky include Marsh Tavern, Sandusky Docks, Second Baptist Church, and Follett House, along with several private "safe houses." However, you can visit Susan Schultz' underground railroad tribute at Facer Park in Sandusky (Water Street, adjacent to Sandusky Bay) anytime. This life-sized statue of a man, his wife, and his child escaping the chains of slavery is surrounded by pedestals with quotes and other illustrations. Admission is charged for the trolley tour. To obtain a schedule and for reservations, call (419) 624–0274; www.sanduskyunderground railroad.org.*

- ***Underground Railroad Tour.*** *103-C Muskingum Terrace, Marietta, OH 45750. With a photo exhibit, maps, and books, the Levee House Cafe is the logical starting point for this exploration. Both the Ohio and Muskingham Rivers served as major routes for fugitive slaves crossing from Virginia. Of the original sixteen underground railroad stations, six sites are available to view, including Henderson Hall Plantation (Route 2, Williamstown, WV 26187; 304–375–2129), Blennerhasset Island Plantation (137 Juliana Street, Parkersburg, WV 26101; 304–420–4800), Putnam House in Harmar Village (519 Fort Street, Marietta), and the John Stone House (110 Stone Road, Belpre, OH 45714), among others. Hours for sites vary; admission may be charged. Tours are conducted by historian Henry Robert Burke. (740) 373–0218; www.mariettaohio.org/undergroundrailroad.*

- **Oberlin.** As Stop 99 on the Underground Railroad—Stop 100 being Canada and freedom—Oberlin was the site of many dramatic events, such as Oberlin-Wellington Rescue of 1858 in which citizens intervened and ensured the safe passage of slave John Price to Canada, and participation in Abolitionist John Brown's historic raid on October 1859 in Harpers Ferry, Virginia, to mention a few. A place to start would be the Oberlin Heritage Center (73½ South Professor Street; 440–774–1700; www.oberlinheritage.org) which offers classes, genealogy and research resources, and guided tours. Included in the latter are Monroe House, the home of General Giles W. Shurtleff, the leader of the first African-American regiment from Ohio to serve in the Civil War and the circa 1836 Little Red Schoolhouse, the town's first public school, integrated in defiance of Ohio's "Black Laws." Other sites of interest are the First Church in Oberlin (106 N Main Street; 440–775–1711; www.firstchuroberlin.org), host to the Oberlin Anti-Slavery Society and shelter to escaping slaves; The Wilson Bruce Evans House (33 E Vine Street), home of black Abolitionist leader Wilson Bruce Evans (1824–1898), who with his brother Henry helped lead many slaves to freedom; and the Underground Railroad Sculpture (90 E College Street, Talcott Hall; 440–774–1700). Designed and installed by students, it resembles a locomotive version of the Led Zeppelin "Stairway to Heaven" song, but the rising railroad tracks symbolize the underground nature of the effort to resist slavery and "lift up" individuals to freedom. Call individual sites for hours; admission may be charged. For more information, visit www.passagetofreedomohio.org.

- **Ripley.** At the opposite end of the state, near the Ohio/Kentucky border is the village of Ripley, where both geography and people were sympathetic to the Underground Railroad cause—creek beds threw off tracking dogs, and hills and valleys provided excellent hiding places and escape routes. Tours include multiple historic residences of two-legged activists, notably the John Rankin House (6152 Rankin Hill Road; 937–392–1627), where the Presbyterian minister and founder of the Ohio Anti-Slavery Society sheltered more than 2,000 escaping slaves. At the Parker House (330 Front Street; 937–392–4188, www.johnparkerhouse.org), visitors will learn about the life and times of freeman John Parker, who purchased his freedom at age 18 and settled in Ripley in the 1840s. Parker built and operated the Phoenix Foundry and Machine Company and was awarded patents for a tobacco press, sugar mill, and soil pulverizer. Other standouts include the First Presbyterian Church (114 Mulberry Street), where Rankin and others preached their anti-slavery doctrine and the Ripley

(continued)

Museum (219 N. 2nd Street; 937–392–4660; www.ripleymuseum.org). Located in an 1850s home, it consists of ten rooms, with furniture, portraits, photographs, clothing, and more illustrating the village's past, Underground Railroad and elsewise. Believe it or not, it also boasts a 1920s beauty parlor but that depicts an altogether different type of slavery. Call individual sites for hours; admission may be charged. For more information, visit www.passage tofreedomohio.org.

music and/or popular hit song and dance revues, an ice skating extravaganza, 80's themed entertainment, and more. Other highlights include:

- **The Kids' Area.** This award-winning section encompasses Nickelodeon Central and Hanna-Barbera Land. Four kids' coasters, twenty-two rides, and photo opportunities with popular Nickelodeon characters in those hot and uncomfortable costumes make this a major draw.

- **Thrill Rides.** Kings Island "scream machines," include The Beast, purportedly the longest wooden 'coaster in the world; Son of Beast, which claims to be the tallest, fastest, and only looping one of its kind; King Cobra, where you can stand up and be lurched; and Face/Off, a looping, forward and backward, face-to-face inverted number. Drop Zone Stunt Tower, the tallest (315 feet) gyro drop tower in the world, and Congo Falls, a boat ride ending in a five-story waterfall plunge, are other stomach-churners.

- **Boomerang Bay.** You can actually "surf" on a boogie board via a wave ride, explore lagoons with dramatic waterfalls, and choose from a variety of wild-to-mild water slides at this Australian-themed water park. A "tipping tub" dumps gallons of H_2O on willing participants and a four-person raft ride simulates a wild white-water passage.

The park also accommodates guests with special needs with access to a limited number of wheelchairs; and a rider safety guide explains entry guidelines and procedures as well as specific information related to each attraction. Additionally, metal detectors are installed at all entrances so lock all nonessential items in your trunk and forget about sneaking in food and, obviously, weapons. Open daily, June through August, and weekends in April, May, September, October, and the first weekend in November. Admission is charged. (800) 288–0808; www.visitkingsisland.com.

The Golf Center at Kings Island. 6042 Fairway Drive, Mason, OH 45040. This twenty-seven-hole Jack Nicklaus–designed course is ideal. Although called the Grizzly, with another eighteen-hole course named the Bruin, it's anything but beastly: This championship course has seen the likes of some of the world's greatest duffers and PGA/LPGA tournaments. It also has a driving range, pro shop, and a competition tennis stadium and courts that host the annual ATP Tennis Championship (www.master-series.com). Open daily. Fee charged. (513) 398–7700; www.thegolfcenter.com.

Alverta Green Museum. 207 West Church Street, Mason, OH 45040. Donated by a long-time resident who is the museum's namesake, this antique-filled home provides a peaceful respite and has historical photographs, documents, and artifacts. It chronicles life in Mason before the 'coaster/water-slide invasion. Open Thursday and Friday; other times by appointment. Free. (513) 398–6750; www.historicalmason.homestead.com.

The Beach. 2590 Waterpark Avenue, Mason, OH 45040. With two million gallons of water, 40,000 square feet of sand, and forty-plus rides and attractions, it's a real beach—for Ohio, anyway. Kahuna Beach, a newer offering, boasts "ocean" waves crashing down around exotic islands, lounge seating amid palm trees, and cabana waiters ready to take your order—hot in more ways than one. Aztec Adventure, which involves 500 feet of twists, turns, and dips through the mouth of a giant jaguar. Or opt for the Cliff—a five-story freefall that's a real hanger. The Banzai is a triple-drop speedslide while Thunder Beach Wavepool will agitate with 750,000 gallons of crashing, ocean-style waves. Or take the spin cycle down the 470-degree helix Watusi. Floaters might better appreciate the Pearl, with its palm trees, waterfalls, and balmy waves; they can also drift and glide along the Lazy Miami River. Open daily from the end of May through August; some weekends in May and September. Admission is charged. (513) 398–7946; www.thebeachwaterpark.com.

where to shop

Aces and Eights. 2383 Kings Center Court, Mason, OH 45040. This 37,000-square-foot motorcycle emporium was named in honor of an 1876 shootout between Cincinnatian Charlie Henry Rich and his "buddy" Wild Bill Hickok. Go "hog" wild with a selection of Harley-Davidsons, apparel, and gear related to modern-day "outlaws," many of whom are doctors and accountants. (513) 459–1777; www.98hd.com.

Kings Mill General Store. 5687 Columbia Road, Kings Mills, OH 45034. This specialized shop features all manner of yuletide dolls, ornaments, and nutcrackers for the year-round Christmas enthusiast. (800) 323–5639; www.kingschristmas.com.

where to eat

Course View Restaurant. 6042 Fairway Drive, Mason, OH 45040. The menu is American bistro, and there are more than fifty-five items to choose from. Dine with great patio and window views of the greens in the summertime or in front of a cozy fireplace in winter. Lunch and dinner only. $$–$$$. (513) 573–3321; www.thegolfcenter.com.

where to stay

Kings Island Resort and Conference Center. 5691 Kings Island Drive, Mason, OH 45030. Recently renovated, this 288-room accommodation offers indoor/outdoor swimming pools, exercise and game rooms, as well as shuffleboard, tennis, volleyball, and basketball courts. There's a restaurant on-site, and outdoor barbecues are available. It's across the street from Kings Island; free transportation to the amusement park is provided. $$–$$$. (800) 727–3050; www.kingsislandresort.com.

Ramada Limited. 9665 Mason-Montgomery Road, Mason, OH 45040. Less than 4 miles from Kings Island, this former Country Hearth Inn offers a variety of room types, indoor swimming pool and whirlpool, in-room recliners, and an incredible breakfast of eggs, pancakes, waffles, cappucino, bagels, and more. $$. (513) 336–7911; www.ramada.com.

day trip 04

southwest

arts and science:
cincinnati

cincinnati

Had Cincinnati kept its original name of Losantiville, would it be as nifty as it is today? Would this gently rolling metropolis still have a funky downtown with 1920s and '30s architecture, pocket parks, and outdoor sculptures? Would it boast two major league sports teams and impressive venues like the new six-story eye candy Contemporary Arts Center (44 East Sixth Street; 513–345–8400), the Aronoff Center for the Arts (650 Walnut Street; 513–721–3344) with its multiple performance spaces, and Riverbend Music Center (6295 Kellogg Avenue; 513–232–6220), which draws top-name acts? Or would it be a one-traffic-light hamlet with a Dari Twist and a gas station?

One will never know, thanks to the Society of Cincinnati, a group of Revolutionary War officers after which the city was named in 1790. By the mid-1800s, it was the sixth largest municipality in the nation and particularly popular with German immigrants, who lived in the now historic Over-the-Rhine neighborhood. And, like many places in Ohio, it served as a stopover for the Underground Railroad.

Although Prohibition resulted in the closure of twenty breweries, Cincinnati kept on truckin', adding new businesses and cultural attractions and rehabbing buildings. Visitors can explore Fountain Square in the heart of the city (on Fifth Street, between Walnut and Vine) or get the best views of downtown and the Ohio River from nearby Mt. Adams, a happening place with unique shopping, clubs, and restaurants. Fans of the arts will find plenty

at the Cincinnati Opera (the second oldest in the United States), the Cincinnati Pops and the Symphony Orchestra, and the world-famous Playhouse in the Park. Or you can gambol over the state line for gambling at the Argosy Casino and Hotel Lawrenceburg (777 Argosy Parkway, Lawrenceburg, IN 47025; 888–274–6797; www.argosy.com) or the Grand Victoria Casino and Resort (600 Grand Victoria Drive, Rising Sun, IN 47040; 800–473–6311).

From Columbus, Cincinnati is a straight shot down I–71 south, about an hour and a half away. Add more time at rush hour or if there's a Reds game at the spanking new Great American Ball Park or the Bengals are playing at Paul Brown Stadium. Hot dogs, anyone?

where to go

Cincinnati Art Museum. 953 Eden Park Drive, Cincinnati, OH 45202. Nearly six millennia of world art is explored here, including paintings, sculpture, decorative arts, costumes and textiles, drawings, and more. With 18,000 square feet of gallery space, the Cincinnati Wing makes the museum the first in the nation to have a permanent exhibition detailing its community's art history. Highlighted artists include painter Frank Duveneck, sculptor Hiram Powers, impressionist John H. Twachtman, and others in addition to a display of decorative arts from the Rookwood Pottery Company. Along with works from ancient Egypt, Greece, and Rome, you'll find art from Native Americans, the Near and Far East, and Africa. Displays encompass works by European old masters and American artists up to the 1980s. Standouts include the only collection of ancient Nabataean works outside of Jordan, a Herbert Greer French accumulation of old master prints, and European and American portrait miniatures. Open daily except Monday. Free. (513) 721–2787; www.cincinnatiartmuseum.org.

Cincinnati Museum Center. 1301 Western Avenue, Cincinnati, OH 45203. Located in Union Terminal, a 1933 art deco structure that served as a railway station until the early '70s, this restored combo attraction houses the following collections as well as the Robert D. Lindner Family OMNIMAX Theater, a five-story domed motion-picture screen with acoustics that make for an all-encompassing experience. Hours vary according to attraction. Admission is charged unless otherwise noted. (513) 287–7000; www.cincymuseum.org.

- **Cincinnati Historical Library.** This regional research center contains books, periodicals, manuscripts, maps, and newspapers dating back to the 1750s as well as thousands of nineteenth- and twentieth-century photographs and rare publications. Free. Open daily except Sunday.

- **Cincinnati History Museum.** Time travel, anyone? This re-creation of Old Cincinnati features settlers who tell visitors what it was like back on the frontier. A 90-foot sidewheel steamboat is also on display. Open daily.

- **Museum of Natural History and Science.** Visitors can explore the Ohio Valley landscape, including a Kentucky limestone cavern and a reproduction of Cincinnati's Ice Age from 19,000 years ago. Open daily.

- **Cinergy Children's Museum.** Kids of all ages can have a wilderness adventure in The Woods, learn about water power at The Water Works, and work with interactive machines in The Energy Zone. Kids' Town and Children Just Like Me provide lessons in making friends locally and globally. Open daily.

Cincinnati Zoo and Botanical Garden. 3400 Vine Street, Cincinnati, OH 45220. With about 600 different animal species and 3,000 types of plants, this is one wild attraction. Not only does it have the most gorilla births of any zoo, but you can also view Komodo dragons, white Bengal tigers, and rare black Sumatran and Indian rhinos. There's a wildlife theater with performing critters and an exotic-cat training program, among other offerings. Camel rides, a renovated birdhouse, and a lush, tropical rain forest round out the exhibits. Open year-round. Admission is charged. (800) 944–4776; www.cincinnatizoo.org.

Krohn Conservatory/Eden Park. 1501 Eden Park Drive, Cincinnati, OH 45202. This 187-acre green space pretty much lives up to its Biblical namesake. In addition to lakes, statues, and a water tower, two groves of trees honor presidents and war heroes, respectively. Other sites of note include the Melan Arch bridge, a pioneering structure built in 1894; the 30-foot-high Ohio River Monument; and the Seasongood Pavilion, which hosts free summertime concerts. The warm weather also brings out flowering trees and a carpet of more than 50,000 daffodils. Completed in 1933 and one of the country's largest public greenhouses, Krohn Conservatory nurtures exotic tropical, desert, and orchid plants encompassing more than 1,000 species from all over the world. Seasonal highlights include Sherwood Forest (one might expect Robin Hood to leap from the heavily wooded oaks, boxwood, cineraria, primula, and blooming bulbs) and a butterfly show wherein thousands of winged wonders are released in a colorful enclosed garden. Open daily. Free, although donations welcome. (513) 421–4686; www.cincinnatiparks.com.

Taft Museum of Art. 316 Pike Street, Cincinnati, OH 45202. Built in 1820, this Federal-style structure served as the home of Anna Sinton and Charles Phelps Taft from their marriage in 1873 until their deaths during the Great Depression. Permanent collections include European and American master paintings, such as works by Rembrandt, Hals, Gainsborough, Sargent, and others; Chinese ceramics, mostly porcelains of the Kangxi reign; and European decorative arts, such as French Renaissance Limoges enamels and seventeenth- and eighteenth-century watches. The museum's $19 million renovation includes expanded educational and exhibition facilities, a performance space, and upgraded gift shop and tea room. Open daily. Free on Wednesday and Sunday; admission charged the rest of the week. (513) 241–0343; www.taftmuseum.org.

National Underground Railroad Freedom Center. 50 East Freedom Way, Cincinnati, OH 45202. Located downtown, near the banks of the Ohio River that separated slave from free states, the Center not only recounts slaves' dramatic journey to freedom but also highlights modern-day slavery. (And it does exist—in the form of prostitution, domestic servitude, use of farm and sweatshop workers and child laborers, among other things). Since opening in August 2004, nearly a million people have toured exhibits and attended programs. A few standouts include:

- A 21 × 30', two-story log slave pen. Built circa 1830, it housed slaves being shipped to auction for a few days to several months. Originally located in Mason County, Kentucky, it was owned by Revolutionary War soldier John Anderson. With eight small windows, the original stone floor, and a row of wrought-iron rings to tether the males, it serves as a chilling reminder.

- The "Suite for Freedom" Theater and "ESCAPE! Freedom Seekers" presentation. The latter, an interactive display about the Underground Railroad, provides school groups and families with choices on an imaginary escape attempt. The theater offers animated films on the nature of freedom throughout human history, particularly as related to the Underground Railroad and slavery in the U.S. Another film, *Brothers of the Borderland,* tells the story of the Underground Railroad in Ripley, Ohio and conductors John Parker and Reverend John Rankin.

- The Family Search Center where visitors can investigate their own genealogy.

Open Tuesday–Saturday. Admission is charged. (877) 648–4838 or (513) 333–7500; www.freedomcenter.org.

Harriet Beecher Stowe House. 2950 Gilbert Avenue, Cincinnati, OH 45206. This Cincinnati home of Harriet Beecher Stowe, author of *Uncle Tom's Cabin,* was restored in 1978 and includes a museum, gift shop, and cultural center. Call for hours. Admission may be charged. (513) 751–0651.

Cincinnati Fire Museum. 315 West Court Street, Cincinnati, OH 45202. Along with teaching fire prevention and management techniques, this attraction lights up the area's 200 years of contributions to the field through illustrations, memorabilia, and equipment. Go out in a blaze of glory and slide down the fire pole, "drive" the big red truck, and ring the antique bell. Closed Monday and holidays. Admission is charged. (513) 621–5553 or 621–5571; www.cincyfiremuseum.com.

Newport Aquarium. One Aquarium Way, Newport, KY 41071. From I–71, take I–471 south to the Newport exit (Route 8) and turn left; it's about five minutes from downtown Cincinnati. Swim with the big fish without getting wet. Although aimed at children, all ages might enjoy the Frog Bog with its interactive exhibits, games, and 20 species from around the world. (Is there a prince in the house?) Along with a daily penguin parade, the Kingdom of Penguins provides a bird's-eye view of their entertaining antics. "Walk" on shark-infested waters and gape at the underwater tunnels that simulate diving in a coral reef. Larger-than-life murals, special effects, and 11,000 marine animals encompassing 600 species create total immersion. Open daily. Admission is charged. (800) 406–3474; www.newportaquarium.com.

where to shop

Jungle Jim's. 5440 Dixie Highway, Fairfield, OH 45014. No quick trips to pick up a few items here: this ginormous food fun house features specialties from 75 countries, along with the usual Pop Tarts and Oscar Meyer wieners. Wild and crazy exhibits highlight the various departments; a 1952 fire truck shrieks the location of the hot sauce and Robin Hood and his band of merry men point the arrow to the English grocery section. So plan on spending a few hours, or even the full day, since there's plenty of food to be had. (513) 674–6000; www.junglejims.com.

Kilimanjaro African Art. 310 Ludlow Avenue, Cincinnati, OH 45220. Since 1980, the proprietor has been carving and importing African art. Sculptures, masks, music and instruments, clothing, jewelry, and more are among the many authentic offerings bursting at the seams of this store. (513) 221–0700; www.africanforus.com.

Hyde Park Square. 2643 Erie Ave. Cincinnati, OH 45208. Along with being a hub for local activity and the arts scene, this neighborhood is a high-traffic shopping district. Among the art galleries, restaurants and apparel emporiums are a Sunday farmer's market from June–Oct; Alligator Purse (2701 Erie Avenue, 513–871–6171) an upscale boutique featuring up-and-coming designer women's clothing, shoes, handbags and jewelry; and Castle House (3435 Edwards Road, 877–505–9431; www.castlehouse.com), which has provided children's clothing for nearly sixty years. No phone; www.hydeparksquare.org.

Kenwood Towne Center. 7875 Montgomery Road, Cincinnati, OH 45236. With more than 180 stores, this is serious shopping. Along with the usual suspects of Macy's, Dillard's, Parisian, Banana Republic, and others, many one-of-a-kind boutiques can be found here. (513) 745–9100; www.shopkenwood.com.

where to eat

Montgomery Inn Boathouse. 925 Riverside Drive, Cincinnati, OH 45202. This eatery boasts an irresistible combination: a wonderful view of the river and terrific ribs, among other menu items. Purchase the sauce to make your own at home. $$–$$$. (513) 721–7427; www.montgomeryinn.com.

Roly Poly Rolled Sandwiches. 425 Walnut Street, Cincinnati, OH 45202. This cafe serves more than fifty gourmet rolled tortilla-and-filling combos and hearty homemade soups. Specialties in the former include grilled egg Rolys for breakfast, the monster veggie, basil cashew chicken, smokehouse turkey, pepper steak, and more. $–$$. (513) 721–4499; www.rolypolyusa.com.

Mt. Adams Fish House. 940 Pavilion Street, Cincinnati, OH 45202. Along with fresh sushi and high-quality seafood, this chic restaurant boasts an extensive wine list, daily specials, and carry-out. $$–$$$. (513) 421–3250; www.mtadamsfishhouse.com.

Rookwood Pottery Bistro. 1077 Celestial Street, Cincinnati, OH 45202. Located in the historic Rookwood Pottery building atop Mt. Adams, this casual, upscale eatery features American cooking with a European (mostly French) flair. $$. (513) 721–5456.

Newport on the Levee. One Levee Way, Newport, KY 41071. Can't agree on a place to eat?' Hop on I-471 North to the Newport Exit (Route 8) to Dave Cowens Drive (Exit 5). Here you'll find a dozen restaurants, from Bar Louie to Mitchell's Fish Market to the Reserve Restaurant and Patio Lounge and all gradations in between. $–$$$. (859) 291–0550; www .newportonthelevee.com.

Camp Washington Chili. 3005 Colerain Ave. Cincinnati, OH 45225. Founded in 1940, this place is deemed "the best" by many. Five-way chili is a Cincinnati thing, more of a spaghetti with spiced meat extravaganza, topped with beans, cheese, and/or onions. Get your fix in a retro '50s diner with a friendly atmosphere. $. (513) 541–0061; www.campwashington chili.com.

where to stay

The Cincinnatian. 601 Vine Street, Cincinnati, OH 45202. The region's only Mobil four-star, AAA four-diamond hotel, this accommodation combines elegant tradition with modern amenities. Full-time concierge, evening turndown, in-room safes, newspapers by request, and twenty-four-hour room service are but a few refinements. $$$. (800) 942–9000; www .cincinnatianhotel.com.

Garfield Suites Hotel. 2 Garfield Place, Cincinnati, 45202. It's all suites, all the time, with personalized service, completely equipped full-size kitchens, separate bedrooms, two-line phones, and health club privileges. With a deli, room service, cable TV, and pay-per-view movies, you will neither starve nor suffer from video deprivation. $$–$$$. (513) 421–3355; www.garfieldsuiteshotel.com.

Wallace House Bed & Breakfast. 120 Wallace Avenue, Covington, KY 41014. Located five minutes south of downtown Cincinnati, this 1905 Queen Anne Victorian offers large and luxurious rooms with private baths and queen-size beds. A hearty, home-cooked breakfast, high-speed Internet access, and a centrally located big-screen TV with movies help seal the deal. $$$. (888) 942–8177; www.wallacehousebb.com.

Cincinnati's Weller Haus. 319 Poplar Street, Bellevue, KY 41073. These two side-by-side Victorian Gothic homes offer uniquely decorated guest rooms with private baths and phones. Breakfast is served by candlelight. $$–$$$. (800) 431–4287; www.weller haus.com.

west

day trip 01

west

>>>

simply capital:
columbus • the districts

columbus

For those who'd rather not travel far, there's Columbus. It's listed among *Fodor's* top picks for overlooked/underrated places to visit during the cold months, but Columbus has plenty to offer year-round.

Downtown alone is worthy of serious touring, although the surrounding areas have major sights, too. Along with several unique and varied districts, there's a replica of the *Santa Maria* in Battelle Riverfront Park (614–645–8760; www.santamaria.org) and numerous arts- and science-type draws. And there are lots of sports, ranging from the Columbus Blue Jackets, the city's NHL hockey team, to Ohio State University's National Championship football team and its always-popular basketball team. In between are the Columbus Crew; the Columbus Clippers minor-league baseball team; the Columbus Marathon, a qualifier for the Boston Marathon; and two—count 'em—race tracks: Beulah Park for Thoroughbred horses (3811 Southwest Blvd., Grove City; 614–871–9600; www.beulahpark.com) and Scioto Downs for harness racing (6000 High Street; 614–491–2515; www.sciotodowns.com).

Thanks to Interstates 270, 670, 71, and 70, U.S. 23 and 33, and SR 315 and 161, Columbus is easily navigable. However, should you visit during road construction season (March until November or even December), it's best to ask a local for an alternate route to avoid singing those orange-barrel blues. Could that be why Columbus is a recommended *winter* diversion?

west day trip 01

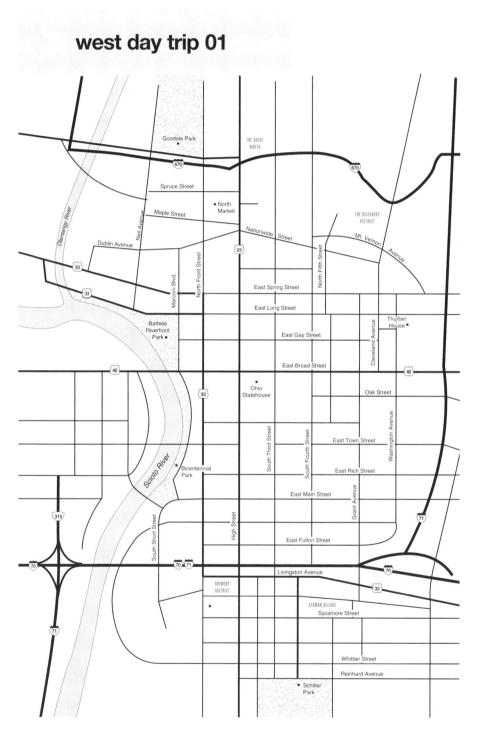

Goodale Park

THE SHORT NORTH

Spruce Street

North Market

THE DISCOVERY DISTRICT

Maple Street

Nationwide Street

Mt. Vernon Avenue

Dublin Avenue

Neil Avenue

Olentangy River

Marconi Blvd.

North Front Street

North Fifth Street

East Spring Street

East Long Street

Battelle Riverfront Park

East Gay Street

Cleveland Avenue

Thurber House

East Broad Street

Ohio Statehouse

Oak Street

Bicentennial Park

South Third Street

South Fourth Street

East Town Street

Washington Avenue

East Rich Street

Scioto River

East Main Street

Grant Avenue

South Short Street

High Street

East Fulton Street

BREWERY DISTRICT

Livingston Avenue

GERMAN VILLAGE

Sycamore Street

Whittier Street

Reinhard Avenue

Schiller Park

where to go

COSI. 333 West Broad Street, Columbus, OH 43215. This learning experience for all ages focuses on a wide spectrum, from Labs in Life, a state-of-the-art laboratory where research on obesity and physical activity is conducted on-site to WOSU/COSI Media Center, a hands-on media center that allows you to create your own videos, among other things. You'll also explore the mystery of life, the ocean, and space, and you can travel through time in a model town as it develops from 1898 to 1962. The little squirts have their own area; traveling exhibition galleries, an outdoor science park, and three theaters, one of which has a seven-story screen and a motion simulator round out the offerings. Open daily. Admission is charged. (888) 819–2674; www.cosi.org.

Columbus Museum of Art. 480 East Broad Street, Columbus, OH 43215. This extensive collection of American and European art from 1850 to 1945 features impressionists, expressionists, cubists, modernists, and "contemporaries" with works by Degas, Monet, Matisse, Picasso, Bellows, Demuth, Hopper, Marin, and O'Keeffe. Highlights include the Russell Page Sculpture Garden, the Ross Photography Center, and an interactive exhibition for children and families, *Eye Spy: Adventures in Art*. The museum also hosts continuous programs of national and international traveling exhibitions. Closed Monday. Admission is charged. (614) 221–6801; www.columbusmuseum.org.

Wexner Center for the Arts. 1871 North High Street, Columbus, OH 43210. A magnet for eclecticism, this venue attracts creative artists and programs from all media, from all over. Constructed courtesy of hometown billionaire Leslie Wexner (of The Limited, Bath and Body Works, and other retail conglomerates), its architecture is an amalgamation of contemporary, modern, and classic designs. Its unconventional appearance is matched by a layout that can be confusing even to those with a good sense of direction. Still, it's worth the visit if only to see something that has been written up in just about every architectural magazine and has been described as "a spaceship that crash landed on the prairies." Open daily. Admission is charged. (614) 292–3535; www.wexarts.org.

Motorcycle Hall of Fame Museum. 13515 Yarmouth Drive, Pickerington, OH 43147. Vroom, vroom . . . in fewer than fifteen years, the Motorcycle Hall of Fame Museum evolved from a favorite of aficionados to a major attraction and caretaker of America's motorcycle heritage, drawing even nonbikers. The twenty-three-acre campus doubles as American Motorcyclist Association headquarters and houses an impressive collection of Harleys, Hendersons, Indians, and Hondas (pre-Acura). The two-story, 26,000-square-foot facility showcases thousands of machines, from early board-trackers and streamliners to competition Superbikes and Motocrossers. Open daily. Admission is charged. (614) 856–2222; www.motorcyclemuseum.org.

Franklin Park Conservatory and Botanical Garden. 1777 East Broad Street, Columbus, OH 43203. Tired of the weather? Here you can go to a different climate year-round in a series of separate zones that represent four regions of the world. Visit the cool Himalayan mountains or tropical forest. Or hit the desert, then head over to a rain forest. You can also plant yourself in traditional rooms housing palm, bonsai, and orchid collections. Two land-scaped courtyards are open during warm weather. Open daily except for Monday (unless it's a holiday Monday). Admission is charged. (800) 214–7275; www.fpconservatory.org.

Columbus Zoo and Aquarium. 9990 Riverside Drive, Powell, OH 43065. Go north on I-270 to the Sawmill Road exit, and go north again. Turn left on Powell Road to Riverside Drive. Talk about animal attraction: Nearly all continents are covered here. There's an Afri-can rain forest; a North American section with prairie dogs, migratory birds, and wetlands; and critters from South America, Asia, and Australia. The Manatee Coast is one of three facilities outside Florida to exhibit these endangered critters. The cheetah and lowland gorilla breeding programs and ever-popular ape exhibit have spawned not only offspring, but also imitators (monkey see, monkey do?). The zoo boasts one of the country's largest collec-tions of reptiles, and the director emeritus, "Jungle Jack" Hanna, is a regular on *Late Show with David Letterman* and other national TV shows. Open daily. Admission is charged.(800) 666–5397; www.colszoo.org.

the districts

One of the neat things about Columbus is that you can explore the following districts 24/7 and not spend a penny if that's your preference or if you're extremely self-disciplined. However, pay close attention to the parking signs and hours in the Short North or you may come back to no car at all and a hefty fine to get it back (the Web site, http://www .shortnorth.org/news.asp?n=12 provides suggestions, tips, and information). And the curbs in German Village can be deadly on tires and bumpers if you park too close (if you can find a space at all).

German Village. Six blocks south of the State Capitol and south of I–70 (Third and Fourth Street exits). Mailing address: German Village Society, 588 South Third Street, Columbus, OH 43215. This restored nineteenth-century community with renovated homes, quaint shops, and unique pubs and eateries has picture-perfect brick-and-limestone cottages and well-tended sidewalks, gardens, and flower boxes as well as lovely green spaces. Rescued from the wrecking ball in 1960 by the above-mentioned society, it is now on the National Register of Historic Places. (614) 221–8888; www.germanvillage.com.

Brewery District. Just to the west and north of German Village in and around High and Front Streets, this fun and funky area contains happening nightspots, cool restaurants, microbreweries, and wineries. Historically, German residents produced beer and ale here, although Prohibition put a drain on that, resulting in a downward spiral, so to speak. How-ever, many of the warehouses and original buildings have been refurbished to their original beauty, allowing for a taste of history as well.

Arena District. Nationwide Arena, 200 West Nationwide Boulevard, Columbus, OH 43215. Go north up High Street and through downtown, turn left on Nationwide Boulevard, and you'll run into Nationwide Arena. Home of the Columbus Blue Jackets, this 20,000-seat multipurpose facility hosts concerts and other events. Huntington Park, the new three-level, 10,000-seat home of the Columbus Clippers, also recently opened here. The Arena District boasts ninety-five acres of sidewalks and paths, an outside giant-screen TV, restaurants, bars, and retail outlets. (614) 246–2000; www.arenadistrict.com and www.nationwidearena .com.

Short North. Mailing address: 1126½-A North High Street, Columbus, OH 43201. Literally a few blocks north of the Arena District, this popular, revitalized neighborhood hosts gallery hops on the first Saturday of each month. Prints, paintings, ceramics, and more from local to international artists can be found, as well as specially crafted home goods, clothing, and jewelry. There are loads of one-of-a-kind restaurants and plenty of clubs with live music. (614) 228–8050; www.shortnorth.org.

University. Ohio State University. Columbus, OH 43210. Go farther north on High Street and you'll run into 16,000 acres with about 50,000 college students. Along with buildings, libraries, and a strip of campus-related shops, bookstores, and restaurants, you'll find Ohio Stadium, home of the Buckeye football team, and a Jack Nicklaus museum, which honors the Columbus-born and OSU-grad golfer. (614) 292–6446; www.osu.edu.

where to shop

North Market. 56 Spruce Street, Columbus, OH 43215. This indoor fresh-produce emporium has been around for almost 125 years. Offerings include vegetables, meats, poultry, and baked goods as well as exotic and ethnic foods. You can even dine here; seating provided. (614) 463–9664; www.northmarket.com.

Book Loft. 631 South Third Street, Columbus, OH 43206. This independent bookstore has more than 100,000 hardbacks and paperbacks in thirty-two rooms in a pre–Civil War structure. Best of all, most titles are discounted, some of them quite heavily. There's also a selection of CDs, cards, and posters, and visitors can enjoy their purchases in a peaceful adjoining courtyard. (614) 464–1774; www.bookloft.com.

Polaris Fashion Place. 1500 Polaris Parkway, Columbus, OH 43240. Just what Columbus needed . . . another mall. It got it anyway, and this version includes Saks, Macy's, JCPenney, Macy's, Sears, and The Great Indoors, plus more than 150 specialty shops and a huge array of restaurants. And it's ginormous, encompassing two levels with more than 1.5 million square feet and four major intersections. Although you may wear out your walking shoes, you're never far from one of more than 80 restrooms and the kids can frolic in a play area that's the largest in the region. (614) 846–1500; www.polarisfashionplace.com.

Easton Town Center. 160 Easton Town Center, Columbus, OH 43219. Recession? What recesson? This state-of-the-entertainment center is why some cultures regard America as the Evil Empire (at least in the sense of materialism). Almost 150 monuments to consumerism in this nicely laid-out outdoor/indoor mall include AMC Easton 30 Movies, Gameworks, Tiffany's, Cheesecake Factory, Nordstrom, Macy's, Funny Bone comedy club, and an open-air venue for various performers. 614) 416–7000; www.eastontowncenter.com.

South Campus Gateway. 1556 N. High Street, Columbus, OH 43201. Perhaps more of a lifestyle choice than an actual shopping experience, this relatively new addition boasts actual (but not free) parking. Located between campus and downtown, stores range from the eclectic but affordable Au Moda (1552 N. High Street; 614–299–6632; www.aumoda .com) to the more usual but interestingly laid out Barnes & Noble (1598 N. High Street; 614–247–2000; www.ohiostate.bncollege.com). There are also lots of funky restaurants, a movie theater, and even places to live if you *really* like it. (614) 298– 8115; www.south campusgateway.com.

Buckeye Corner. 1315 West Lane Avenue, Upper Arlington, OH 43221. The locus for all things Ohio State, this official retail partner of the OSU Alumni Association has expanded from the above "corner" to four Columbus locations. The go-to place for scarlet & gray dog jerseys, block "O" earring sets, infant cheerleader rompers, Ohio State logo boxer shorts, and much, much, much more. (614) 486–0702; www.buckeyecorner.com.

where to eat

Mitchell's Steakhouse. 45 North Third Street, Columbus, OH 43215. From one extreme to the other: This cosmopolitan, upscale steak and chop house offers the finest hand-cut, aged, corn-fed USDA prime. Other specialties include lobster tails, fresh bread, and housemade soups, dressings, and sauces. And the decor is as sublime as the food. $$$. (614) 621–2333; www.mitchellssteakhouse.com.

Columbus Brewing Company. (CBC). 525 Short Street, Columbus, OH 43215. This menu covers the full gamut: wood-fired pizzas, pasta, steaks, chicken, chops, seafood, salads, and more. No "specials of the house" here; everything is good. $$–$$$. (614) 464–2739; www.columbusbrewing.com.

The Rusty Bucket Tavern. 1635 West Lane Avenue, Upper Arlington, OH 43221. With several locations in and around Columbus, you're rarely far from a "Bucket." Not only is the decor comfortable, welcoming, and spacious, but the menu covers all bases. Simple comfort foods like meatloaf are offered alongside peel-your-own shrimp, with plenty of soups, salads, sandwiches and blue-plate specials in-between. $$. (614) 485–2303; www .rustybuckettavern.com.

Rosendales. 793 North High Street, Columbus, OH 43215. Located in a renovated circa 1924 auto showroom, this is food as theater, both in atmosphere and offerings. Dine on the balcony or, weather permitting, outdoors; oversized windows offer prime people watching. The menu changes seasonally but many items are traditional with a touch of the contemporary. Some off-the-wall offerings include a goat cheese sorbet with beets. Or play it relatively safe with sea bass in soaked in soy sauce or the short ribs with risotto. $$$. (614) 298–1601; www.rosendales.com.

Elevator Brewery & Draught Haus. 161 North High Street, Columbus, OH 43215. Located in the historic Clock Restaurant and close to many downtown attractions, this eatery is dark wood and stained-glass intensive. Handcrafted microbrews and other beverages complement house-cut steaks, fish, chicken, and pork. There's also a nifty bar area and accompanying munchies like corn brats, chicken wings, and quesadillas. $$. (614) 228–0500; www.elevator brewing.com.

where to stay

The Lofts. 55 East Nationwide Boulevard, Columbus, OH 43215. This example of nineteenth-century architecture has evolved into a high-falutin' experience. Originally a warehouse, accommodations here include exposed brick walls, beams, and ductwork; New York subway-style tile in the bathroom; and custom designed lighting, furniture, and accessories. They also have high-speed Internet access, personal butler service, and cell doors from the Ohio Penitentiary. Go figure. $$$. (614) 461–2663; www.55lofts.com.

Westin Great Southern. 310 South High Street, Columbus, OH 43215. The only nineteenth-century hotel building still in use, this lodging boasts classy chandeliers, a spectacular stained-glass ceiling, and magnificent marble floors. All rooms have cherrywood furnishings, luxurious baths, personalized voice mail, and a fitness center. $$$. (614) 228–3800; www.westincolumbus.com.

Short North Bed and Breakfast. 50 East Lincoln, Columbus, OH 43215. Situated in the Short North, this renovated mid-city retreat boasts seven guest rooms each with a queen-size bed, full bath, and cable TV (some also have an extra twin bed).There are accommodations for your car as well, and a full Continental breakfast for the owners. $$$. (800) 516–9664.

Harrison House Bed and Breakfast. 313 West Fifth Avenue, Columbus, OH 43201. Located in historic Victorian Village, a suburb full of rehabbed Victorians—houses, not people—this residence is close to downtown, Ohio State, and other local areas of interest. Along with original cut-glass windows, ornate woodwork, lace curtains, and more, four guest rooms include private baths and amenities such as cable and phone. Full breakfast included; those leaving the table hungry do so by choice. $$. (800) 827–4203; www .harrisonhouse-columbus.com.

day trip 02

west

fun in the sun and snow:
west liberty • zanesfield •
bellefontaine • lakeview

For diversity, Logan County is tough to beat: Along with skiing and snowboarding in the winter, you can romp at the lake and go horseback riding during the warm months. There are two caverns and two castles, and a few miles east of Bellefontaine is Mount Campbell (actually Campbell Hill, according to the map), a whopping 1,550 feet above sea level. Bellefontaine also lays claim to the first concrete street in America and the shortest road (McKinley Street, just 17 feet long). So many rarities, so little time.

west liberty

About an hour northwest of Columbus, the region can be reached a couple of ways. Those wishing to go directly to West Liberty can take I–70 west to SR 68 north. Or you can opt for the more picturesque (i.e., circuitous) route via I–270 to U.S. 33, then north to SR 245 west, which leads directly to attractions such as Ohio Caverns and the Piatt Castles.

where to go

Ohio Caverns. 2210 East SR 245, West Liberty, OH 43357. Discovered in the late 1800s by a farmhand, this truly cool (54 degrees, no matter what the outside temperature) underground cave quickly became a tourist draw. Its crystalline stalactite and stalagmite formations, including the humongous 5-foot Crystal King, are ever-evolving, kaleidoscopic, and varied, making each visit a little bit different. Well-lit paved walkways, a gift shop, and shelter

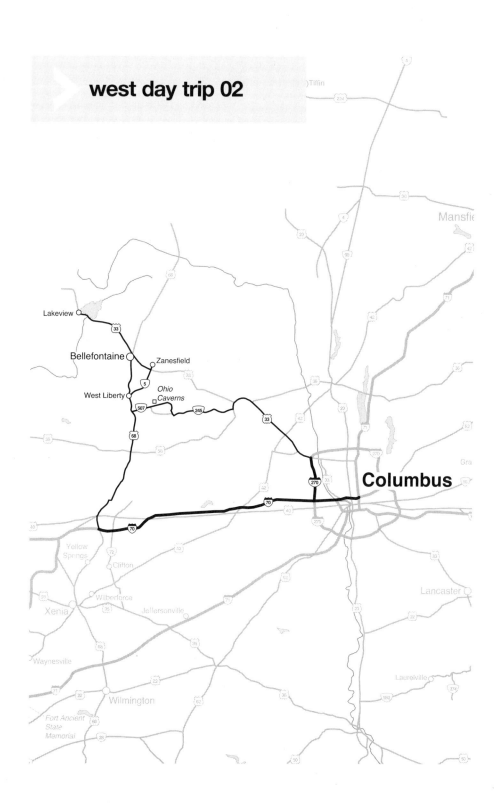

house/picnic tables make for a pleasant diversion. Open daily. Admission is charged. (937) 465–4017; www.ohiocaverns.com.

Piatt Castles. 10051 Township Road 47, West Liberty, OH 43357. Two locally prominent brothers, General Abram Sanders Piatt and Colonel Donn Piatt, decided that their home should truly be their castle(s). In the late 1800s, Abram built Mac-A-Cheek, while Donn constructed Mac-O-Chee. Both were decorated and frescoed by French artist Oliver Frey. "Cheek" has remained in the Piatt family for five generations and sits atop a hill amid awe-inspiring surroundings. "Chee" has extraordinary painted walls and ceilings and unusual architecture. Both are loaded with antiques, Native American artifacts, and relics from the Civil and Mexican Wars, and host various special and seasonal programs. Open March through October, Thanksgiving through New Years; other times by appointment. Admission is charged. (937) 465–2821; www.piattcastles.org.

where to shop

Marie's Candies. 311 Zanesfield Road, West Liberty, OH 43357. This sweet success story started in 1956 and has continued to grow, just like consumers' waistlines. More than eighty varieties of chocolates are sold in this historical train depot, and before buying, you get to sample the merchandise. (866) 465–5781; www.mariescandies.com.

Pioneer House. 10245 Township Road 47, West Liberty, OH 43357. The historic log home of the Piatt brothers' parents is now a gift shop. Elizabeth Piatt, their mother, sheltered fugitive slaves whenever her husband, a federal circuit court judge, was out of town. He sent a messenger to warn of his return so the slaves could move to the next stop and she could avoid arrest for her "illegal" activities. Today's tamer ambience includes Yankee candles (how appropriate), tinware, quilts, lace linens, antiques, and other Americana. (937) 465–4801.

Global Crafts. 106 N. Detroit Street, West Liberty, OH 43357. This truly international selection ranges from handcrafted reed baskets to Kenyan carvings to textiles, boxes, jewelry, and soapstone from India. Global Crafts is a nonprofit branch of the Mennonite Central Committee, a relief and development agency. (937) 465–3077.

zanesfield

From West Liberty, take CR 5 north about 8 miles to Zanesfield.

where to go

Mad River Mountain Ski Resort. 100 Snow Valley Road, Zanesfield, OH 43360. With an elevation of 1,460 feet, this place has lots of altitude. There are more than twenty trails for skiing or snowboarding. A major snowmaking system covers 125 acres in case Mother

Nature decides not to cooperate. Trails range from gentle slopes for children and beginners ("Placid Trail," "Big Easy") to "most difficult" and "experts only" with shiver-making names like "The Chute" and "Peril." Those who prefer sled riding can take advantage of the tubing park. Lessons, a beginner's area, accessory shop, and cafe round out the offerings. Open daily, December through March. Admission is charged. (800) 231–7669; www.skimadriver.com.

Marmon Valley Farm. 7754 SR 292, Zanesfield, OH 43360. With 480 acres of fields, woods, hills, and streams, these riding stables offer English and Western options on more than one hundred horses and ponies. It also hosts summer camps, barn dances, sledding, and sleigh-riding activities as well as church retreats. Hours vary. Call for reservations and fee information. (937) 593–8000; www.marmonvalley.com.

where to stay

Myeerah's Inn. 2875 Sandusky Street, Zanesfield, OH 43360. Formerly a stagecoach stop and goods store in the early 1800s, this large two-story brick structure now boasts three guest rooms furnished with Ohio antiques. Fresh flowers, mints, and a hearty French country breakfast are other niceties. Bonus: The proprietor's husband is the county coroner. $$. (937) 593–0000.

bellefontaine

Just 5 miles from Zanesfield, Bellefontaine can be reached by going west on U.S. 33.

where to go

Zane Shawnee Caverns. 7092 SR 540, Bellefontaine, OH 43311. This a"maze"ing conglomeration of chambers and corridors consists of three levels of varied formations of stalactites and stalagmites. Ohio's only "cave pearls," created from dripping mineral-laden water, can be found here. The caverns also have the somewhat creepy distinction of being a hibernation center for bats. Located in Southwind Park and owned and operated by the Shawnee Nation, the site also features a Native American museum. Open daily. Admission is charged. (937) 592–9592; www.zaneshawneecaverns.net.

Orr Mansion/Logan County Historical Museum. 521 East Columbus Avenue, Bellefontaine, OH 43311. In 1908 a local lumber baron built this neoclassical mansion, which also serves as the county museum and archives. Highlights include two-story columns, a third-floor porch, and oak woodwork, with vintage furniture, clothing, musical instruments, and more scattered throughout. Local railroad items, an antique toy collection, and military artifacts share space with a one-room school and general store. Open Wednesday and Friday through Sunday, May through October; Friday and Saturday, November through April. Admission is charged. (937) 593–7557; www.logancountymuseum.org.

where to stay

Whitmore House. 3985 SR 47 West, Bellefontaine, OH 43311. This century-old Victorian home sits amid four acres of lawns and gardens. Three bedrooms and a restaurant are provided; a full breakfast can be purchased. $. (937) 592–4290; www.whitmorehouse.com.

Mountain Top Inn. 308 North Main Street, Bellefontaine, OH 43311. This friendly, family-owned motel has fifty rooms with all the usual suspects: A/C, cable, microwave, refrigerator, laundry, and outdoor pool. $–$$. (937) 593–9622; www.mtttopinn.com.

lakeview

From Bellefontaine, Lakeview is a straight shot northwest on U.S. 33, less than 15 miles.

where to go

Indian Lake State Park. 12774 SR 235 North, Lakeview, OH 43331. A fancy resort at the turn of the last century, Indian Lake was once labeled the Midwest's Million Dollar Playground. Now a public park and the state's second largest artificially made body of water, its 5,800 acres of H20 are ideal for boating, fishing, and picnicking. A nature center offers up historical displays, a wildlife room, aquarium, and hands-on area. Two beaches, campgounds, sevenmiles of easy walking trails, and a paved bike path add to the big puddle's appeal. Open daily. Free. (937) 843–2717; www.dnr.state.oh.us.

where to eat

Brothers Bar & Grill. 11977 SR 235, Lakeview, OH 43331. This unassuming eatery specializes in burgers, fried fish sandwiches, chicken gizzards, and bar food, and hosts live local entertainment. $. (937) 843–3449.

Cranberry Resort. 9667 SR 368, Huntsville, OH 43324. It sounds like a hotel but is actually a restaurant/club. Along with appetizers, a huge selection of sandwiches, salads, pies, and a kids' menu, there's a full lineup of local entertainment. Beer 'n' ribs are a feature on Thursday. Patrons can arrive by land or by boat and just pull up at the dock. $. (937) 842–4947; www.cranberryresortindianlake.com.

Froggy's at the Lake. 11065 County Road 293, Lakeview, OH 43331. Recently renovated and expanded, Froggy's leaps with live entertainment, a pool with swim-up bar, boat docks, and more. The menu includes broasted chicken, large sandwiches, pizza, and other items. Ready to party? This is the place. $–$$. (937) 842–5580; www.froggys-online.com.

where to stay

Indian Lake State Park Campground. 12774 SR 235 North, Lakeview, OH 43331. Three hundred seventy sites for tents and RVs and seventy-three nonelectric hookups can be found at this first-come, first served area. Showers, flush toilets, laundry facilities, miniature golf course, and bike rental are included. Or you can rent a tepee, camper cabin, or tent. $. (937) 843–2717; www.ohiodnr.com.

day trip 03

west

another alternative:
yellow springs • xenia • wilberforce • clifton

Those looking for a change of pace would do well to visit this area. Along with what some might call hippie-dippy Yellow Springs, there's an old mill stream, Rails-to-Trails hiking and biking, plus an African-American history museum.

yellow springs

Although it's only about an hour from Columbus, Yellow Springs could be in an alternate universe. A hotbed of radicalism during the Vietnam era, the home of Antioch College (795 Livermore Street, Yellow Springs, OH 45387, 937–769–1000; www.antioch-college.edu) which itself has been undergoing a revolution and is temporarily (or maybe not) closed, YS retains its patina of cutting-edge unconventionality through its shops, artistic life, and political interest groups, whose flyers and brochures seem to proliferate from every bulletin board and telephone pole. This is the place to go if you want to revisit the '60s—sort of.

To get to Yellow Springs, take I–70 west, and go south on U.S. 68, a total of about 60 miles.

where to go

John Bryan State Park/Clifton Gorge State Nature Preserve. 3790 SR 370, Yellow Springs, OH 45387. This spectacular example of your geological forces at work encompasses Clifton Gorge, a designated national natural landmark with distinctive rock

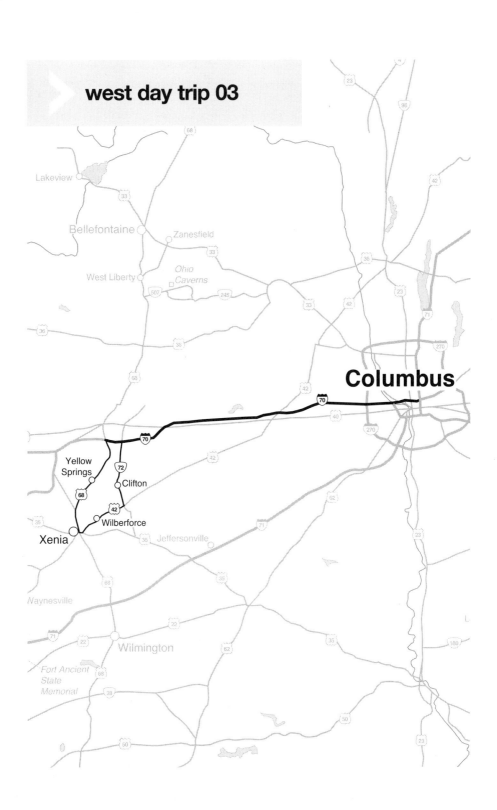

west day trip 03

Lakeview

Bellefontaine
Zanesfield

West Liberty
Ohio
Caverns

Columbus

Yellow
Springs
Clifton

Wilberforce

Xenia
Jeffersonville

Waynesville

Wilmington

Fort Ancient
State
Memorial

formations, massive trees, and varied, lacy stands of wildflowers. The park itself has hundreds of oaks and maples, as well as various shrubs, flora, and birds, making it a scenic
event no matter what the season. Camping, fishing, boating, hiking, rock climbing, and
more are available. Open daily. Free. (937) 767–1274; www.johnbryan.org.

Glen Helen Nature Preserve. 405 Corry Street, Yellow Springs, OH 45387. With 1,000
acres of thickets, forests, meadows, and rivers, this is the point from which Yellow Springs'
namesake waters, once believed to be a cure-all, originate. There's also an ecology institute, outdoor education center, raptor center, and trailside museum, as well as beautiful
walking and hiking terrain, making it a favorite of nature lovers and inquiring minds of all
ages. Open daily. Donations welcome. (937) 767–7375; www.antioch.edu/glenhelen.

Young's Jersey Dairy. 6880 Springfield-Xenia Road, Yellow Springs, OH 45387. Along
with indulging in arguably the best milk shakes and ice cream around, visitors can pet and
visit farm animals, play eighteen holes of miniature golf, and hone their putting and batting
skills. Depending on the time of year, you can watch cows being milked, wander through
a cornfield maze, take a hayride, or participate in holiday-themed events. Altogether an
udderly moo-ving experience. Open daily. Admission may be charged. (937) 325–0629;
www.youngsdairy.com.

Little Miami Scenic Trail. Yellow Springs station: on the bike path between Xenia Avenue
and Dayton Street. Mailing address: Rails-to-Trails Conservancy, Ohio Field Office,10 South
High Street, Suite A, Canal Winchester, Oh 43110. The Yellow Springs to Xenia route runs
about 10 miles over scenic natural surroundings, ending on Third Street in Xenia. Many of
the paths originated from unused tracks and are part of the national Rails-to-Trails program.
Expect to encounter all ages and levels of fitness on the trail itself, from senior citizen hikers
and moms with new babies to serious cyclists who zip by at amazing speeds. Constructed
from railroad buildings and refurbished, both the Yellow Springs and Xenia stations provide
restrooms, concessions, and displays, and serve as a stopover. Open daily. Free. (937)
837–6782; www.miamivalleytrails.org/miami.htm.

where to shop

Yellow Springs has an abundance of specialized and eclectic stores, many of which have
been around for well over twenty years. You can spend an hour or a day, and prices are
generally reasonable. The shops feature compelling and unusual items from a regional
colony of artists who, like shopkeepers and other locals, have found permanent refuge in
the alternative lifestyle.

Angelic Devas. 245 1/2 Xenia Avenue, Yellow Springs, OH 45387. Seekers of environmental spiritualism will be enlightened by books, classes, gifts, and more. (937) 767–7273; www
.angelicdevas.com.

Bonadies Glasstudio. 220 Xenia Avenue, Yellow Springs, OH 45387. This emporium specializes in custom stained-glass windows, lamps, and other art, along with restoration of existing items. One of the best facilities of its kind. (937) 767–7021; www.bonadies glasstudio.com.

Dark Star Books. 237 Xenia Avenue, Yellow Springs, OH 45387. With more than 40,000 used fiction and nonfiction tomes in all categories, you'll never run out of reading material. Comic books, gaming and trading cards, and even bumper stickers are also tendered. (937) 767–9400; www.darkstarbookstore.com.

Earth Rose. 221 Xenia Avenue, Yellow Springs, OH 45387. Who needs mall-wear when you can choose from among Birkenstock shoes, Indian print and handwoven clothing, tapestries, and imported gifts? (937) 667–8165.

Epic Bookshop. 120 1/2 Dayton Street, Yellow Springs, OH 45387. Bone up on self-development, Buddhism, and Yoga; selections include memoirs and children's books. Leather journals, incense, statues, prayer flags, toys, yoga mats, meditation cushions, and goddess jewelry can also be purchased. (866) 876–6896; www.epicbookshop.com.

No Common Scents. 1525 Xenia Avenue, Yellow Springs, OH 45387. But lots of nice smells, including 175 essential and aromatherapy oils. This shop has more than 250 herbs and spices, including twenty-five spice blends. In addition to twenty varieties of teas, there are five green teas and nearly two dozen special and potpourri combinations. (800) 686–0012; www.nocommonscents.com.

Julia Ettas Trunk. 100 Corry Street, Yellow Springs, OH 45387. Unique women's apparel covers all ages, sizes, and styles. Some items are pricey; others are deeply discounted. (937) 767–2823.

Ohio Silver. 245 Xenia Avenue, Yellow Springs, OH 45387. The name aptly describes this huge selection of earrings, rings, bracelets, and other accessories. Some gold and items in other media can be found. There's also an in-store cat to visit while contemplating purrchases. (937) 767–8261.

Organic Grocery. 230 Keiths Alley, Yellow Springs, OH 45387. No weekly specials or piped-in music, just healthy, natural, and often hard-to-find foodstuffs that are good for you (taste may be another story, however). (937) 767–2654.

Yellow Springs Pottery. 222 Xenia Avenue, Yellow Springs, OH 45387. Selections originate from a consortium of potters (as opposed to a pot cooperative, which is illegal, even in this town). Works of art are colorful, functional, and make for distinctive and useful gifts. (937) 767–1666; www.yellowspringspottery.com.

where to eat

Golden Jersey Inn. 6880 Springfield-Xenia Road, Yellow Springs, OH 45387. Specialties of the fresh and varied menu range from omelettes to baked potato soup to a variety of sandwiches. Dinner serves up bacon-wrapped pork chops, meat loaf and mashed pota-toes, barbecued pork ribs, char-grilled ham steak, and more. $–$$$. (937) 324–2050; www .youngsdairy.com.

Winds Cafe. 215 Xenia Avenue, Yellow Springs, OH 45387. This gourmet eatery features seasonal items and flavorful combinations. Regular menu changes ensure that each visit is a different dining experience. Special dinners and beer and wine tastings are also offered. $$–$$$. (937) 767–1144; www.windscafe.com.

Sunrise Cafe. 259 Xenia Avenue, Yellow Springs, OH 45387. Three squares, Yellow Springs–style, include a portabello and spinach omelette with fontina cheese; pasta with handcrafted sauce; tabouli; thai peanut tofu; and moon plate (rice, beans, vegetables, and salad), to mention a few. $–$$. (937) 767–7211; www.sunrisecafe-ys.com.

where to stay

Springs Motel. 1801 Xenia Avenue, Yellow Springs, OH 45387. Constructed in the 1950s, this clean but no-frills lodge has twelve rooms and has been recently refurbished with such essentials as new showerheads and data ports. $. (937) 767–8700; www.the springsmotel.com.

Hearthstone Inn & Suites. 10 South Main Street, Cedarville, OH 45314. From Yellow Springs, take SR 343 East to SR 72 South; it's about ten minutes away. Everything new is old again: this recently established country inn features twenty guest rooms that combine traditional furnishings with all the amenities. The lobby boasts high ceilings, stone fireplaces, and comfy sofas while outside is a wooded park with baseball, tennis, jogging, and picnic facilities. $$–$$$. (877) 644–6466; www.hearthstone-inn.com.

xenia

Xenia and nearby Fairborn are known for Wright Patterson Air Force Base and tornadoes. Although Wright-Pat is located in Dayton (see West Day Trip 4), many of its personnel reside in Greene County. So when aliens are mentioned, it may be in the context of little green men and not green cards. Plucky Xenia suffered through two major twisters in 1974 and again in 2000. Although fatalities, injuries, and major property damage resulted, the town continues to offer cultural and recreational opportunities. From Yellow Springs, continue on south U.S. 68 about 10 miles to Xenia.

where to go

Greene County Historical Society. 74 West Church Street, Xenia, OH 45385. Relive the story of Greene County through permanent and special displays, which include a 1799 log house and an 1876 Victorian dwelling. Along with a general store and railroad memorabilia, the collection encompasses farm equipment, china, books, toys, and furniture. Hours vary; closed Monday. Admission may be charged. (937) 372–4606.

***Blue Jacket.* Caesar's Ford Amphitheater.** 520 South Stringtown Road, Xenia, OH 45385. Or *How a Guy Named Marmaduke Van Swearingen Became a Shawnee War Chief.* This outdoor drama, played out on what was originally the tribe's sacred ground, depicts the Revolutionary War–era struggle of Native Americans, frontier settlers, and escaping slaves. Horses, cannons, flaming arrows, and more add excitement and authenticity. Dinner and backstage tours available. June through September only. Admission is charged. (877) 465–2583 or (937) 376–4358; www.bluejacketdrama.com.

where to stay

Alpha House. 758 Alpha Road, Alpha, OH 45434. Alpha is in Beavercreek, just a few minutes west of Xenia on U.S. 35. Guests get the run of a two-story brick Federal-style home built in 1843. Formerly a general store and post office, the inside has been refurbished and is full of antiques, along with having a piano and record player. Some rooms come with private baths; a full breakfast is included. $$. (800) 337–2852; www.alphahousebandb.com.

wilberforce

Wilberforce is just a few miles northwest of Xenia on U.S. 42.

where to go

National Afro-American Museum and Cultural Center. 1350 Brush Row Road, Wilberforce, OH 45384. Located next to Central State University, this 50,000-square-foot center includes a museum and galleries. Focus is on research and education; the permanent exhibit explores African-American history from the end of World War II to the Voting Rights Act of 1964. Recorded narratives, gospel tunes, and artifacts such as jewelry, clothes, sports equipment, and consumer products breathe life into a '50s-era barbershop, beauty salon, and church interior. Changing exhibitions encompass art, music, inventors, and other aspects of black heritage. Open Tues–Sat. Admission is charged. (800) 752–2603; www.ohiohistory.org.

clifton

More history can be found in nearby Clifton. Take U.S. 42 east to SR 72. Drive north about 4 miles to Clifton.

where to go

Historic Clifton Mill. 75 Water Street, Clifton, OH 45316. Built in 1802 and one of the largest working gristmills remaining in the United States, this well-preserved attraction gets down to the real nitty-gritty with a detailed tour. Other points of interest include a Christmas light display, a Santa Claus collection (3,000 Santas, from 1850 to the present), and a restaurant. Open daily. Admission may be charged. (937) 767–5501; www.cliftonmill.com.

where to eat

Millrace Restaurant. Clifton Mill, 75 Water Street, Clifton, OH 45316. Home-cooked breakfast and lunch includes pancakes and corn bread made right in the mill. Breads, pies, and cookies are also baked fresh daily. Menu encompasses hearty country eggs and pork product combos, sandwiches, salads, soups, and desserts. $$. (937) 767–5501.

day trip 04

west

>>> **a wright outing:**
dayton

dayton

In addition to being the birthplace of aviation, Dayton has spawned inventions such as the automatic car self-starter, the heart-lung machine, the cash register, and the room air-conditioner. Along with the Wright Brothers, Dayton innovators include the late humorist Erma Bombeck, actor Martin Sheen, baseball star Mike Schmidt, and well-known word-smith John Jakes.

Thanks in part to the one-hundredth anniversary of flight, which expanded many existing historical attractions, Dayton has undergone a renaissance. Added to the truly nifty culture magnets such as the Victoria Theatre (138 North Main Street, Dayton 45402; 937–228–3630; www.victoriatheatre.com), a fully renovated, exquisite Italian marble- and brass-laden venue built in 1866, is the Schuster Performing Arts Center (Second and Main Street; 937–228–7591; www.schustercenter.org). Home of the Dayton Opera, Dayton Phil-harmonic, and Broadway Series, this jewel of the Gem City boasts a towering glassed-in Wintergarden, which features art-deco accents and palm trees. Also reminiscent of '30s elegance is its 2,300-seat Mead Theatre, whose domed ceiling re-creates the fiber-optic star-scape of December 16, 1903, the evening of Wilber and Orville's first powered flight.

Another sparkler is Fifth Third Field (220 North Patterson; 937–228–2287; www.dayton dragons.com). Playground of the single-A baseball team, the Dragons, this 7,200-seat stadium is modeled after such American classics as Wrigley Field and has enjoyed major

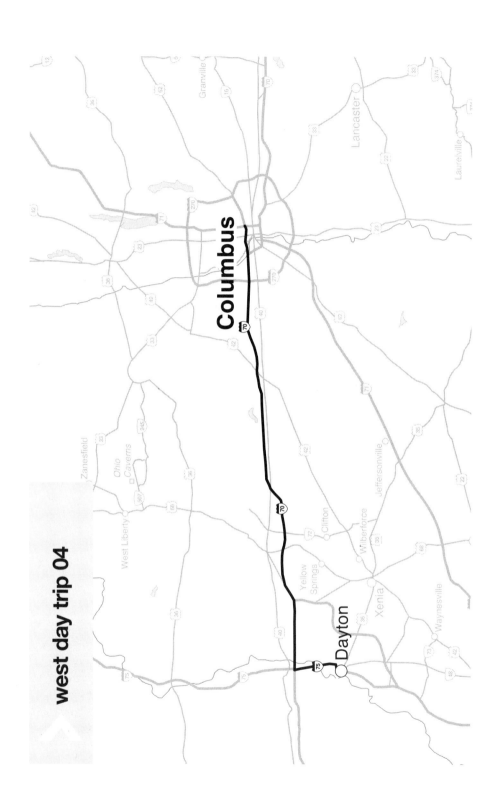

west day trip 04

Columbus

Dayton

success, with sold-out games and several promising players making the leap to the major leagues.

From Columbus, take I–70 west and go straight; you'll run right into the outskirts (to get downtown, take I–75 south). Dayton's about 100 miles away, an easy ride of about an hour and a half. Unless, of course, it's summertime and the highway gods have chosen a section of the interstate for construction, something that occurs with amazing regularity on this particular stretch. Then it's anyone's guess.

where to go

National Museum of the United States Air Force. 1100 Spaatz Street, Wright-Patterson Air Force Base, OH 45433. This is on the way to Dayton, so get off I–70 at exit 44A and take I–675 south to exit 15, Colonel Glenn Highway. Follow Colonel Glenn Highway to Harshman Road/Wright Brothers Parkway and turn right. Turn right again at Springfield Pike; the museum is on the right. The oldest and largest military aviation museum in the world houses more than 300 aircraft and missiles. Highlights include Wright Brothers memorabilia, World War II artifacts, the *Apollo 15* capsule, and diaries and medals from the early 1900s to the present. Galleries focus on the Air Force's early years, the Korean War, modern and space flight, and more. The addition of a third hangar includes aircraft from Desert Storm and other recent conflicts; there's a flight simulator as well. Experimental and presidential aircraft—including the Air Force One that flew JFK's body from Dallas back to Washington D.C.—and rotating special displays as well as a six-story IMAX theater make this a high-flying experience and the best deal in town. Open daily. Museum is free; admission is charged for IMAX. (937) 255–3286; www.nationalmuseum.af.mil.

National Aviation Hall of Fame. Located at the Air Force Museum, 1100 Spaatz Street, Wright-Patterson Air Force Base, OH 45433. This new attraction features interactive exhibits emphasizing scientific and historical contributions of air and space pioneers. An induction ceremony is held each year to recognize outstanding aviators in the United States; honorees range from such legends as the Wright Brothers, Amelia Earhart, Chuck Yeager, and John Glenn to lesser-known names like Marion E. Carl, the first Marine helicopter pilot, and Albert Lee Ueltschi, founder of FlightSafety International and other organizations. Admission may be charged. Call for hours. (888) 383–1903; www.nationalaviation.org.

Wright B Flyer. 10550 Springboro Pike, Miamisburg, OH 45342. From I–70, take I–675 south to Springboro Pike and go south. Want to experience the "Wright" stuff? Take a spin on this replica of the world's first mass-produced airplane (circa 1910) designed by Orville and Wilbur Wright. (Not to worry, previous flight problems such as those encountered at Kitty Hawk have been corrected.) Built by a group of aviation aficionados and run by volunteers, this "B" is housed in a hangar at the Wright Brothers Airport. Open Tuesday, Thursday, and Saturday. Museum is free, but flights do cost. (937) 885–2327; www.wright-b-flyer.org.

Dayton Aviation Heritage National Historical Park. Various locations. On October 16, 1992, Congress established this national park to honor Wilbur and Orville Wright and Paul Laurence Dunbar, who also happened to be childhood friends. Visit the park's Web site at www.nps.gov/daav. The following sites are included:

- **The Wright Cycle Company.** 16 South Williams Street, Dayton, OH 45407. This shop, operated by the Wright Brothers from 1895 to 1897, has been completely restored and contains period bicycles and machinery. A just-opened interpretive center features a Wright-Dunbar timeline, a collage on inventions and technology, a reproduction of Hale's Grocery, and Dunbar memorabilia, among many other things. Open daily from Memorial Day to Labor Day, Wednesday through Sunday the rest of year. Admission is charged. (937) 225–7705.

- **Dunbar House State Memorial.** 219 North Paul Laurence Dunbar Street. Mailing address: P.O. Box 1872, Dayton, OH 45401. The Paul Laurence Dunbar home in Dayton has been restored to appear as it did when he lived there, including rooms furnished with his own possessions. In addition to the library and a Native American artifact collection, a standout is a bicycle given to Dunbar by the Wright Brothers. The site also hosts frequent programs on Dunbar, his legacy, and African-American history. Open daily. Admission is charged. (937) 224–7061.

- **Carillon Historical Park.** 2001 South Patterson Boulevard, Dayton, OH 45409. Sixty-five wooded acres of buildings, attractions, and exhibitions include the 1905 *Wright Flyer III,* the world's first craft capable of controlled (this being a key word here) flight. Several automobiles manufactured in Dayton such as the Stoddard and the Maxwell, vintage bicycles, a 1930 print shop, and a ninety-seven-year-old schoolhouse can also be found. Bonus: Deeds Carillon, Ohio's largest bell tower, a real chimer. Closed Monday. Admission is charged. (937) 293–2841.

- **Huffman Prairie Flying Field,** Wright Memorial and Interpretive Center. To access the field, take Route 444, Wright-Patterson Air Force Base, OH 45433. Accessed through Gate 12A. The interpretive center is also off 444. After their first successful powered flight in 1903, the Wright Brothers erected a hangar for their plane on the Huffman Prairie outside of Dayton; a replica stands there today. They used this farmland to perfect their flying skills in 1904 and 1905, and as the site of the Wright Company School of Aviation/Wright Exhibition Company from 1910 to 1916. The newly opened interpretive center features additional information, books, and friendly rangers who will fill you in with the "Wright" lore. Open daily during daylight hours. Free. (937) 425–0008.

Woodland Cemetery and Arboretum. 118 Woodland Avenue, Dayton, OH 45409. This is a sort of A-list of the Dayton dead. Along with the Wright Brothers and their parents and sister, Paul Laurence Dunbar, his mother, and Erma Bombeck are buried here. Along with ornate headstones and a Tiffany stained-glass window in the stone chapel, there are more than 200 species of trees on these heavily wooded grounds. Open daily. Free. (937) 228–3221; www.woodlandcemetery.org.

Sunwatch Prehistoric Indian Village. 2301 West River Road, Dayton, OH 45418. This re-creation provides insight into the Fort Ancient Native American tribe that settled along the banks of the Great Miami River more than 800 years ago. Along with a reconstructed village, you'll find what has been described as an elaborate wooden counterpart to England's Stonehenge. Posts placed in the center of the village provided a complex system of charting time and seasons and were used to schedule planting and harvesting. Open Tues through Sat. Admission is charged. (937) 268–8199, www.sunwatch.org.

Boonshoft Museum of Discovery. 2600 Deweese Parkway, Dayton, OH 45414. A learning experience for kids of all ages: Hands-on activities consist of water tables, a two-and-a-half-story climbing tower and slide, and a zoo featuring live animals. A state-of-the-art digital planetarium features a variety of shows and special effects matinees. Environmental exhibits and science programming are also emphasized; there's an early childhood area as well. Open daily. Admission is charged. (937) 275–7431; www.boonshoftmuseum.org.

Dayton Art Institute. 456 Belmonte Park North, Dayton, OH 45405. The permanent collection of this historic Italian Renaissance building includes works by Claude Monet, Edgar Degas, and Andy Warhol, as well as various media in American, European, and Asian galleries. Special exhibits focus on Africa, regional artists, and exploring the human body in art as well as photography, painting, and glass sculpture. EXPERIENCENTER, an interactive showcase, is geared toward children. Open daily. Free, but admission may be charged for special exhibits. (937) 223–5277; www.daytonartinstitute.org.

Riverscape Metropark. 111 East Monument Avenue, , Dayton, OH 45402. Located downtown, this popular gathering spot features a multicolored fountain, which shoots colored streams of water hundreds of feet into the air. "Invention stations" provide insight into the workings of such great minds as Charles Kettering and the Wright Brothers and everyday minutiae like Dayton-originated ice-cube trays, pop-top cans, cash registers, and more. Several "walks" highlight local luminaries and history. Hydro-bikes, pedal boats, roller blades, and regular bicycles are also available for rental, and a sidewalk Interactive Fountain provides "blasts" of H_2O for all ages. Open daily. Free. (937) 274–0126; www.riverscape.org.

Citizen's Motorcar Company: America's Packard Museum. 420 South Ludlow Street, Dayton, OH 45402. This fully restored 1930s Packard dealership re-creates the glamour of the era through an art-deco showroom and more than twenty completely refurbished automobiles. Artifacts from the Packard Motorcar Company can also be found. This favorite of old-car buffs and preservationists has won several awards. Open daily. Admission is charged. (937) 226–1710; www.americaspackardmuseum.org.

where to shop

Feathers. 440 East Fifth Street, Dayton, OH 45402. Located in the Oregon District, here you'll find vintage clothing, art-deco items, and 1950s "modern" memorabilia. (937) 228–2940.

Rutledge Gallery. Kettering Tower Lobby, 40 North Main Street, Dayton, OH 45423. Along with contemporary art, sculpture, paintings, and drawings, this enterprise hosts work from both local and international artists. Framing services are also available. (937) 226–7335; www.rutledge-art.com.

Dayton Mall. 2700 Miamisburg-Centerville Road, Dayton, OH 45459. One of the region's first megamalls, this conglomeration boasts 160 stores, including anchors Macy's, JCPenney, Elder-Beerman, and Sears. (937) 433–9833; www.daytonmall.net.

Town and Country Shopping Center. 300 East Stroop Road, Kettering, OH 45429. From I–675, take exit 10 and go west; turn left on Stroop Road. Favorite hunting grounds of local shoppers include classy stores such as Stein Mart, Books & Co., and the Secret Ingredient. (937) 293–7516; www.daytontownandcountry.com.

The Mall at Fairfield Commons. 2727 Fairfield Commons, Beavercreek, OH 45431. From I–675, go south on North Fairfield Road. This new addition to the area's mall-stellation includes 150 shops. Selections range from anchors like Parisian, Sears, Macy's, Elder-Beerman, and JCPenney to specialty shops, including Northern Reflections, Bath & Body Works, and The Museum Store. (937) 427–4300.

The Greene Town Center. 51 Plum Street Beavercreek, OH 45440. Take US 35 to I-675 S to exit 10. Consider this Easton Town Center lite. Dozens of entertainment, retail, and dining options line pedestrian-friendly streetscapes, open-air gathering spaces, fountains, and parks for children. Here you'll find Eddie Bauer, Joey & Eric, Artisans, Envy XOXO, and McCormick & Schmick's, and even a few places that the Columbus cousin lacks such as Jennaclaire Handbag Studio, Jule boutique, Von Maur department store, and others. (937) 490–4990; www.thegreene.com.

where to eat

The Trolley Stop. 530 East Fifth Street, Dayton, OH 45402. Eclecticism abounds in the atmosphere, food, staff, clientele, and music. Enjoy vegetarian entrees, homemade soups, and sandwiches while sitting in the New Orleans–style courtyard in the Oregon District. $-$$. (937) 461–1101; www.trolleystopdayton.com.

Stockyards Inn. 1065 Springfield Street, Dayton, OH 45403. This is a great place for your basic steaks, ribs, prime rib, and fresh seafood. $$-$$$. (937) 254–3576.

The Pine Club. 1926 Brown Street, Dayton, OH 45409. This is the town's most popular steak house, so expect to wait. But the locals keep coming back, and with good reason. $$–$$$. (937) 228–5371; www.pineclub.com.

Citilites. 109 N. Main Street, Dayton, OH 45420. This eatery features such comfort foods as grilled cheese with tomato bisque and fish and chips along with more chi-chi fare like bang-bang chicken, and a warm cheese dip and tomato relish combo for bruschetta. Pick your poison, er calories with a wide assortment of desserts and bar drink specialties. $$–$$$. (937) 222–0623; www.victoriatheatre.com/dining/dining.php.

Jay's Seafood Restaurant. 225 East Sixth Street, Dayton, OH 45402. Located in an 1852 gristmill and the site of the historic Pony House Saloon, the most excitement that occurs now is the arrival of fresh fish, flown in daily. Entrees can be served gussied up with sauces, baked, char-grilled, or blackened. Poultry and steak are also available. $$–$$$, (937) 222–2892; www.jays.com.

where to stay

Crowne Plaza Hotel. 33 East Fifth Street, Dayton, OH 45402. Get connected to the Dayton Convention Center and many of the sites via a walkway to this 280-plus-room hotel which features such amenities as an airport shuttle, fitness center, and pool. Free parking's also available—almost unheard-of in a downtown city—and room rates can be very reasonable if you ask about specials. $$. (937) 224–0800; www.cpdayton.com.

Hawthorn Suites Dayton North. 7070 Poe Avenue, Dayton, OH 45440. One- and three-room suites feature a fully equipped kitchen as well as a living area with a fireplace and pull-out sofa. Other suite types are also available, covering a wide range of budgets. Bonuses: complimentary hot breakfast buffet daily and Wednesday evening social hour. $–$$$. (937) 898–7764; www.hawthorn.com.

SpringHill Suites Dayton. 417 Springboro Pike, Dayton, OH 45449. Another "suite" option is this new property. Each space has a living room/seating area with a sofa and armchair, large work desk with ergonomic desk chair, 32" swiveling flat-screen, WiFi, and more. A complimentary hot breakfast buffet, indoor pool and whirlpool, and other amenities add even more sugar. $$–$$$. (937) 432–9277 or (888) 287–9400; www.marriott.com/DAYSH.

My Grandfather's Garden Bed & Breakfast. 251 Green Street, Dayton, OH 45402. Dayton's oldest operating B&B (or so the Web site says) can be found in this fully renovated 1850s home in the Oregon District. But not to worry, this crib has all the fixin's. Rooms are fully soundproofed with private baths, central air-conditioning, Internet connectivity, and feather beds. Plus you get great views of the quiet, residential 'hood with its historic homes and gardens. $$. (937) 228–6385; www.mygrandfathersgardenbandb.com.

festivals and celebrations

Ohio seems to have cornered the market on festivals, especially those concerning food. Subjects of adulation range from popcorn to tomatoes to pumpkins, with melons, walleye, and bratwurst thrown in for good measure. Some may not be in day-trip locales discussed in this book, but they might be worth the detour, particularly if you like to chow down on a particular item.

Among this cornucopia you'll also find festivals that celebrate different cultures, the arts, even autos. For more information and to obtain a list, contact the Ohio Department of Development, Division of Travel and Tourism, 77 South High Street, Columbus, OH 43216; (800) 282–5393; www.discoverohio.com. Additionally, local convention and visitors bureaus and chambers of commerce publish detailed information on area festivals, and there's a resource dedicated to all festivals, all the time: The Ohio Festivals and Events Association, 2055 Cherokee Drive, London, OH 43140; (419) 668–5231; www.ofea.org. Call for admission prices, dates, and times.

january
African Culture Fest, Cincinnati Museum Center, Cincinnati. African drummers and dancers, storytellers, and cuisine make for a fun wintertime diversion. (513) 287–7000.

february
Snow Trails Ski Carnival, Mansfield. Shiver your timbers. Events include a bikini race, shovel cup event, slope style competition, team cross-skiing, and more. (800) 644–6754.

march
Maple Syrup Festival, Indian Lake State Park, Lakeview. Take a wagon ride through the sugar bush and stop off at a production shack to watch park staff boil the sap. You get to sample the results. (937) 843–2717.

Great Midwest Quilt Show and Sale, Lebanon, Warren County Fairgrounds. Quilters from all over the United States display their handcrafted wares. Antique quilts are featured as well. (513) 932–1817.

april

Geauga County Maple Festival, Chardon. A rite of spring, this festival celebrates the production of maple syrup, a leading agricultural moneymaker. There are two—count 'em, two—parades, maple syrup judging and auction, queen pageant, photo contest, sap run, bathtub races, and more. (440) 286–3007; www.maplefestival.com.

may

Wild Turkey Festival, McArthur. Just in time for spring gobbler season, this gathering features car and quilt shows, crafts, rides, games, and food. A queen is crowned, but she's no turkey. (740) 596–4945.

Moonshine Festival, New Straitsville. A working moonshine still display, local history museum, moonshine burgers, and moonshine pie are but a few highlights. Other temptations include carnival rides and games, free entertainment, food, souvenirs, talent show, fiddle and banjo contest, and car/truck display. (740) 394–2838.

Port Clinton Walleye Festival, Perry Street, Port Clinton. Along with enjoying the fruits of the "Walleye Capital of the World," you can stroll down a midway filled with rides, games, arts and crafts, and vendors of both the food and non-edible kind. (419) 734–7600; www.walleyefestival.com.

Feast of the Flowering Moon, Downtown & Yoctangee Park, Chillicothe. Despite its almost Zen-sounding name, this gathering features a mountain-man encampment, a Native American Powwow and juried craft shows along with many commercial exhibits. (740) 887–2979; www.feastofthefloweringmoon.com.

june

Columbus Arts Festival, downtown Columbus. Hundreds of fine artists and craftspeople are selected from a large pool of talented individuals. Add music, arts activities for all ages, food from the city's most popular restaurants, and special exhibitions and you have one of the top arts festivals in the United States. (614) 224–2606; www.gcac.org/fest.

International Washboard Festival, Logan. "Clean up" with washboard-based live music and wandering minstrels, along with street vendors and Hocking Hills cuisine (nonroadkill category). This colorful and entertaining festival highlights the historic downtown, culminating in a free tour of the Columbus Washboard Company, the only manufacturer of guess-whats in the United States (740) 380–3828; www.washboardmusicfestival.com.

Lancaster Old Car Club Spring Festival, Fairfield County Fairgrounds, Lancaster. Antiques, classics, and hot rods share space with a flea market featuring more than 300 vendors. Old auto parts, steam and stationary engines, antique tractors, and more can be found here. (740) 654–9434; www.lancasteroldcarclub.org.

Banana Split Festival, Wilmington. What better excuse to celebrate summer than by digging into the festival's namesake? Other indulgences include collectibles from the 1950s and '60s, arts and crafts, games, and muscle cars from the post-World War II era. (877) 428–4748; www.bananasplitfestival.com.

Avon Heritage Duct Tape Festival, Avon. Among the 1001 uses here are sculptures, fashion, games, even a parade. As the home of Duck brand duct tape and the self-proclaimed "Duct Tape Capital," Avon has found its "calling" and is sticking to it. (866) 818–1116; www.avonducttapefestival.com.

Coshocton Hot Air Balloon Festival, Coshocton. Fly high for two days, weather permitting. There are also rides, arts and crafts displays, merchandise, food and beverage stands, and live entertainment. (740) 622–5411 or (800) 589–2430.

Strawberry Festival, London. Formerly known as the Marigold Festival, this event recently switched its focus. Events include two parades; the crowning of a queen; a 5K race; car, motorcycle, and antique tractor shows; live entertainment; a strawberry recipe bake-off; and other diversions. (740) 857–1417; www.londonstrawberryfestival.com.

july

Lancaster Festival, Lancaster. More than seventy-five events consist of classical and popular music, jazz, dance, and art exhibits by international artists and musicians. Highlights include Splendor in the Brass, Candlelight Chamber Music Concert, Farm Fare Day, the Young People's Concert, and evening fireworks. (740) 687–4808; www.lanfest.org.

Ohio Hills Folk Festival, Quaker City. This tradition began over a century ago when festivals were just an excuse for generic parades, queens, craft demonstrations, fireworks, and so on. This one's stayed the course, and also offers tours of a farm museum, country store, and Quaker Meeting House. (740) 679–2704.

Miami Valley Steam Threshers Association, Plain City. With steam engines, antique tractors, gas engines, shingle mills, veneer mills, drag saws and more, it's a gearhead's sixteen virgins in heaven. The less mechanically inclined can check out the blacksmith shop, flea markets, arts, crafts, and food. Along with tractor pulls, the schedule calls for frequent wheat threshing, which sounds much kinkier than it actually is. (614) 270–0007, (614) 266–5466; www.miamivalleysteamshow.org.

august

Ohio State Fair, Ohio State Fairgrounds, Columbus. This granddaddy of all fairs features agriculture and horticulture, livestock, and youth activities, as well as culinary and craft offerings. Along with learning how to milk a cow, get the most out of your admission by cruising the midway with more than seventy rides, by seeing big-name entertainers as well as a variety of shows for children and adults, and by taking the world's longest portable sky ride, to mention but a few options. Foodstuffs range from sausage sandwiches to elephant ears to french fries to funnel cakes. (614) 644–3247; www.ohiostatefair.com.

Dublin Irish Festival, Dublin. Recognized as one of the best of its kind in the United States, this fast-growing event features vendors, Irish entertainers and dancers, international and local bands, as well as cultural and children's activities. (614) 410–4545; www.dublinirish festival.org.

Sweet Corn Festival, Millersport. This "ear-resistible" happening is hot buttered sweet corn heaven with more than eighty food and game concessions. There's also a parade, free entertainment stages, and several contests. (740) 467–3639; www.sweetcornfest.com.

Bucyrus Bratwurst Festival, Bucyrus. Perfected by local butchers whose families emigrated from Germany, bratwurst from Bucyrus has a unique flavor and is roasted over an open fire. Parades, continuous entertainment, crafts and art shows, rides, games, beer gardens, and friendly folks make for a spicy diversion. (419) 562–2728; www.bratfest.org.

Obetz Zucchinifest, Lancaster Park, Obetz. Finally, a festival celebrating a healthy vegetable! Along with the usual arts and crafts and games, there's a pageant (zucchini queen for a day?) as well as zucchini burgers, fudge, bread, and other products. (614) 497–2518; www.obetzzucchini.com.

Twin Days, Twinsburg. This somewhat redundant experience focuses on socializing, celebration, and fun, and draws multiple submissions in the form of twins, triplets, and so on from around the world. (330) 425–3652; www.twindays.org.

Renaissance Festival, Harveysburg (runs through October). Step back into sixteenth-century Elizabethan England. Thirty acres encompass more than 150 costumed performers and one hundred daily shows. Surely they joust, as well as offer crafts, feasts, and theater-in-the-ground (as in encounters of the muddy kind). (513) 897–7000; www.renfestival.com.

Milan Melon Festival, Town Square, Milan. This well-rounded experience includes an elaborate car display, a tractor pull, muskmelon ice cream, and watermelon sherbet as well as plenty of the fresh stuff. (419) 499–9929; www.milandmelonfestival.org.

september

Oktoberfest, German Village, Columbus. Voted a top event by the American Bus Association, this venerable and popular gathering boasts authentic German music, dancing, food, and crafts, even though it is held in September. (614) 221–8888; www.germanvillage.com/oktoberfest.

Wellston Coal Festival, Wellston. Strip away modern-day cares with coal-miner Olympics, a coal dust sundae-eating contest, coal-mine memorabilia, coal crafts, and rides, as well as exhibits and live performers. The final immersion: a tour of a working coal mine. (740) 384–5141; www.wellstoncoalfestival.com.

Mantua Potato Festival, Buchert Park. This rural farming community celebrates its moneymaking spuds with live entertainment, food, rides, and games. Along with the crowning of a festival queen and her court, there's a 15K Potato Stomp and 1-mile fun run. (330) 274–0770.

Geneva Area Grape Jamboree (JAM-boree, get it?), Geneva. Have a "grape" time sampling grapes, freshly squeezed grape juice, wine, and other products. You can even stomp them for free when not partaking of the art show, craft fair, grape culinary contest, concession booths, farmer's market, antiques, ethnic foods, amusement rides, street dancing, and much more. (440) 466–5262; www.grapejamboree.com.

Reynoldsburg Tomato Festival, Civic Park, Reynoldsburg. OK, so maybe free tomato juice sounds rather bland, but there are fried green tomatoes, an agricultural exhibit, a Grand Champion Tomato Contest, and a talent show. Attack of the killer tomatoes, anyone? (614) 866–2861; www.reynoldsburgtomatofestival.org.

Marion Popcorn Festival, downtown Marion. Explosive excitement includes popcorn sculpture and a trip to the Wyandot Popcorn Museum at Heritage Hall. There's free entertainment; arts, crafts, and food; a 5K run, and a Popcorn 100 bike tour. (740) 387–3378; www.popcornfestival.com.

Ohio Swiss Festival, Sugarcreek. Holey cow! Attractions in this Alpine setting include Swiss music, costumes, and tons of cheese from eleven manufacturing facilities. There's also Steinstossen (stone throwing), Schwingfest (Swiss wrestling), and polka dancing as well as a children's parade. (888) 609–7592; www.sugarcreekohio.org.

october

Circleville Pumpkin Show, Circleville. Ohio's oldest festival has two daily parades and a world's largest pumpkin contest as well as foodstuffs such as pumpkin fudge (which tastes much better than it sounds). Squash, gourds, fruits, and vegetables are also welcome. (740) 474–7000; www.pumpkinshow.com.

Ohio Gourd Show, Mt. Gilead. Fruit or vegetable? This question may never be answered, but you can learn about gourds and gourd craft in five buildings. Demonstrations on cleaning, carving, wood burning, painting, and more are also offered. (419) 547–0025; www .americangourdsociety.org/ohiochapter.

november

Buckeye Book Fair, Wooster. More than seventy authors from in and around the state autograph their tomes at a discount. And it's just in time for the holiday season. (330) 262–3244; www.buckeyebookfair.com.

december

Dalton Holidays Festival, Dalton. Along with handcrafted treasures, this Christmas-themed gathering features entertainment, a country-style breakfast, Mrs. Claus's pantry, a fireman's ham dinner, and Christmas Parade. The entire village participates with lights and other seasonal displays. (330) 828–2323.

Winterfair, Ohio State Fairgrounds, Columbus. All manner of unique arts, crafts, jewelry, and more can be found here, making it the ideal shopping opportunity for the hard-to-satisfy giver and receiver. (614) 486–7119; www.ohiocraft.org/fairs_wf.html.

regional information

north

day trip 01

Lake Erie Shores and Island Welcome Center—East
(Sandusky/Erie County Visitors & Convention Bureau)
4424 Milan Road, Suite A
Sandusky, OH 44870
(800) 255-3743
www.shoresandislands.com

Cedar Point
One Cedar Point Drive
Sandusky, OH 44870
(800) 237-8386
www.cedarpoint.com

day trip 02

Lake Erie Shores and Island Welcome Center—East
(Sandusky/Erie County Visitors & Convention Bureau)
4424 Milan Road, Suite A
Sandusky, OH 44870
(800) 255-3743
www.shoresandislands.com

Lake Erie Shores and Island Welcome Center—West
(Ottawa County Visitors Bureau)
770 SE Catawba Road
Port Clinton, OH 43452
(800) 441-1271
www.shoresandislands.com

Kelleys Island Chamber of Commerce
General Delivery
Kelleys Island, OH 43438
(419) 746-2360
www.kelleysisland.com

Convention and Visitors Bureau of Windsor, Essex County and Pelee Island
333 Riverside Drive West, Suite 103
Windsor, ON N9A 5K4
(800) 265-3633
www.visitwindsor.com

Port Clinton Chamber of Commerce
110 Madison Street, Suite C
Port Clinton, OH 43452
(419) 734-5503
www.portclintonchamber.com

Put-in-Bay Chamber of Commerce
148 Delaware Avenue
Put-in-Bay, OH 43456
(419) 285-2832
www.put-in-bay.com

Marblehead Peninsula Chamber of Commerce
5681 East Harbor Road, Suite C
Marblehead, OH 43440
(419) 734-9777
www.marbleheadpeninsula.com

The Lakeside Association
236 Walnut Street
Lakeside, OH 43440
(419) 798-4461
www.lakesideohio.com

day trip 03

Milan Chamber of Commerce
P.O. Box 422
Milan, OH 44846
(419) 499–9929
www.milanohio.com

Seneca County Convention and Visitors Bureau
114 South Washington Street
Tiffin, OH 44883
(888) 736–3221
www.senecacounty.com

Bellevue Area Tourism and Visitors Bureau
P.O. Box 63
Bellevue, OH 44811
(419) 483–5359
www.bellevuetourism.org

Sandusky County Convention and Visitors Bureau
712 North Street
Fremont, OH 43420
(800) 255–8070
www.lakeeriesfavoriteneighbor.com

northeast

day trip 01

Malabar Farm State Park
4050 Bromfield Road
Lucas, OH 44843
(419) 892–2784
www.ohiodnr.com

Mansfield and Richland County Convention and Visitors Bureau
124 North Main Street
Mansfield, OH 44902
(800) 642–8282
www.mansfieldtourism.org

day trip 02

Holmes County Chamber of Commerce and Tourism Bureau
35 North Monroe Street
Millersburg, OH 44654
(330) 674–3975
www.visitamishcountry.com

day trip 03

Canton Stark County Convention and Visitors Bureau
222 Market Avenue North
Canton, OH 44702
(800) 552–6051
www.visitcantonohio.com

Zoar Community Association
P.O. Box 621
Zoar, OH 44697
(33) 874–2646
www.zca.org

Tuscarawas County Convention and Visitors Bureau
124 East High Avenue
New Philadelphia, OH 44663
(800) 527–3387
neohiotravel.com

day trip 04

Akron/Summit Convention and Visitors Bureau
77 East Mill Street
Akron, OH 44308
(800) 245–4254
www.visitakron-summit.org

day trip 05

Hale Farm & Village
2686 Oak Hill Road
Bath, OH 44210
(800) 589–9703
www.wrhs.org

Peninsula Area Chamber of Commerce
1619 West Mill Street
Peninsula, OH 44264
(330) 657–2788
www.explorepeninsula.com

day trip 06

Positively Cleveland and Visitors Center
The Higbee Building
100 Public Square, Suite 100
Cleveland, OH 44113-2290
(800) 321–1001
www.positivelycleveland.com

east

day trip 01

Granville Information
141 East Broadway, P.O. Box 514
Granville, OH 43023
(740) 587–0707
www.granville.oh.us

Licking County Convention and Visitors Bureau
455 Hebron Road
Heath, OH 43056
(800) 589–8224
www.lccvb.com

Greater Buckeye Lake Chamber of Commerce
P.O. Box 5
Buckeye Lake, OH 43008
(740) 928–7100
www.buckeyelakecc.com

day trip 02

Longaberger Main Office
One Market Square
1500 East Main Street
Newark, OH 43055
(740) 322–7800
www.longaberger.com

Dresden Welcome Center
414 Main Street, P.O. Box 707
Dresden, OH 43821
(800) 315–1809
www.basketvillageusa.com

day trip 03

Wheeling Ohio County Convention and Visitors Bureau
1401 Main Street
Wheeling, WV 26003
(800) 828–3097
www.wheelingcvb.com

southeast

day trip 01

Hocking Hills Tourism Association
13178 SR 664 S
Logan, OH 43148
(800) 462–5464
www.1800hocking.com

day trip 02

Athens County Convention and Visitors Bureau
667 East State Street
Athens, OH 45701
(800) 878–9767
www.athensohio.com

day trip 03

Marietta/Washington County Convention and Visitors Bureau
Putnam Commons
121 Putnam Street
Marietta, OH 45750
(800) 288–2577
www.mariettaohio.org

day trip 04

Jackson Area Chamber of Commerce
234 Broadway Street
Jackson, OH 45640
(740) 286–2722
www.jacksonohio.org

Gallia County Convention and Visitors Bureau
61 Court Street
Gallipolis, OH 45631
(800) 765–6482
www.visitgallia.com

south

day trip 01

Adams County Travel and Visitors Bureau
110 N. Manchester Street
West Union, OH 45693
(877) 232–6764
www.adamscountytravel.org

southwest

day trip 01

Prime Outlets Jeffersonville
8000 Factory Shops Boulevard
Jeffersonville, OH 43128
(800) 746–7644
www.primeoutlets.com

Clinton County Convention and Visitors Bureau
13 North South Street
Wilmington, OH 45177
(877) 428–4748
www.clintoncountyohio.com

day trip 02

Warren County Convention and Visitors Bureau
Triangle Office at Kings Mill
5412 Courseview Drive, Suite 220
Mason, OH 45040
(800) 791–4386
www.ohioslargestplayground.com

Waynesville Area Chamber of Commerce
P.O. Box 281
Waynesville, OH 45068
(513) 897–8855
www.waynesvilleohio.com

day trip 03

Kings Island
6300 Kings Island Drive
Kings Island, OH 45034
(800) 288–0808
www.visitkingsisland.com

Warren County Convention and Visitors Bureau
313 East Warren Street
Lebanon, OH 45036
(800) 433–1072
www.ohio4fun.org

Cincinnati Visitors Bureau
525 Vine Street, Suite 1500
Cincinnati, OH 45202
(800) 543–2613
www.cincyusa.com

day trip 04

Cincinnati Visitors Bureau
525 Vine Street, Suite 1500
Cincinnati, OH 45202
(800) 543–2613
www.cincyusa.com

west

day trip 01

Greater Columbus Convention and Visitors Bureau
277 W. Nationwide Blvd., Suite 125
Columbus, OH 43215
(800) 354–2657
www.experiencecolumbus.com

day trip 02

Logan County Convention and Visitors Bureau
100 South Main Street
Bellefontaine, OH 43311
(888) 564–2626
www.logancountyohio.com

day trip 03

Yellow Springs Chamber of Commerce
101 Dayton Street
Yellow Springs, OH 45387
(937) 767–2686
www.yellowspringsohio.org

Greene County Convention and Visitors Bureau
1221 Meadowbridge Drive, Suite A
Beavercreek, OH 45434
(800) 733–9109
www.greenecountyohio.org

day trip 04

Dayton/Montgomery County Convention and Visitors Bureau
1 Chamber Plaza
Suite A
Dayton, OH 45402
(800) 221–8235
www.daytoncvb.com

Dayton Web site
www.dayton.com

Index

about the author

Sandra Gurvis (www.sgurvis.com, www.booksaboutthe60s.com) is the author of twelve books, including *Careers for Nonconformists* (a selection of the Quality Paperback Book Club), *Where Have All the Flower Children Gone?* and the novel, *The Pipe Dreamers* as well as hundreds of magazine articles and essays. Her newest titles are *Ohio Curiosities,* (Globe Pequot, 2007); *Management Basics,* 2nd ed. (Adams, 2007); and *Managing the Telecommuting Employee* with Michael Amigoni (Adams, 2009). She is currently finishing her second novel, *Country Club Wives* and working on a postsecondary biography on Paris Hilton (Greenwood Publishing, in press).

Her books have been featured in newspapers, television, and radio stations across the country and have been excerpted in magazines. Sandra has also written extensively on business and medical topics and lectures frequently on writing, the '60s, and her books. She has been selected for residencies and fellowships and is a member of the American Society of Journalists and Authors (ASJA) and the American Medical Writers Association (AMWA). She lives in Columbus, Ohio.